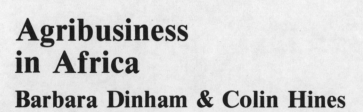

Agribusiness in Africa
Barbara Dinham & Colin Hines

First published 1983

Earth Resources Research Ltd
258 Pentonville Road
London N1 9JY

© 1983 Earth Resources Research Ltd

Typeset and printed by
Russell Press Ltd.

Cover design by Reg Boorer,
Graphics by Bill Sanderson

Trade distribution:
Third World Publications
151 Stratford Road
Birmingham B11 1RD

Dinham, Barbara,
Agribusiness in Africa,
1. Agriculture — Economic aspects — Africa
2. International business enterprises
   I. Title   II. Hines, Colin
      338. 1 8 096   HD2117

ISBN 0 946281 00 9

EARTH RESOURCES RESEARCH

Earth Resources was established in 1973 to investigate contemporary environmental and resource management issues. It is a small versatile research group, specialising in the fields of energy, agriculture, transport and wildlife. Registered as a charity, it is an independent organisation with a qualified staff backed up by outside specialists. The aim is to provide thorough challenging research directly applicable to current policy.

The majority of our work is concerned with UK or European issues, but occasionally we undertake projects with a Third World focus. This book reports the results of one such study, details of other publications in print appear on the inside back cover. Further information about the organisation and enquiries about this report should be sent to the address below. Comments and suggestions are always welcome.

David Baldock
Executive Director
Earth Resources Research Ltd
258 Pentonville Road
London N1 9JX

ACKNOWLEDGEMENTS

This book would not have been written without the inspiration derived from the works of Susan George, Frances Moore Lappé and Joe Collins. It also owes much to their assistance as well as that of Ann Marie Holenstein, Al Imfield, Tina Georgiadis and others in the International Peace Research Association's Food Policy Study Group.

In practical terms it would not have been possible without a generous grant from the Joseph Rowntree Charitable Trust, for which we are very grateful. We also received valuable supporting grants from The Catholic Fund for Overseas Development, The Methodist Church's Division of Social Responsibility, and Trocaire, the Catholic Agency for World Development. In addition a travel grant from The Commonwealth Foundation allowed a visit to Africa.

We are particularly grateful to David Baldock and Greg Lanning for the substantial help they gave by reading and editing the text. Others who made valuable contributions are: in the United States Doug and Steve Hellinger, Fred O'Regan and staff of the Development Group for Alternative Policies, Joe Belden, Erik Eckholm, Harris Gleckman, Guy Gran, Cathy Lerza, Linda Starke, Bruce Stokes, Atul Wad and the staff of the Institute for Food and Development Policy and the African and Middle East Branch of the United States Department of Agriculture. In Tanzania: Frank Ellis, University of Dar-es-Salaam and Martha Honey. In Kenya: the staff of the Coffee Board of Kenya, the Ministry of Agriculture and the National Council of Churches of Kenya. In the United Kingdom: Raphie Kaplinsky, Michael Cowen, Nicola Swainson and others at the Institute of Development Studies, Steven Iaino, Iain McDonald, Paul Richards and the staff of the International Coffee Organisation..

Finally we would like to thank Heather Laughton, Kim Chisholm and Clare Cherrington for the typing of the seemingly innumerable drafts and Greg Lanning for untiring patience, typing and childminding. While we appreciate all the help and support received, we alone are responsible for the views expressed and any errors that remain.

Barbara Dinham
Colin Hines
Earth Resources Research
November 1982

THE AUTHORS

Barbara Dinham is Australian and lived and worked in Africa for four years before working for Friends of the Earth and later Earth Resources Research. She has been active in food politics campaigns and the women's movement. Previous publications include co-authoring the Directory of Social Change, Education and Play, and she also edited a Women's Directory in the same series. She lives in South London and has two daughters.

Colin Hines has been actively involved in environmental and developmental issues for the last 12 years. In 1974 he was the co-author of the ERR report, *Losing Ground,* a critical assessment of British agriculture. Before joining the ERR research staff in 1977 he was food campaigner for Friends of the Earth, and for the past eight years he has been a part-time lecturer in environmental studies at London's Polytechnic of the South Bank.

In addition to research on agribusiness, he has been a consultant to the United Nations Environment Programme and the United States Department of Agriculture co-authoring a report on the changing structure of European agriculture for the latter.

Colin Hines has also worked on the social impact of new technology, and is co-author (with Graham Searle) of *Automatic Unemployment,* published by ERR in 1979.

Contents

List of Tables

List of Figures

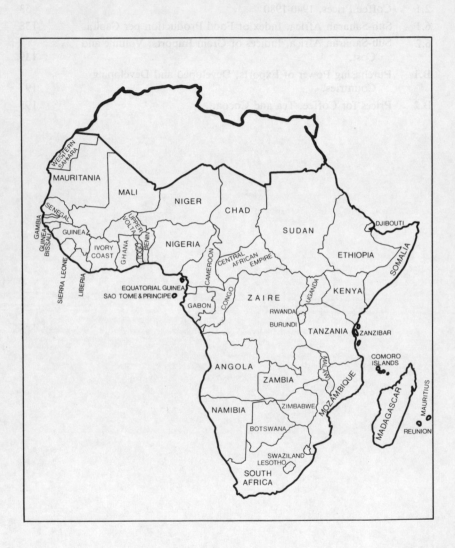

Introduction

There have been great changes in agricultural production in both industrialised and underdeveloped countries since the end of the Second World War. Throughout the world, agricultural production, formerly largely in the hands of peasants or small farmers, is increasingly dominated by big corporations. Agribusiness is the term given to these companies. It is a word which emphasises the broad reach of these large companies which can be involved in several aspects of food production, including the agricultural inputs sector, the farm, the food processing industry and the transport and distribution of food. This study is concerned with the activities of agribusiness transnationals* in African countries south of the Sahara, except for South Africa, which has been excluded because of the entirely different political and economic situation existing within that country. The book examines some of the consequences of companies' involvement for Africa.

The subsidiaries of agribusiness transnationals spread across all sectors. They own plantations, management companies and consultancies, fertiliser and agrochemical plants, animal feedstuff compounders, sales organisations, shipping companies, insurance companies, brokers and auctioneers, export and import companies, merchant banks, farm equipment distributors, research organisations, factories making processing equipment, food and drink processing companies, packaging and labelling plants, distributing organisations, and even the supermarkets selling the final product. Many of the companies have familiar names, including Unilever, Nestlé, Tate & Lyle, Heinz, Brooke Bond, and British American Tobacco (BAT). Even names not generally associated with agriculture — ICI, Hoechst, Shell, BP, all large chemical and oil transnational corporations — are involved in agribusiness activities producing fertilisers, improved seed varieties and agrochemicals, which are among their most profitable activities.

Traditional, and often more balanced, agricultural practices usually involved the recycling of nutrients produced on the farm back into the soil, the practice of crop rotation as a means of reducing attacks from pests, and the replacement of nitrogen lost from the soil by growing

---

* The term 'transnational' has been used throughout this report in preference to 'multinational'. The prefix *trans* means across nations, rather than simply *of*, or *within*, many nations, which the term 'multinational' implies. 'Transnational' is therefore a more accurate description.

legumes. These practices have been all but abandoned in modern Western agriculture, but are still among the traditional techniques of millions of peasant farmers in the Third World. They allow small farmers a greater degree of autonomy and independence than modern techniques and are often more appropriate for African soils. By contrast, agribusiness methods are capital intensive, and place extensive emphasis on the application of new technologies to increase yields, requiring expensive inputs in the form of fertilisers, irrigation, pesticides and herbicides.

Western models may have advantages in rich industrialised countries, where by comparison with the third world, a strong manufacturing and employment base exists. However, these models cannot be transferred wholesale to African countries where, with few exceptions, 75 per cent of the people live on the land, depend on it for their living, have no money for expensive inputs, and, if they lose their holdings, become landless[1] with a poor chance of finding waged work as a substitute.

Vertically integrated and centrally organised, the agribusiness corporations take decisions based on their own criteria of economic rationality. Their search for profits has been driving small farmers off the land in America, Europe and parts of the Third World. Although they claim that they can help to feed the world in an era in which millions of people do not have enough to eat, this is not their primary aim. Indeed, suggesting that agribusiness can 'feed the world' implies that inadequate food production is the basic reason for starvation. This is a simplistic assumption, which ignores entirely the question of poverty: without sufficient incomes, poor people cannot buy food, particularly not the expensive food normally produced by agribusiness.

Africa — the Unequal Partner

By their very nature, agribusiness companies are concerned with finding a profitable means of involvement in food and agricultural production, not with the transformation of peasant agriculture. The central focus of the companies remains in the industrialised countries, and Africa is seen primarily as a source of commodities and a market for manufactured inputs and technical expertise. Many of the strategies for increasing agricultural production devised by agribusiness merely emphasise the development of one economy to meet the needs of another. In this they are following an established tradition.

For over a century the resources of Africa have been exploited to meet European needs, and this is reflected in the economies of the 43 countries considered here, over half of which depend for their major source of foreign exchange on the export of agricultural products consumed in industrialised countries, as shown in Table 1. (The remainder are dependent mainly on mineral exports). Cash crops are vitally important in Africa. Twelve countries are dependent on just one main crop for over 70 per cent of their income, and a further eleven countries depend on only two crops for well over half their income (see Appendix A). Gambia, for example, is an extreme case, where 90 per cent of export revenue is earned from selling groundnuts. Groundnuts occupy 73 per cent of the country's arable land and Gambians depend on imports for their staple foods.

Africa's trade in agricultural commodities is almost entirely with the industrialised world, as trade between African States on the continent is minimal, in most years amounting to less than 10 per cent of total exports (excluding petroleum products).[2] Although the United States is increasing its share of trade with Africa, trading links with the former colonial powers tend to be dominant, and *without exception* there is an adverse balance of trade with these former rulers.

Agricultural exporters are inevitably vulnerable to the vagaries of the world market, but some measure of control can be gained, as well as an economic advantage, by exporting products in a processed form, rather than as raw materials. One way to ease this problem could be to increase the extent to which export crops are processed within Africa itself, since raw materials increase in value significantly at each stage of processing, as they are turned into consumer products, packaged, labelled, and sold under brand names. However, agribusiness companies seek to control the processing and marketing stages of production themselves and so it is in their interest to ensure that the only processing carried out in Africa is the minimum necessary to preserve the crop. While African governments have tried to increase their processing and marketing capacity, they lack the necessary technical expertise and access to markets, which remain in the hands of the companies.

Cash Crops and Food Crops

Crops produced for export are known as cash crops, and although a small quantity of such crops may be consumed locally, by and large they are grown to meet the demands of the industrialised world. Africa's major export crops are coffee, tea, cocoa, cotton, palm products (kernels and oil), groundnuts, rubber, tobacco, sisal, timber and sugar. Of these, coffee, tea and cocoa are grown entirely for export; palm oil, groundnuts, tobacco and timber are consumed locally, but the majority is grown for export. Sugar is grown mainly to achieve self-sufficiency, but most sugar-growing countries hope to export a surplus.

The purchasing power provided by agricultural exports rarely keeps pace with the price of the manufactured products which Africa imports. The consequence of this is that ever larger quantities of agricultural pro-

Table 1
Africa — the Importance of Agriculture to the Economy

Country	Popu-lation 1981	% in Agri-culture 1979	GNP per Capita 1978	GDP in Agri-culture 1977[d]	Agr. Exp. as a % of Export Earn'gs
	Million	%	US$	%	%[d]
Angola	6.8	60	300	29	28
Benin	3.4	47	230	39	72
Botswana	.7	86[b]	620	27	31
Burundi	4.8	84	140	64	94
Cameroon	8.6	87	460	33	40
Central African Repub.	2.0	88	250	37	79
Chad	4.5	85	140	52	80
Congo	1.6	35	540	15	26
Djibouti	.2	f	n.a.	n.a.	n.a.
Equitorial Guinea	.4	76	n.a.	n.a.	99
Ethiopia	33.5	80	120	50	90
Gabon	.6	77	3580[g]	25	8
Gambia	.5	78	230	65	90
Ghana	11.7	51	390	49	63
Guinea	5.5	81	210	43	28
Guinea-Bissau	.9	83	180	n.a.	92
Ivory Coast	8.8	80	840	25	83
Kenya	16.2	78	330	30	79
Lesotho	1.4	84	280	38	67
Liberia	1.9	70	460	29	23
Madagascar	8.8	84	250	29	86
Malawi	6.2	85	180	45	95
Mali	6.8	88	100	38[e]	70[+]
Mauritania	1.6	84	270	35	13
Mauritius	1.0	28	760	30	95
Mozambique	10.6	65	140	45	80
Namibia	1.3	50	n.a.	12	3
Niger	5.4	89[c]	560	47	25
Nigeria	85.3	54	560	23	4
Rwanda	4.8	90	180	52	82
Senegal	5.8	75	340	28	50
Sierra Leone	3.4	66	210	32	42
Somalia	4.0	81	130	31	85
South Africa	29.9	29	1480	9	Min.
Sudan	18.9	78	320	41	90
Swaziland	.6	74	590	41	63
Tanzania	18.3	82	230	45	73
Togo	2.6	68	320	25	40
Uganda	13.6	81	280	55	90
Upper Volta	6.0	82	160	34	High
Zaire	29.0	75	210	16	25
Zambia	5.8	68	480	14	1
Zimbabwe	7.6	60	480	16	n.a.

Sources: New African Yearbook, 1979, 1981-82, Department of Trade, fact sheets, World Bank Atlas 1979.

a. Food imports are shown for the latest year available, but these vary substantially from year to year, e.g. a drou year will increase food imports. See Appendix C for a fuller picture.
b. The vast majority are women — the figure is an under-estimate because of migrant workers.
c. Including 18 per cent nomadic herders.

Imports of Food as a % of Total Imports[a]	Major Cash Crops Exported Latest year available given in brackets (% = Percentage of export earnings)
9%	(1978) Coffee 8%, sisal 2%, crude oil 49%, diamonds 41%[h]
13%, mainly staple foods	(1979) Cotton 28%, cotton seed 3%, cocoa 24%, palm produce 12%, groundnuts 5%
13%	(1979) Beef 18%, diamonds 52%, copper nickel matte 17%
17%	(1979) Coffee 93%
9%	(1979) Cocoa 17%, coffee 25%, timber 7%, palm produce, bananas, sugar, cotton
Some food imported	(1978) Coffee 29%, cotton 6%, wood 16%, diamonds 37%
Food imported during drought	(1976) Cotton 80%
20%	(1977) Timber 17%, coffee 4%, cocoa 3%. sugar 2%, crude oil 54%, potash 7%,
22%	n.a.
17%	(1970) Cocoa 66%, coffee 24%, timber
—	(1979) Coffee 69%, hides and skins 17%, pulses 3%, oilseeds 1%
85%	(1975) Wood 8%, oil 78%
Imports rice, staple food	(1976) Groundnuts 90%, fishing increasing
Imports food	(1977) Cocoa 61%, wood 8%, gold, diamonds, manganese, bauxite
Imports food grains	(1976) Coffee 5%, pineapples 23% (in 1975), palm kernels 1%, bauxite 72%
26%	(1977) Groundnuts 60%, palm kernels 12%, shellfish 6%, wood 1.5%
11%, including staple foods	(1979) Coffee 31%, cocoa 23%, wood 16%, bananas 1%, palm oils 2%, cotton 2%
Mostly self-sufficient but currently imports grain	(1979) Coffee 27%, tea 15%, petroleum products 18%, pyrethrum 1%, sisal 1%, hides and skins 3%
23%, including maize	(1973) Wool and mohair 50%, occasionally exports wheat
12%, including staple food	(1977) rubber 17%, timber, coffee, cocoa, palm kernel, products, iron ore
Imports staple food rice	(1979) Coffee 45%, cloves 18%, vanilla 4%, some sugar, sisal, fish
11%	(1979) Tobacco 55%, tea 16%, sugar, cotton, groundnuts, rice
Food imported since drought (1972)	(1978) Cotton 47%, livestock, groundnuts 1%, fish 2%
Food imported since Sahel drought	(1977) Fish 13%, gum arabic 0.2%, iron ore 80%
20%	(1979) Sugar 68%, tea
15%	(1977) Cashew nuts 21%, sugar 12%, shrimps 10%, tea 8%, cotton 6%, sisal, coconuts
Staples imported from South Africa	(1977) Cattle 10%, fish 7%, skins 7%, minerals 76%
Food imported since Sahel drought	(1976) Groundnuts 2%, cattle, uranium 64%
11%, and increasing rapidly	(1978) Cocoa 6%, cotton, rubber, palm produce, timber, coffee, petroleum 89%
—	(1978) Coffee 71%, tea 13%, tin 5%, wolfram
Over 50%, including staples	(1977) Groundnuts 37%, phosphates 10%
14-22%	(1979) Cocoa 12%, coffee 2%, palm products, fishing, diamonds 63% bauxite 5%
15%	(1979) Live animals 71%, bananas 12%, hides and skins 8%
—	(1979) Mainly minerals, gold 39%, diamonds 8%
—	(1979) Cotton 65%, groundnuts 4%, sesame 3%, gum arabic 8%
—	(1975) Sugar 54%, citrus, rice, cotton, maize, pineapples (total 9%)
Imports in some years	(1978) Coffee 35%, cotton 11%, tobacco 6%, sisal 6%, tea 5%, cashew nuts 6%, diamonds
Usually self-sufficient	(1976) Cocoa 17%, coffee 16%, phosphates 52% (coffee usually only about 5%)
Usually self-sufficient	(1979) Coffee 27%, cotton 11%, sisal 6%, tea, copper, diamonds
Imports staple foods	(1978) Cotton 32%, karite nuts 9%, live animals 37%, groundnuts
20%, mainly staple foods	(1979) Coffee 10%, copper 36%, cobalt 46%, diamonds 7%
Imports staple maize in some years	(1978) Copper is main export, some tobacco
Self-sufficient	(1979) Tobacco, beef, sugar and minerals (details not yet available)

d. 1977 figures where possible, some earlier figures used.
e. Plus livestock 20 per cent.
f. nomadic.
g. Depending on population, between $1.355 and $3,580.
h. Per cent of major exports, therefore over-estimate of total exports.

duce must be exported in order to buy a constant quantity of manufactured goods. The general movement of commodity prices, as experienced by African producers, points to some of the problems associated with declining or fluctuating prices (see Appendix B). Even a 'good' year brings problems, for it encourages investment to increase the output of a crop, although there is no guarantee that the price will be sustained, and every chance that it will fall if all exporters increase their production.

Table 1 covers the main cash crops and for each one shows its importance to the main producing countries, expressed as a proportion of their total export revenue. The table also shows the percentage of the total population engaged in agriculture. This generally means subsistence agriculture, since only a small minority are likely to be growing cash crops. For example, Kenya has an estimated 78 per cent of its population engaged in agricultural production, but only 12 per cent of these grow cash crops.[3] Thus only a small proportion of peasant farmers is likely to benefit from any gains brought about through the production of cash crops.

While Africa is heavily dependent on exports of cash crops for foreign exchange earnings, there has recently been an increase in imports of staple food grains, bought mainly from the industrialised nations. Appendix C sets out the major African food importing countries, and shows the percentage of their total imports devoted to food. Domestic food production is inevitably affected by food imports, which can both depress local prices and allow governments to ignore the fundamental problems facing peasant producers, and it is particularly worrying that Africa's food deficit is predicted to continue growing.*

Agribusiness in Africa

This report attempts to show the role that transnationals have assumed in Africa, particularly in relation to cash crops, and to explore the impact of their escalating presence. The first chapter reviews the existing role of transnationals in Africa, from their roots as plantation companies, or purchasers of peasant-produced cash crops, to the adaptations which the corporations have made since independence. It attempts to answer the questions: Can agribusiness increase Africa's wealth? Who benefits from their presence? What happens when companies become involved in processing food for consumption in Africa? What conflicts arise between

---

* Food imports inevitably fluctuate, for example the Sahelian countries' food imports rose during the drought of the late 1960s and early 1970s. However, it should be noted that Senegal, which generally requires substantial food imports even when not affected by drought, was exporting fresh vegetables to Europe at the height of the Sahelian drought,[4] and at a time when 55 per cent of the country's arable land was producing groundnuts for export.

the companies and governments, or indeed, between governments and peasant farmers?

Two cash crops receive special attention — coffee and sugar. Coffee is the major export of thirteen African countries, but only a minute proportion of Africa's output is consumed on the continent. Even in the West coffee is something of a luxury product, and consumption drops if the price rises too high. Most coffee is grown in Africa by smallholders, not by companies, but the chapter shows both the complexity of the market and the weakness of Africa's bargaining position. The large coffee manufacturing companies have acquired almost total control of coffee processing, where much of the value of the final product is added.

Sugar, which is developing fast as a cash crop in Africa, is unusual in that it is grown as much for internal consumption as for export. Nonetheless, the transnational corporations still play a major role, both shaping the development of the industry by means of their consultancies and management contracts, and by providing through their subsidiary companies such inputs as irrigation schemes and factories.

The report then contrasts two countries with different approaches to development. The first of these is Kenya, which has used private foreign investment as a way of raising capital funds for development, and at the same time built up a thriving smallholder sector growing cash crops for export. The second is Tanzania, where the government has emphasised the needs of its rural population, involving peasant farmers in development and, as far as possible, excluding private foreign investment. Can either approach bring rewards to Africa? Against what odds are African governments operating? The report shows how poverty stands in the way of some solutions and examines the extent to which governments have reduced poverty, inequality and unemployment.

Finally, the implications of the increasing role of agribusiness in African domestic food production are discussed, and there is a critical look at the current trend towards investment in modern large-scale food production schemes.

The concept of 'development' has been used extensively throughout this report, however, a concise definition has not been attempted. This is partly because development can only be defined in relation to the development goals of the particular country concerned, and partly because the report is not a study of underdevelopment, but of the activities of agribusiness in underdeveloped African countries. Inevitably, however, certain assumptions are made. For Dudley Seers, measuring development means asking certain questions:

'What has been happening to poverty? What has been happening to inequality? What has been happening to unemployment? . . . if these are getting worse it would be strange to call the result development, even if per capita income had soared.[5]

It is in this spirit that this report examines the role of agribusiness in Africa.

CHAPTER 1

Agribusiness in Africa

Export crops are important to the economies of most African countries, but few of these countries exercise any influence over the price they receive for their produce. Transnational corporations are dominant in supplying the inputs such as fertilisers, pesticides, farm machinery, processing equipment; in growing the crops; in buying, shipping, selling, processing and marketing Africa's primary products.

This chapter is an overview of agribusiness in Africa, and has drawn out the problems associated with attracting foreign private investment to develop African resources in the agricultural sector. There is no easy route for underdeveloped African countries to reduce their dependence on cash crop production, and build self-reliant economies. Debts, balance of payments problems and the need for foreign exchange create a pressure to expand agricultural production and the most obvious solution involves turning to the sources of capital, technology and expertise most readily available: that offered by transnational agribusiness companies.

This survey tries to answer some of the questions relating to the advantages or disadvantages of such investment. Questions such as the effect of transnational corporations on local enterprise and local processing of cash crops; the extent of pressure to expatriate capital and profits; the degree of control exercised by African governments; the technological choices made by foreign companies and their relevance for underdeveloped countries; whether foreign investment increases or decreases the agricultural policy choices open to African governments; whether the priorities of agribusiness coincide with those of African governments or, indeed, those of peasant farmers.

To do this, the Chapter traces historically the growth of agribusiness in Africa, showing how it came to dominate agricultural production and helped to re-shape it away from food crops to favour export crops. The role of plantation companies has been important, and they have tenaciously retained their African interests to the present day. As plantation agriculture has become impossible or less profitable, the companies have specialised in developing agricultural consultancies and management subsidiaries, as well as extending control over the food processing industry. Where possible, the interests of companies in particular countries, crops and food industries are detailed in a quantitative form. However, this information is difficult to trace and impossible to present comprehensively. The next two chapters attempt to rectify this with a detailed examination of the coffee and sugar industries.

Africa becomes a Producer of Cash Crops

Before the colonial era, food production was the primary function of African agriculture, with most settled societies cultivating their own particular staple crops. Food security and self-sufficiency were common, for example in Upper Volta, the populations always had three harvests in reserve as an insurance against drought, and it was socially unacceptable to eat grain that had spent less than three years in the granary.[1] In many areas, the technology of subsistence agriculture used iron tools, such as the hoe, and there were highly developed farming practices, including irrigation, terracing, crop rotation, green manuring, mixed and swamp farming. Cultivation was based on an experienced evaluation of soil potential,[2] essential on a continent where the soils are extremely delicate and easily destroyed by intensive farming. Agricultural surpluses were common, and were traded for other goods, moving along the many trade routes crossing the continent.[3] Other food surpluses went to specialist workers who produced not food, but articles for use. In the Niger delta, communities supported groups of wood-carvers, smith, salt-makers, potters, traders, diviners-and-doctors, and many other activities.[4]

The domestic economies of African societies were enclosed and largely self-sufficient, and trade with other continents was mainly in luxury products and guns. However, from the 16th century onwards internal stability and self-reliance were increasingly undermined by the activities of the European slave trade which, in 300 years, brought devastation to all but a few corners of the Continent. There was immense depopulation, estimated at between 30 and 100 millions, and those Africans sold as slaves so systematically over this period were the youngest and strongest women and men. Cheap European goods flooded into Africa in payment for the slaves, and replaced locally produced cotton goods, metalware, and other products. Local economic structures were broken by the onslaught, while in England profits earned from the trade financed the industrial revolution. David and Alexander Barclay used their gains from the slave trade to set up a bank, similar profits helped James Watt to produce his famous engine. Funds for the Great Western Railway came from Bristol slave merchants, and innumerable iron, and later textile, works were built from the proceeds.[5] The slave trade ended only slowly from 1807 onwards.

In West Africa, European slaving merchants had established bases on the coast, and although inland societies suffered, the coastal states had prospered. The ending of the trade plunged some of these city states into an economic crisis. Slowly, but only partially, this crisis was eased as the states switched to the export of palm oil and other raw materials.[6] Those Africans who had profited from slaving developed plantations, traded and chartered ships and crews to transport the crops to Europe. Palm oil became the major export, with "Europe needing more and more soap as her factories grew in number and her cities in filfth".[7] Merchants at the old slave-trading port of Liverpool responded quickly and switched to palm oil early in the 19th century when slaving became difficult or impossible.[8] The exports grew rapidly: for example on the Guinea Coast trade expanded from a few tons in 1800 to several thousand tons a year by the 1830s.[9] The European merchants on the Coast, however, were determined to displace the African monopoly over the palm oil trade with their own, and began to press their governments to supply political and military support, for consuls and territorial annexations. Inevitably, British rule in Africa followed the traders. Although initially this was somewhat reluctant, after the 1880s the consuls needed less urging, and the army and navy were frequently used to secure the traders' interests.[10]

While in West Africa the move to cash crops was initiated and controlled by Africans, the region was dominated by a smaller number of trading and mining companies. By 1864, 21 British firms had trading stations in the Niger delta, and within seven years five British steamers were operating in the river. These companies played a key part in fixing the terms of trade: both the prices African producers got for their produce, and the prices they had to pay for the European goods they bought.[11]

The experience of Eastern, Central and Southern Africa was different. Large areas of these regions were annexed by settlers, frequently without the initial encouragement of a colonial power. But territorial imperatives ensured that colonial administrations were established. Across the continent, land was alienated from the African population — not without long and protracted struggles — and the settlers grew crops for export. In many cases, such as that of coffee in Kenya, Africans were forbidden to grow cash crops, and this lucrative market remained in the settlers' hands.

In other colonies, where there were no settlers and peasant farmers were reluctant to grow crops required by the colonial power, coercion was not uncommon. In the Portuguese colonies, in Tanganyika under German rule, in French Equatorial Africa and in French Sudan, Africans were forced, in some cases with guns, to grow Europe's supplies.[12] A practice which continued in some forms until at least the Second World War.

However, perhaps the most iniquitous form of European intervention during the late 19th century was that of concession companies. These companies were 'given' by the colonial powers sole rights to the land, labour, and even the fruits of the forest and the soil over huge areas of Africa. The policy affected Central, Eastern and Southern regions, but the Equatorial territories suffered most from the concession company system, and it was here that some of the worst forms of plantation agriculture flourished. One of the major concession companies was that of King Leopold of Belgium in the Congo Basin. This yielded rich profits, especially after 1895, from the export of rubber and ivory collected by a brutal system of forced labour. The effects were appalling, with the population estimated to have halved between the 1880s and 1908 — a far greater loss to the region than during the slaving era. The concession companies also controlled French and German equatorial Africa around 1900. Chad, Gabon, the Central African Republic and Congo-Brazzaville, were divided among 40 such French companies with a 30-year charter. In 1898 the South Cameroons company, with mainly Belgian capital, received nearly 20 million acres, where it could collect rubber, without payment, for eternity.[13]

By the end of the 19th century, the mining and concession companies had staked their claims to Africa, along with settlers and the colonial governments. For 300 years African societies had been weakened by the slave trade, and over large areas of the continent the new demands for land and labour further destroyed the economic, social and political structures which had held African societies together. Extensive regions were annually denuded of a significant proportion of their 'fit adult males', and the effects were often disastrous. The removal from the rural economy of the more able-bodied young men left women to take total responsibility for agriculture. While in most of Africa, women have traditionally shouldered the major burden of work, particularly in food production, they had not previously done so alone. In many tribes, the men were responsible for capital formation in the rural economy, for example through the improvement and extension of the community's farms.[14] But the colonial authorities, the mining companies and the plantation owners persisted in regarding Africans as a giant reserve of cheap labour. Labour policies were enforced by imposing poll or hut taxes, thus compelling people to earn cash to pay them; as well as through enclosure acts, and by discourging or outlawing African enterprise such as trading.[15] The parts of Africa most affected by these policies include modern day Angola, Botswana, Burundi, Congo, Kenya, Lesotho, Malawi, Mozambique, Rwanda, Tanzania, Zaire, Zambia, and, perhaps with the most far-reaching consequences, South Africa.

This is the background against which big European companies turned to Africa to establish plantations in the early 20th century.

Plantation Companies

Plantations were designed to secure regular and reliable supplies of raw materials for the companies' factories in the industrialised centres. Through their own plantations, with centralised control, the companies could plant on the scale required, pick crops at the ideal moment, and carry out processing essential for preservation on the spot. Such supervision is essential for quality control, and hence the potential for greater profits. For example, plantation agriculture produced oil palm fruit sufficiently free of fatty acids to make good quality soap, margarine and cooking oils. Poorer quality fruits, or those bruised before processing, may only make poor quality soaps, candles, and anti-corrosion oils. Above all, plantations guaranteed the enormous quantities of agricultural produce needed for the scale of production of European factories.

In 1911, William Hesketh Lever established one of the first plantations owned by a foreign company in Africa. W.H. Lever was the dominant force behind Lever Brothers — now Unilever, the world's biggest food business.* Since the turn of the century, Lever had been determined to secure control of palm oil supplies for the company's Port Sunlight soap factories, and about ten years later signed a contract with the Belgian colonial authority to develop plantations in the Congo (now Zaire). Lever Bros. established a subsidiary, Société Anonyme des Huileries du Congo Belge (HCB), which was given the right to choose 74,000 hectares of palm-bearing land, and rights to an additional 200,000 hectares after ten years. under the terms of this agreement, HCB could take over a maximum of 750,000 hectares of freehold property after 25 years.[16] This land was appropriated for Lever from the local population, although some was deserted at the time as a result of the massive depopulation of the Congo under Belgian rule. In contrast to the impoverishment of the Congolese, Lever Bros. flourished, later adding plantations in Ghana, Nigeria, Cameroon and Gabon and extending its interests into coffee, tea and cocoa production. Through its various subsidiaries, it became the major plantation company in Africa.

The advantages of controlling agricultural supplies had to be offset against the costs of establishing plantations. These costs are high and it takes some time to see a return on investment: 3-4 years for palm oil or tea, 5 years for coffee, up to 10 years for cocoa. But the negligible cost of land; the minimum wages paid for labour; and the low running costs of established estates, meant that they still represented a cheap source of supply. With such favourable terms, the companies could only benefit. For example, in 1926, the Firestone Rubber Company signed a concession with the Liberian government for *one million acres* at a rate of $0.04 cents per acre developed. Firestone brought 80,000 acres into producton to form the largest single rubber plantation in the world,[17] and

*See Unilever company profile.

Liberia became so dependent on the company that it was for many years known as the 'Firestone Republic'. Even so, Liberia gained little from its resources.

"In 1927, to pay off Liberia's existing debts, the government concluded the infamous loan agreement with a Firestone subsidiary, the Finance Corporation of America. Only half the loan, for up to $5 million over 40 years at 7 per cent interest, was ever issued; but service charges and advisers' salaries cost over $270,000 a year which was 20 per cent of government revenues in 1928 and 50 per cent in 1931."[18]

Plantation agriculture in Africa expanded as more companies sought to control the total production process by not only manufacturing, marketing and distributing a product, but also growing the crop. For example, tea became a major plantation crop in Africa when, in the early 1920s Brooke Bond Ltd set up the first such plantation in Kenya. Brooke Bond has established tea plantations in India, Pakistan and Ceylon (Sri Lanka) at about the same time as Unilever opened its oil palm plantations in the Congo, and now sought to diversify its sources of supply even further with seeds smuggled out of India.[19] The company later added plantations in Uganda, Tanzania and Malawi. Other British companies also dominated the tea trade and they quickly followed Brooke Bond in establishing tea plantations in Africa. These include: James Finlay group (Kenya); Walter Duncan & Goodricke (Malawi) and its subsidiary Eastern Produce (Kenya and Malawi); Warren Plantations (Kenya); George Williamson (Kenya and Malawi); McLeod Russell (Zimbabwe); Inchcape (Kenya); Mitchell Cotts (Kenya and Uganda); Unilever (Nigeria and Zaire).[20]

Companies setting up plantations were seeking to supply the lucrative European markets, but some companies also foresaw the scope for expanding sales in Africa itself. Brooke Bond actively promoted tea drinking within Kenya, and opened a sales office in Mombasa in 1928. Six years later Brooke Bond was supplying all Kenya's teas and had succeeded in making it the most popular drink in the country.* New patterns of concentration emerged as companies sought to dominate African markets and tightened their grip on trade. Unilever's interests increasingly extended beyond plantations, as it built up, or took over, a network of subsidiary companies, which imported and distributed a wide range of goods, not only their own products. In 1920 they bought the Royal Niger Company, and in 1929 combined 37 firms into the United African Company, "henceforth a giant which colonial governments, as was remarked by a British economist in the 1940s, were quite powerless to deal with . . . by 1936 the United Africa company had more than 56 per cent of all Nigerian exports of palm-oil and kernels, cocoa and

---

*In fact, Brooke Bond retained this local monopoly right up to the 1970s when local sales were eventually taken over by the Kenya Government.

peanuts."[21] In the more prosperous countries with large markets, such as Nigeria, Unilever also opened soap manufacturing subsidiaries, using local palm oil supplies. Unilever in particular has benefited greatly from its central position in African trade:

"Africa is now a market . . . for all kinds of goods, from frozen peas (Birds Eye, Unilever subsidiary), to motor cars. Unilever's centre of gravity lies in Europe, but far and away its largest member (the UAC)* is almost wholly dependent for its livelihood . . . on the well-being of West Africa."[22]

In the tradition established by the mining and concession companies, thousands of men were drawn to work on plantations. Once again, women shouldered alone the major responsibility for growing food, caring for the elderly and bringing up children. As farmers the families may have been poor, but were broadly self-sufficient.[23] They now became dependent labourers, receiving low wages from the plantation companies which justified this on the basis that the workers did not have families to support. This meant that the labour of women and children on the land subsidised the low wages that companies paid to workers on the plantations (a practice which still continues today).[24] Meanwhile, the constant flow of workers off the land made it more difficult to farm adequately, as well as creating other social pressures. An official report of 1935 on the consequences of migrant labour in Nyasaland (Malawi) stated:

"The whole fabric of the old order of society is undermined, when 30 to 60 per cent of the able-bodied men are absent at one time . . . Emigration (i.e. labour migration), which destroys the old, offers nothing to take its place, and the family community is threatened with complete dissolution."[25]

The Post-Colonial State and Plantations

In 1957, Ghana was the first African country to win independence and by the mid-1960s most colonies had followed, with the exception of the Portuguese colonies and southern Africa. In the colonial period African resources of land and labour had been exploited for European demands, for example growing luxury crops like tea, coffee, cocoa and cotton, often building whole economies on one crop such as sisal in Tanzania. In general, Europe's needs prevailed. There was, for example, a huge shortage of vegetable oils in Europe after the Second World War and large tracts of the Dodoma region of Tanzania were planted with groundnuts, under a highly mechanised system, to meet the shortage. Little was known of delicate tropical soils, the effect of heavy machinery, the difficulties of maintenance, or of local conditions, and the scheme was totally ineffective and destroyed the soil for many years. With few

*Previously United Africa Company, now UAC International Ltd.

exceptions, African needs for food, housing, education and management training were neglected.[26]

Independent African governments faced the problem of ensuring that before wealth was drained from their countries it was first shared more equally among the labour which created it. Could a politically independent state wrest economic power from the foreign companies which continued to control their export crops? The strategies open to independent governments were limited and experience soon showed that measures to acquire immediate control by nationalisation led to retaliation from the companies involved. Most countries opted for more modest legal and financial controls, for example laws governing the amount of foreign exchange a company could export, tighter fiscal measures, or the compulsory acquisition of local shareholdings. These measures did not drive the companies out — nor were they particularly intended to do so, for the companies were by now crucial to many African economies. The measures were intended to assert more local control, but did not succeed in aligning the companies' aims and interests with those of the newly independent states.

For example, Sena Sugar Estates in Mozambique, a plantation company based in the United Kingdom and Portugal, dropped production steadily after Independence in 1974, having made healthy profits up to this time. It then ran up debts with the Bank of Mozambique, the US Eximbank and the South African Industrial Development Corporation. The company claimed that its losses were solely due to the low sugar prices then prevailing. However the Mozambique government was sceptical, particularly when it discovered that the company had left 70 per cent of its 1977 cane crop unharvested.[27] Such an action is in fact not uncommon, since companies may well not find it profitable to harvest a crop in a particular year, despite the fact that from the government's point of view harvesting and exporting the crop may be essential for employment or foreign exchange purposes.

The larger companies have much greater economic strength and more powerful friends than the governments of the countries where they operate. Even governments sympathetic to foreign investment, such as that of President Mobutu in Zaire, cannot direct the activities of such companies to their entire satisfaction. The story of the oil palm plantations in Zaire illustrated one such conflict of interests and its outcome.

Oil Palm Plantations in Zaire

The oil palm tree is native to Zaire and is an important local product, used in cooking and food preparation. After Independence the plantation companies ran down their estates to a point where, in 1978, a

World Bank report found that the country would be importing palm oil within 12 years unless the local industry was revived.[28] Until Independence, these companies had been free to take profits out of the country without interference from foreign exchange controls. Were they unable — as they maintain — or merely unwilling to maintain investment levels and prevent the decline of the palm oil industry?

Zaire attained Independence in 1960 when the Belgians conceded free elections and immediate independence, hoping to retain their vast economic interests.[29] After Independence, however, Zaire was far from a stable country: it had been devastated by years of brutal exploitation, both physical and financial, and from 1964 to 1966 internal struggles for political control culminated in large-scale uprisings. Mobutu took control in an army coup in 1965 and has ruled the country since, showing more sympathy to foreign investors than to Zairean workers and peasants.* However, the 1960s did not provide a favourable investment climate and Unilever, for example, vacated many of its estates temporarily during this period.[30] At the same time, Unilever further increased its investments in Malaysian palm oil plantations. The geographic climate was more suitable and the political climate less explosive than in Zaire. Palm oil production in Malaysia rose from an average yearly production of 120,400 tons between 1961 and 1965 to 620,000 tons in 1970.[31] Production of palm oil on Zaire's commercial estates declined steadily from 240,000 tons in 1959 and by 1976 amounted to only 125,000 tons a year,[32] a reflection of the companies' reluctance to invest in the Zairean plantations.

In 1973, the Zaire government attempted to revive the neglected palm oil industry and took over the commercial estates from the companies. The companies did not co-operate and there was insufficient local technical or managerial expertise to run the plantations, despite the fact that 60 years had now passed since the first plantation (Unilever's) was established. Nor did Zaire have the capital necessary to invest in a rehabilitation programme and in 1975 the plantations were handed back to the original owners with the proviso that 40 per cent of the shares were transferred to local interests, still leaving the companies with a controlling stake.[33]

In 1976, alarmed by the deteriorating state of the plantations and the prospect of importing palm oil, the government formulated a 'Plan d'Urgence', focusing on rehabilitating these commercial oil palm plantations. The Plan carried no reference to such alternatives as small scale peasant production. Also in 1976, a World Bank official proposed an 'Oil Palm Development Project'[34] and, at the request of the

*Mobutu is reputedly one of the richest men in the world, with his personal fortune amounting to around £100 million.

government, asked three major companies, representing two-thirds of Zaire's commercial oil palm industry, to draw up plans for rehabilitating their existing plantations. These companies were:[35]

> *Plantations Lever du Zaire* (PLZ) (Unilever subsidiary), with four palm plantations in the Northern Equator and Haut Zaire regions and three in the Bandundu region. It cultivates some 34,000 hectares of oil palm as well as 12,000 hectares of rubber, cocoa and tea. The company wanted to close or sell off its Bandundu plantations, which were less suitable for new high yielding varieties of palm.
>
> *Compagnie de Commerce et de Plantations* (CCP) (a subsidiary of OLFICA). CCP grows about 4,300 hectares in the Equateur region and operates four mills in Bandundu for fruit collected from natural palm groves.
>
> *Enterprises Agricoles et Industrielles de la Busira au Lomami* (BUSIRA) (a subsidiary of AGRICOM). In the pre-independence years, BUSIRA had cultivated about 13,000 hectares of oil palm in what was considered to be the most productive land in Zaire. However, the company neglected production in the mid-1960s and in 1978 was cultivating only 3,800 hectares of palm, along with plantations of rubber (4,300 hectares) and coffee (400 hectares).
>
> Both OLFICA and AGRICOM are in turn subsidiaries of the Belgian holding company, Compagnie Generale, which has extensive interests in Zaire.

The World Bank accepted the companies' report, without alteration, for the palm oil rehabilitation project, and made it an official Bank document after a meeting in Paris in December 1977. Although the Bank is not permitted to lend money to private companies by its constitution, it accepted the companies' investment proposals and negotiated the terms of a loan with representatives of the three companies, as well as Mr Mukendi, Director General of the Zairean Department of Agriculture and the other three development financing organisations, the African Development Fund (ADF), the Arab aid bank BADEA (Banque Arabe pour le Developpement Economique en Afrique) and Caisse Central de Co-operation Economique (CCCE). A loan was then arranged with the International Development Agency, the World Bank's soft loans division, which provides finance on more favourable terms than the Bank itself. Repayments were to be over 15 years, including a 5-year period of grace and the interest rate was set at 10 per cent per annum. To comply with its constitution, the IDA contribution of $9 million to the palm oil rehabilitation project was formally lent to the government, which in turn lent it on to the companies. Of the total project cost, amounting to US $47.4 milion, US $23.7 million was lent by aid-giving agencies (the contribution from ADF, BADEA and CCCE totalling US $14.7 million).

The companies' total financial contribution amounted to 44 per cent of the project, or US $21 million. However, under the terms agreed, this capital was able to be entirely raised from within Zaire, with the result that local resources which might otherwise have been lent to Zaireans were diverted to foreign companies. Consequently one of the political advantages of involving foreign companies in a project — their ability to provide overseas capital — was eliminated at the request of the companies themselves.

Before agreeing to participate in the project, the companies negotiated a number of highly favourable terms, for example:[36]

* Taxes on imports needed for the project were to be waived;
* Companies were to be allowed to buy all the foreign exchange necessary to operate their existing oil palm plantations and installations efficiently;
* Non-Zairean nationals were to be allowed to remit abroad as much of their salaries as was needed to attract them (a further drain on foreign exchange);
* If one of the companies withdrew support for the seed development element in the project, the government was obliged to guarantee to meet the demand for good quality seeds;
* Smallholder cultivation schemes were to be established adjacent to the plantations to help 'attract and retain sufficient labour *by supplementing wage income with food crops and livestock'* (our italics), and the cost of this was to be borne by the government.

The final point is particularly revealing, as it is made clear throughout the World Bank report that the working conditions on the plantations were such that the companies had found it virtually impossible to attract sufficient labour and their recurring worry was that the project would fail for lack of labour. Nevertheless, the companies were not prepared to raise wages substantially and the government agreed to subsidise this scheme to the extent of US $2.4 million. This continues a long tradition in Africa, whereby foreign investors use unpaid labour in the subsistence farming sector to supplement low wages, in this case with the formal support of the government.

In effect, oil palm plantation companies in Zaire first ran down their estates and then virtually wrote their own terms for reviving the industry. Funds from the world's largest development agency, the World Bank, were made available for the revival of plantation agriculture under foreign control. While this was possible because Mobutu and the Zaire government were prepared to support the companies, in this case the government agreed to do so only after they had failed to enlist the companies' co-operation in reviving a nationalised palm oil industry.

Retaining Plantation Interests

While plantations remain profitable, companies are unlikely to relinquish control unless forced to do so. They still represent the ultimate in vertical integration and many transnationals believe that 'the only way to be in the market 52 weeks a year is to control your production'.[37]

Plantations require less new investment than manufacturing or distribution divisions, and generally have a high profit to turnover ratio. In 1978, for example — admittedly a year of peak prices for coffee and tea — Brooke Bond made a profit of £23 million on a turnover of £799 million in its trading, manufacturing and distribution activities, whereas it made almost the same amount, £20.6 million, on a turnover of only £43.8 million in its plantation activities.[38]

In general, companies do not report in detail on their plantation interests and activities and it is difficult — if not impossible — to obtain a comprehensive picture of the remaining privately controlled plantations in Africa, although some of these are set out in Table 1.1. It is quite possible that direct investment is now less than during the colonial period, although this is not always clear. For example, in 1961 Unilever owned a total of about 87,000 hectares of plantations in Africa (Cameroon, Gabon, Ghana, Nigeria, Zaire) and Asia (Malaya and the Solomon Islands).[39] The company now owns 90,000 hectares of plantations, divided between Asia and four African countries: Cameroon, Ghana, Nigeria and Zaire.[40]

In some African countries (for example, Zaire, Ivory Coast, Swaziland, Liberia, Malawi and Mauritius) there has been no fundamental political objection from the government to the production of cash crops by foreign companies. However, this is not the case in other independent African countries, where governments have responded by nationalising plantation companies, by taking a majority interest, or by adopting more limited policies as in Kenya, where further expansion of agribusiness plantations has been restricted. As is shown below, undoubtedly the trend is for companies to move away from direct investment and into estate management.

Curbing the expansion of foreign-owned plantations has the advantage that the exodus of foreign capital and expertise can be limited, while the government can concentrate on supporting smallholder schemes for growing the cash crops on which the country has become dependent. This strategy has been applied to major African cash crops such as tea, coffee and cocoa where local knowledge of production and marketing exists. For example, Kenya, Tanzania and Ivory Coast have established authorities with responsibility for these crops, and gained a great deal of knowledge and expertise in both production and marketing, so becoming less dependent on foreign companies for these aspects of production. In Kenya, the government allowed plantation companies such as Brooke Bond, Finlays and Socfinaf (a French-owned company growing coffee) to continue estate production on land held at independence. At the same time, smallholder coffee and tea production received investment and encouragement from government schemes.

There are, however, an increasing number of 'new' agricultural

Table 1.1

Selected Transnationals with Controlling Interest in Plantations in Africa 1980

Company	Crops	Countries	Other details
Brooke Bond Liebig, UK	Tea, coffee, flowers, vegetables, tara, cinchona, cattle ranches	Kenya, Malawi, Tanzania, Zimbabwe	
Cadbury Schweppes, UK	Cocoa	Cameroon	600 ha. In general Cadbury's buys rather than grows its cocoa requirements.
Eastern Produce UK.	Tea	Kenya, Malawi	
James Finlay & Co, UK	Tea	Kenya	
Firestone Rubber, USA	Rubber	Ghana, Liberia	24,000 ha in Ghana now the largest private rubber plantation in the world
HVA, Netherlands	Sugar, palm kernels, rubber, palm oil	Nigeria, Zaire, Kenya	Also has plantations growing natural fibres, cassava, fruit, vegetables, coffee, rubber, tobacco.
Inchcape & Co. Ltd., UK.	Tea	Kenya	
Libby's (Nestlé) Switzerland	Pineapples	Swaziland	
Lonrho Ltd., UK	Tea, sugar, food crops and livestock, coffee, timber, tobacco, wattle	Kenya, Malawi, Mauritius, Zambia, Zimbabwe	
Mitchell Cotts Ltd.,UK.	Tea, cotton, pyrethrum, coffee, dairy farms	Kenya, Uganda	
R.J. Reynolds	Pineapples	Kenya	
Rivaud Group & Cie Financière pour l'Outre Mer, France	Rubber and palm oil	Cameroon	
Socfinaf Co. Ltd., France	Coffee	Kenya	
Tate & Lyle, UK	Sugar	Zimbabwe	Manages numerous other estates
Unilever, UK/Nld	Palm kernels, palm oil, tea, cocoa, copra, rubber	Cameroon, Ghana Nigeria, Zaire	66% of all plantations grow palm oil.
United Brands, USA	Bananas	Cameroon, Ivory Coast, Somalia	
Warren Plantations Holdings Ltd., UK	Tea, coffee, rubber	Kenya, Nigeria	

Sources: Annual Reports, company information, various articles.

markets. In Europe, the demand for tropical fruits, and off-season fresh fruit, vegetables and flowers is booming. Foreign companies once again dominate the production of crops for this specialised market.

Plantations: the New Luxury Crops

The production and export of some fresh produce is far from new: bananas are a long-standing plantation crop and are one of the five most important exports from poor countries. Three US conglomerates dominate the market, sharing 61 per cent of the world banana trade. These are United Brands (29 per cent), Castle & Cooke (19 per cent), and Del Monte (13 per cent).[41] United Brands has plantations in Ivory Coast, Cameroon and Somalia and in Somalia bananas are a major foreign exchange earner.* However, African bananas form an insignificant proportion of the world trade.

In the 1960s, transnationals began to enter the pineapple industry on a large scale, when the three leading firms, Del Monte, Castle & Cooke and Nestlé stepped up their activities in the Third World. The most important industry growth in Africa took place in Kenya (Del Monte) Swaziland (Nestlé's) and in the Ivory Coast (a French company, SCOA) and the story of Del Monte's interests in Kenya is examined in Chapter 4.

Since the early 1960s transnationals have also acquired substantial interests in the fruit and vegetable processing industries of under-developed countries. Thirty-three leading food processing firms now have more than 140 investments in fruit and vegetable processing concerns, serving both export and local markets. In Africa, these investments are to be found in Benin, Angola, Uganda, Liberia, Ivory Coast, Senegal, Zambia, Tanzania, Ghana, Zimbabwe, Kenya and Nigeria.[42] Their presence in the processing industry has led several companies to expand into the market — the production of fresh horticultural products for consumption in Europe and North America. At present, industrial countries import about 90 per cent of all traded horticultural products, of which Third World countries ship 30-40 per cent. Trade is dominated by citrus fruits, potatoes and tomatoes, but in Africa an increasing amount of land is being cultivated to supply European markets with a variety of fresh flowers and out-of-season vegetables and fruit — either dried or flown fresh.

In such non-traditional crops, foreign companies dominate. In Kenya, Brooke Bond responded to regulations encouraging local re-investment of profits and preventing further enlargement of its tea and coffee plantations, by expanding into this market. In 1978, Brooke Bond Kenya

---

*In 1977, the United Brands plantation in Somalia paid its workers US$0.67 per day, a lower rate than on any of its other plantations. Workers on the company's Ivory Coast plantations received US $1.87 a day, and in Cameroon US $1.60 a day.

took over the Sulmac Company from a Danish firm which had established this business, growing vegetables as well as flowers (carnations, chrysanthemums and ferns) for flying fresh to Europe. The activities of this subsidiary are examined in more detail in Chapter 4. European and US companies without a tradition of investing in African plantations are also expanding into these markets.

Two examples are typical, that of Bruecker Werker in Kenya, and Castle & Cooke in Senegal.

Pan African Vegetable Products

Pan African Vegetable Products is a company set up by the Bruecker Werker company of West Germany, with part of the equity held by Barclays Overseas Development Company, the Industrial Co-operative Development Corporation (ICDC) of Kenya, the Industrial Development Bank, and the Safida Investment Company of Switzerland. The company grows carrots, turnips, beans, leeks, potatoes, dill, red and savoy cabbages, capsicum, swedes and celery. The vegetables are dehydrated and sent to West Germany and other European countries at the rate of 36,000 tons a year. The company itself owns one farm and leases another, cultivating over 800 acres of irrigated crops, or half the vegetables required. The other half are supplied by more than 5000 outgrowers. These growers depend totally on the company: it approves and provides seeds, pesticides and herbicides to listed growers on a credit basis, against the crops being grown for the factory. Over 90 per cent of the factory's production is exported[43] and it runs all year round, working six days a week, 24 hours a day, employing between 450 and 650 people, depending on the season.

Because the ICDC has a shareholding in the venture, the company was able to raise local funds to operate. The Commercial Bank of Africa, which must, under government regulations, reserve 17 per cent of its loans for agriculture, financed *all* the company's working capital through overdraft facilities and also guaranteed a long-term loan in 1975.[44] While it is true that the Kenya government is encouraging export-oriented industries, the Kenyan banks have demonstrated more willingness to use limited local resources to capitalise foreign expertise than to finance indigenous enterprise.

Bud Senegal

In 1972, Bud Antle Inc., a large California-based food conglomerate (taken over in 1978 by Castle & Cooke, a US transnational with plantations in Latin America and Asia) formed a joint enterprise with the Senegalese government. The subsidiary, Bud Senegal, is an affiliate of the House of Bud in Brussels.

Bud Senegal grew vegetables using a virtually labour-free drip irrigation system, with plastic tubes continuously supplying water to each plant individualy, tapping the vast reserves of water just below Senegal's dry soil.[45] Three times a week, from early December until May, a DC-10 cargo jet would take off from Senegal loaded with green beans, melons, tomatoes, aubergines, strawberries and paprika. the destinations were Amsterdam, Paris, Stockholm. The vegetables were not marketed locally, but in any event most Senegalese do not have enough money to buy them. One year, green bean prices in Europe dropped below the cost of picking, packaging and air freighting Bud's big crop. But this did not mean cheap green beans for the Senegalese: the company destroyed the entire crop.[46] In 1974, as the Senegalese starved in the middle of one of the worst droughts for decades, European governments reacted to a vegetable glut at home by buying up and destroying over £53 million worth of vegetable products.[47]

Local people gained few jobs from the project, and in laying out its 450 hectare plantation, Bud uprooted the indigenous baobab trees which were an important village resource, having previously provided local families with rope, planting materials, fuel and wind erosion protection. Other villagers fared even worse: the government provided police to evict them from their land to make way for Bud's plantation.[48]

Undertakings such as this are regarded by overseas aid agencies as 'development', and qualify for 'soft' loans, so that agribusiness firms need to use virtually none of their own capital (as in the palm oil rehabilitation project in Zaire). Finance for Bud Senegal was provided by the World Bank and Swiss and Dutch development funds, as well as the Senegalese government, which was a stockholder. The project was taken over by the Senegalese government in 1976, when the project ran into financial difficulties. By this stage the project had virtually failed, and the government was left with eroded soil and imported machinery which could not be maintained. Although the state could attempt to grow vegetables, the transport and marketing networks were out of its control, and transport had been a persistent problem.[49] In 1979, the government could no longer maintain the project, and the company closed completely. Meanwhile, Castle and Cooke has moved into Gambia, Nigeria, Ivory Coast and Mali, and announced plans to expand into the rest of Africa.

In Senegal in 1979, Kissinger called for a multi-million dollar anti-hunger programme to 'roll back the desert'.[50] This project attempted to do so, but in using high technology to produce export crops it has done almost nothing to alleviate hunger.

The market for fresh flowers, fresh fruit and vegetables may never reach the scale of the traditional African exports of coffee, tea, cotton and so on, but nevertheless contributes to the constant pressure to develop African agriculture to meet overseas requirements. On the other hand more African countries are asserting control over their traditional agricultural export industries, through smallholder developments or joint ventures in plantation agriculture, but they continue to have little influence over the marketing and distribution of the products.

Controlling the Crops

The companies are in a powerful position to control the crops on which Africa depends. Their control comes not primarily from owning plantations, but from their vertical integration, which stretches across the whole production process. A plantation subsidiary may make less profit when prices are low, but this is only one element of a transnational's total operations. The companies derive their strength and most of their profits not from producing commodities, but from processing, trading, transport, marketing and distributing activities.

A quick glance through those companies which grow crops in Africa reveals the full extent of this integration. The range of subsidiaries covers businesses of almost every kind: management and consultancy companies; processing factories and mills (most of the tea, palm oil and sugar companies own their own factories or mills, e.g. the Dalgety subsidiary Spillers owns flour mills in Zimbabwe and Zambia); buying organisations, auctioneers and brokers (nearly all transnationals have a broking and/or buying subsidiary); shipping companies (Unilever's Pamol Line, Tate & Lyle, Booker Line, Gill & Duffus, Lonrho's 'Watergate' Line); insurance; fertiliser, pesticide and seed subsidiaries; animal feedstuffs; agricultural machinery supplies or distribution agencies (Unilever, Lonrho); packaging; shopkeeping (Unilever, Lonhro, Booker McConnell); engineering (Tate & Lyle, Booker McConnell, Unilever); licensing and trademarks (all companies with brand names only allow these to be used under licence and charge for the use of trade names); export and import companies; merchant bankers (Finlays and Guiness Peat International); research groups (nearly all transnationals have their own research organisations, especially the big oil and chemical companies, e.g. ICI, Shell, Hoechst and Ciba-Geigy, which are deriving a growing percentage of their profits from agribusiness); warehousing; marketing and distribution (including retail outlets in industrialised countries).

Looking at the crops which are important to Africa, Table 1.2 shows that the position which a few major companies occupy on the world market has far-reaching implications for the bargaining power of producing countries. Just four major corporations (Gill & Duffus, Cadbury-Schweppes, Nestlés and Rowntree) control 60-80 per cent of

Table 1.2

Transnationals Which Dominate The World Market In Africa's Most Important Crops

Crop	Company/Companies	Comments and Details
Cocoa	Cadbury-Schweppes, Nestles, Gill & Duffus, Rowntree	These four companies control 60-80% of world cocoa sales.
Tea	Brooke Bond, Unilever, Cadbury-Schweppes J. Lyons (now Allied Breweries subsidiary), Nestle's (all European) and Standard Brands, Kellogg's, Coca Cola (all USA)	Jointly hold about 90% of tea marketed in Western Europe and North America
Coffee	Nestle, General Foods	Jointly hold around 20% of the world market.
Sugar	Tate & Lyle	This company buys about 95% of cane sugar imported into the EEC, although the market is threatened by European beet sugar.
Molasses	Tate & Lyle	The company's subsidiary, United Molasses Co., controls 40% of world trade.
Palm Oil	Unilever UK/Nld, and Lesieur, French	Unilever dominates trade in palm oil.
Tobacco	BAT (UK), R.J. Reynolds (USA), Phillip Morris (USA), Imperial Group (UK), American Brands (USA), Rothmans (UK/South African)	Together control between 89%-95% of world leaf tobacco trade
Cotton	Velkart, Cargill, Bunge Ralli Brothers (all USA), Soga Shosho (Japan), Bambax, Blanchard	Are major transnationals in the cotton trade, and together with nine other multi-commodity trading groups they dominate 85-90% of world cotton trade.

Sources: UN Centre on Transnational Corporations report, F. Clairmonte in the *Guardian,* 13.8.79, Mike Muller, *Tobacco and the Third World: Tomorrow's Epidemic,* various company Annual Reports and company publications; Fibres & Textiles, Dimension of Corporate Marketing Structure, UN 1981–, TD/B/C.1/219.

cocoa sales.[51] Five European firms (Brooke Bond, Unilever, Cadbury-Schweppes, Nestlés and the Allied Breweries subsidiary J. Lyons) and three US-based processors (Standard Brands, Kellogg's and Coca Cola) are jointly responsible for about 90 per cent of tea marketed in Western Europe and North America.[52] Although there are few coffee plantations in Africa, it being largely a smallholder crop, Nestlé and General Foods are the world's major coffee buyers, and together hold around 20 per cent of the world market. Altogether, the eight largest coffee processors control around 55-60 per cent of world sales.*[53] Tate & Lyle's subsidiary, United Molasses Co., controls 40 per cent of the world molasses trade[54] and almost all cane sugar coming into Britain is purchased by Tate & Lyle.** Unilever dominates the world trade in palm oil and controls one-third of world margarine and table oil sales. The French company, Lesieur, is also an important trader, particularly in Africa. Between them, Unilever and Lesieur dominate the palm oil industry in the major African producing countries of Cameroon, Gabon, Ghana, Kenya, Liberia, Malawi, Nigeria, Senegal and Zaire.[55] Six transnational leaf-buying companies control 80-95 per cent of the international leaf tobacco trade.[56] The cotton trade is only slightly more diverse, 15 commodity trading groups dominate 85-90 per cent of the market. The major companies also trade in other commodities, eg. Velkart in coffee, Cargill and Bunge in grains, Ralli Brothers in tropical hardwoods, grain, coffee, tea, rubber, metals and hard and soft fibres, and Soga Shosho in many commodities, in both manufactured and raw material form. The New York Cotton Exchange is the major market place, and this futures market, through its hedgers and speculators, is an important determinant of price.[57]

As African governments introduce controls on foreign ownership of agricultural land and seek to own, or encourage smallholders to produce the export crops, the dominance of big foreign companies over the market means that these companies can adapt and usually profit from the changes. Some big companies feel that it is better to let others take the risk involved in growing crops and that it is more profitable to trade in commodities than to grow them. Tate & Lyle has increasingly moved in this direction. Low or fluctuating commodity prices are an incentive to manage rather than own estates, concentrating on selling commodities and 'collecting juicy commissions', as one financial writer on plantations expressed it.[58] It is a marked trend in Africa, when ownership is transferred to local interests, to maintain influence and a degree of control through technical, service and management agreements.

*See Chapter 2, Coffee.
**See Chapter 3, Sugar.

Management and Service Contracts and Consultancies

Although many newly independent African governments nationalised or acquired a majority shareholding in foreign companies operating within their territory, they had neither the knowledge nor the expertise to run the companies or the estates. Management posts were preserved by the foreign companies for Europeans and, although after Independence many jobs slowly became Africanised, the companies were careful to retain European staff in essential positions (it is said that the last job to be Africanised is always the post of accountant). European directors were retained on the board, and only those Africans who had proved their loyalty to the company, or their sympathy to foreign investment, were appointed to management positions. African governments therefore needed the companies' management expertise and knowledge of the industry. Tanzania, for example, was careful to pay full compensation for nationalisation so that companies would not be antagonised and withdraw their management.

Sugar in particular is being 'developed' in Africa by using transnational consultancies and management contracts.* The companies, particularly Tate & Lyle, Booker McConnell and Lonhro, manage several sugar estates (some of which were previously owned outright by the companies) in which the government now has a majority shareholding. In other sugar estates the same companies have little or no direct stake, but provide management services under contract. Under this system, they influence the development of an estate, and are in a strong position to use inputs (e.g. factory and irrigation equipment) from their own UK-based subsidiaries. A number of foreign companies now manage estates growing food crops, since several African governments have been persuaded to devote considerable resources to the development of large-scale food production rather than be reliant on peasant farmers. Tate & Lyle and the giant South African company, Anglo American Corporation, both manage food crop farms in Zambia, for example. Table 1.3 sets out some other companies with management contracts in Africa.

Management or service fees may include a percentage of profits. But it is important to realise that while profits must be distributed on a *pro rata* basis between various shareholders, the service fees go only to the company. Both management and service fees remain a fixed obligation, payable to the parent company and able to be remitted out of the country free of foreign exchange controls. In contrast, profits on agricultural production fluctuate and are subject either to taxation, or to controls designed to encourage local investments.

It is important for big companies to retain control of their capital and to move it to areas of most efficient and profitable investment. In

* See Chapter 3, Sugar.

Table 1.3

Selected Transnational Corporations Managing Agricultural Schemes in Africa (as at 1981)

Company	Country/ Countries	Projects
Anglo-American Corp (S.Africa)	Zambia	Food crop management.
Booker McConnell Ltd, (UK)	Kenya, Nigeria, Senegal, Somalia	Mostly sugar, but developing expertise in a wide range of crops. (See Table 3.5).
Dalgety (UK)	Liberia	Rice development; with the UK construction company Taylor Woodrow Ltd, are expanding their management interests.
Guinness Peat International (UK)	Sudan, Liberia	Select livestock fattening and processing project in Sudan. Fattens cattle and sheep for slaughter and export to the Middle East; in Liberia the company manages a rubber processing factory.
HVA International (Netherlands)	Ethiopia, Ghana, Tanzania, Kenya, Nigeria, Sudan	Mainly in sugar, but also manages tea estates and factories in Kenya and palm kernel extraction in Nigeria.
Lonrho Ltd (UK)	Ivory Coast, Malawi, Zambia	Various sugar development schemes in Zambia, and 2 large schemes producing cotton, soya beans and wheat.
Mitchell Cotts Ltd, (UK)	Ethiopia, Kenya	Cotton, tea, cattle fattening.
Tate & Lyle (UK)	Ghana, Ivory Coast, Swaziland, Zambia	Mostly sugar, but developing management of a wide range of crops. (See Table 3.4).
Taylor Woodrow (UK)		(See Dalgety).
Technisucre (France)	Ivory Coast, Kenya	Mainly sugar.

Source: Annual Reports, various magazine and newspaper articles.

general, managements dislike any controls over where their profits must be reinvested. To avoid this, it appears that many companies operating in Africa try wherever possible to minimise their profits and channel their surpluses into remittable fees, thus escaping taxation and other controls.

The table below compares the trends in the after-tax profits and service fees of the two Kenyan subsidiaries of foreign-owned companies. The first, CPC Kenya, is concerned with the production of cooking oils and has a US patent. The second, Food Specialties, is a subsidiary of Nestlé.

	1972 £	1973 £	1974 £	1975 £	1976 £
CPC Kenya					
After-tax					
profits	11,755	22,165	(3,130)	(35,525)	(8,693)
Service Fees	1,472	8,788	8,952	7,933	7,380
Food Specialties					
After-tax					
profits	50,149	12,407	66,193	(178,045)	197,084
Service Fees	111,250	189,873	120,978	N/A	170,630

( ) means after-tax loss.

Source: Personal communication to the authors.

Management, service and technical fees drain surpluses away from the host country, and often prolong dependency on foreign inputs, foreign expertise and foreign markets (because of the export-orientation of most companies). But from a government's point of view, such agreements frequently are the most convenient means of exploiting domestic agricultural resources.

Estate management allows agribusiness to tie up sources of supply without tying up capital in ownership. Because the State typically either owns or holds a majority interest in the developments concerned, it is eligible for funding from aid agencies, and in this way cheap finance is funnelled into the production of export crops. Since the estate is now a national enterprise, the government pays for infrastructure such as roads, housing for labour, etc, even if this investment is of more benefit to the export market than to the local population.

Some companies are involved in management agreements and consultancies on a massive scale. Tenneco is a highly diversified US company, the subsidiaries of which market chemicals, oil, pipelines and farm equipment (David Brown), and off land-management and packaging services. Among other projects, it is involved in a major agricultural development scheme in Sudan, which aims at developing a plan covering Sudanese crop selection, irrigation construction, care and feeding of farm workers and crop marketing strategies. The scheme is intended to start by bringing 250,000 acres into production, later to be exanded to 750,000 acres over 15 years, at a cost of about US $1 billion.

However, Tenneco will not supply the capital: it is encouraging Sudan to establish a national development corporation and to employ the company as management consultants. Tenneco's Executive Vice-President, S.T. Ellis, foresees that the company could make a lot more money in this way, as well as opening to itself a huge market: 'the hope of feeding the Arab world'.[59]

Consultancies, rather than the direct management of agricultural enterprises, are becoming an increasingly common and profitable way of influencing the development of African agriculture, providing companies with a convenient opportunity to set a style of development which matches their own interests. Usually, this means large-scale developments, whether on an estate basis (owned by the State or a State corporation), or through outgrower schemes, where farmers are provided with the necessary inputs (on credit) and grow the crop themselves on their own land. A centralised factory (either with or without a 'nucleus' estate) generally processes the crop.

Many large agribusiness transnationals have subsidiaries operating as agricultural consultants, for example:
* Unifeeds International Ltd (Unilever).
* International Crop Protection Consultants (ICI).
* Shell Agriculture International.
* Tate & Lyle Agribusiness Ltd.
* Adra (Renault).
* Mitchell Cotts Agricultural Service.
* Dalgety (apart from its Spillers subsidiaries, the company is involved in Africa almost entirely through management and consultancies).
* Taylor Woodrow (although mainly a construction and engineering company, it increasingly works on a consultancy basis with other agribusiness companies in Africa, e.g. on a Liberian rice scheme with Dalgety, and a sugar project in Ghana with Tate & Lyle).
* HVA International (Dutch agribusiness group, particularly involved in sugar, with 90 per cent of its income coming from Africa).
* Imperial Foods International Technical Services (Imperial Group).

There is also a large number of specialist consultancies with an orientation to African agriculture. These include MacDonald & Partners (UK), irrigation consultant engineers, responsible for numerous agricultural projects in Africa, particularly covering dam building and irrigation aspects; and Minster Agriculture, which also has major agricultural consultancies such as an oilseed development scheme in Sierra Leone for the production of groundnuts and related crops.

Unquestionably, advantages accrue to agribusiness operations through such consultancies, as well as through the adoption of Western styles of agricultural development, which depend on inputs supplied mostly by the companies. Many of the companies which provide managerial and technical expertise are also in a good position to supply inputs such as plant, equipment, fertilisers and pesticides from other subsidiary companies within their group. The centralised organisation of these companies means that supplies may sometimes be purchased more cheaply through subsidiaries; but, conversely, plant and equipment may be more expensive than could otherwise be obtained by 'shopping around' other manufacturers. When technology is sold within firms in this way, it enables profits to be shifted around to suit the companies rather than the countries.

Through management and consultancies, agribusiness retains control of their technological capabilities, making it difficult for governments to foster, monitor or control their own industrial growth.[60] In certain circumstances, companies are able to use consultancies to build up demand for their products, although this is sometimes achieved indirectly, through service or supply agreements. In one case in the 1970s, Hoechst, the giant pharmaceutical company, signed an agreement with the Tanzanian government to supply insecticides and spraying equipment to cotton growers. Hoechst sells insecticides and pumps to a Farmer's Co-operative Union, which in turn loans pumps to farmers, and supplies the insecticides on credit, recovering the price through cotton sales. Hoechst uses government extension officers to supervise the spraying. The officers receive an extra salary from the company, but in turn Hoechst *can remove the extension officers from their jobs if they are not supervising correctly*. This means that the local extension service actually encourages the consumption of Hoechst's insecticides.[61]

Another common practice involves company support for training projects. Demand for tractors has been stimulated in this way by companies like Deere, Massey Ferguson, Caterpillar and Fiat. In Tanga, Tanzania, farmers were taught basic implement maintenance in a project designed to establish tractor rehabilitation centres.[62] This project was established by the UN Food & Agricultural Organisations, and grew out of its Industry Co-operative Programme (ICP).* The Deputy Executive Secretary of the programme, Walter W. Simons, had said of the tractor rehabilitation centres: "These agro-mechanisation centres, which we hope to expand elsewhere, also provide the companies with long term potential for developing their business". Both East and West Africa are now major markets for Massey Ferguson and the company increased its sales in Africa by 50 per cent in 1980, supplying one in four tractors sold there.[63]

Consultancies, management, technical and service agreements and similar arrangements are part of the response of foreign companies to African demands for control over land ownership and other agricultural

*See following page.

resources. However, while African governments continue to use the services provided by foreign companies, the development of agricultural production is likely to remain export oriented, large scale and capital intensive. This may not be critical in itself, if it can be shown to benefit African countries. The companies benefit by securing supplies of export crops, and by expanding a market for their products, particularly agricultural inputs. Whether Africa also benefits from such a heavy reliance on the services and expertise of foreign companies is open to question.

In many instances, the United Nations and other aid agencies advance the interests of foreign companies in underdeveloped countries.

Big Business and Aid Agencies

The closest link between transnational corporations and United Nations agencies was the United Nations Food and Agricultural Organisation's (FAO) Industrial Co-operative Programme (ICP), established in 1966, where over 100 agribusiness companies were directly involved in providing advice for FAO projects and activities. Its objective was "to demonstrate that far-sighted and responsible business contributes to social and economic development by means of fostering profitable private enterprise".[64] The ICP was in fact wound up at six months' notice following the exposé of its existence and the self-interest of the companies involved by, amongst others, Susan George in her book *How the Other Half Dies,* published in 1976.[65] But a similar organisation, the Industrial Council for Development (ICD), resurfaced and in 1980 received formal status as advisor to the UN Development Programme. It is currently playing an active part in establishing increased control by agribusiness of the world's seed supplies.[66]

Before this, however, the ICP's largest achievement was probably its involvement in the setting up of a $2 billion UNFAO tsetse fly eradication project in parts of Western, Central and Eastern Africa. The FAO launched the programme in 1975, following the 1974 World Food Conference, with the intention of eradicating the tsetse fly from seven million square kilometres so that African beef production could be increased.

The FAO set up a task force to direct the campaign, with fifteen representatives of agribusiness companies specialising in pesticides and veterinary drugs. The co-chairman was Fritz Bauer, then a German director of the giant chemical company Hoechst AG, and the task force was part of the ICP.[67]

The tsetse project has been criticised on a number of levels. Firstly it has enabled the manufacturers of pesticides banned or restricted in the West to dump some of their products in Africa. These include DDT, dieldrin (produced by Royal Dutch Shell) and the endosulfon marketed by Hoechst (under the name 'Thiodan'). This form of dumping in under-developed countries was already widespread when the project was started, so much so that in 1977 a speaker at the Second International Conference on Environmental Futures in Reykjavik said that at least as much and maybe more DDT was being manufactured in the West than before it was banned.[68]

The tsetse eradication scheme benefits both the agribusiness companies involved in pesticide production and those involved in the international beef market. The $2 billion plan spread over 40 years could, it is claimed, extend over a seven million square kilometre area, clearing it of tsetse fly and thereby making it possible to carry 120 million head of cattle, producing 1.5 million tons of meat a year, worth about $170 million. The money for the project is to be channelled by national, bilateral and international assistance and the FAO estimated that about $350 million had been committed by 1979.[69]

The project is likely to result in enormous debts for the African countries involved yet the beef produced will mostly be consumed by the richer beef-importing countries. Some local elites will benefit, but the cost of beef will put it out of the reach of the average African in the region. The large companies which control the ranching, packing, distribution and hamburger chains are likely to be the real beneficiaries.[70]

In addition to these disadvantages, other problems have emerged. Firstly, FAO officials privately admit that the area of tsetse fly infesta-tion has actually increased since the spraying programme began, spreading in both Uganda and Zambia. Officially, the FAO no longer refers to an 'eradication programme' but a 'control programme'. Secondly, grave worries have been expressed by local wildlife experts, environmentalists and health authorities about the side effects of pesticide spraying.

Lastly, the emphasis on such large-scale 'technological fix' solutions means that the FAO has virtually ignored the solution to animal protein deficits most favoured by conservationists, i.e. wildlife management or 'bush meat'.[71] Game, unlike cattle, is not affected by the tsetse fly, and if the right species were properly cropped they could represent an enormous meat potential for Africans, both rich and poor.

'Downstream' Agribusiness and African Markets

Although transnational corporations are principally concerned with developing African resources for overseas markets, this does not prevent them from establishing or consolidating their interests in local African markets by opening local processing subsidiaries. Brooke Bond developed a taste for tea in East Africa, and Unilever processed oils and soaps throughout Africa from an early date. Such forms of vertical integration are called 'downstream activities', or 'forward linkages'.

Consumption of some products is near to saturation levels in industrialised markets and Third World countries have become the major focus of future market growth. For example, in the oil and fat sector underdeveloped countries now consume about 40 per cent of world output while only producing about 33 per cent themselves.[72] Consumption is almost static in industrialised countries, but in poorer countries growth is projected at about 4.4 per cent a year.

In many food and beverage industries, third world countries are becoming important areas of market expansion, and transnationals are moving into processing and distribution there. Taking beverages as an example, a recent United Nations report[73] showed that forecasts for growth range from 3.5 per cent a year for cocoa products to 6.8 per cent for coffee. Other major growth areas are meat products, animal feeds and wheat flour, reflecting demand from urban consumers and the more affluent. The major food processors would like to acquire a share of this growth and there is great potential: at present only 10-20 per cent of food raw material in developing countries is commercially processed, in contrast to industrial markets where 80-85 per cent of farm produced raw material is processed before reaching consumers.[74]

By the mid-1970s, over 100 transnationals had more than 600 investments in developing country subsidiaries processing and marketing branded foods locally. Most subsidiaries — over 100 — were in the dairy industry, but other important areas were canned fruit and vegetables, dried soups, breakfast cereals, margarine and table oils, confectionary, soft drink concentrates, beer, coffee and cocoa products. Apart from tropical fruit processing, which is generally for export, all these products are for sale within the host country, and although investment is less in Africa than in the Arabic, Asian and Latin American countries, it is nevertheless growing rapidly. Table 1.4 (which is by no means comprehensive) gives some indication of the extent to which large transnational food processing firms have established subsidaries in Africa. These figures suggest that, for the 16 industries covered, the African countries which have attracted most foreign investment are Kenya (14), Zimbabwe (12), Nigeria (11), Ghana (7), Ivory Coast (6) and Zambia (6). Other important markets are Liberia, Zaire and Cameroon.

Because of the added value which products acquire through processing, and the consequent contribution which agriculture can make to industrial development, underdeveloped countries generally attempt to maximise the amount of downstream processing carried out within the country. However, if the intention is to substitute previously imported goods with locally produced products, countries frequently find that the cost of importing capital equipment and paying foreign expertise is

44

Table 1.4
Selected Food Processing Industries TNCs with Subsidiaries in Africa

Name of Company & Where Based | *African Operations*

COFFEE:

Brooke Bond Liebig, UK	Kenya
East Asiatic, Denmark	N/A
Nestle, Switzerland	Ivory Coast

COCOA PRODUCTS:

Cadbury Schweppes, UK	Kenya, Ghana, Nigeria
Gill & Duffus, UK	Ghana
Interfood, Switzerland	Ivory Coast
Hershey Foods, USA	Ghana
Nestle, Switzerland	Ghana, Kenya, Zimbabwe

TEA*:

Brooke Bond Leibig, UK	Kenya, Malawi, Tanzania
J. Finlay, UK	Kenya
Lonrho, UK	Malawi
Unilever, UK	Nigeria

(*Note: This may only indicate basic processing necessary to preserve the crop)

OILS, FATS, MARGARINE, COOKING OILS:

East Asiatic Co., Denmark	N/A
Lesieur, France	Senegal
Lonrho, UK	Nigeria
Unilever, UK/Nld	Cameroon, Ghana, Gabon, Kenya, Malawi, Nigeria, Zaire, Zimbabwe

FRUIT AND VEGETABLE PROCESSING:

Beecham, UK	Nigeria
Brooke Bond Liebig, UK	Kenya, Nigeria, Zimbabwe
BSN-Gervais Danone, France	N/A
Castle & Cooke, USA	Senegal
CPC, USA	Kenya
Del Monte (now Reynolds), USA	Kenya, Liberia
Nestle, Switzerland	Ivory Coast, Kenya, Nigeria, Swaziland
SCOA, France	Ivory Coast, Senegal
Unilever, UK/Nld	Kenya, Zimbabwe

SUGAR:

Tate & Lyle, UK	Nigeria, Zambia, Zimbabwe
Lonrho, UK*	Malawi, Mauritius, Swaziland
Booker McConnell, UK*	Malawi, Nigeria (16%)

*All manage further factories

WHEAT FLOURS AND MIXES:

Dalgety UK	Zambia, Zimbabwe
Associated British Foods, UK	Between them, these companies have
Continental Grain, USA	subsidiaries in: Cameroon, Lesotho,
Grand Moulin de Paris, France	Liberia, Nigeria, Sierra Leone,
Seaboard Allied Milling, USA	Upper Volta, Zambia, Zaire, Zimbabwe
Tiger Oats, South Africa	

CORN MILLING:

CPC, USA	Kenya

BREAKFAST CEREALS & BAKERY:

Nestle (breakfast cereals), Switzerland	Ghana, Kenya, Zimbabwe
Associated British Foods (bakery), UK	Zimbabwe

ANIMAL FEEDS:
(generally a by-product of processing grains, sugar or other food products)

CPC, USA	Kenya
Dalgety, UK	Zambia, Zimbabwe

MEAT INDUSTRIES (Packing and Canning):

Brooke Bond Liebig/Lyons (Joint Venture) }	Kenya, Nigeria, Sudan, Zambia,
Brooke Bond Liebig, UK	Zimbabwe
Imperial Foods (Poultry), UK	Kenya
Unilever, UK/Nld	Nigeria
Pfizer, USA (Poultry)	Nigeria

DAIRY INDUSTRY:

Carnation, USA	Cameroon, Ivory Coast, Senegal
BSN-Gervais Danone, France	Nigeria
Co-op Condensfabrick Friesland, Nld	Nigeria
East Asiastic, Denmark	Nigeria
Foremost-McKesson, USA	Nigeria
Unigate, UK	Kenya, Nigeria
Unilever, UK/Nld	Ghana, Kenya, Malawi, Nigeria, Zaire, Zimbabwe
Nestle, Switzerland	Ghana, Ivory Coast, Kenya, Nigeria, Senegal, Swaziland, Zimbabwe

FISHERIES:

Ralston Purina, USA	Ghana, Ivory Coast, Senegal, Sierra Leone
Heinz, USA	Congo, Ghana, Liberia, Senegal
Ward Foods, USA	Ivory Coast, Liberia, Nigeria
General Mills, USA	Liberia
Nippon Suisan Kaisha, Japan	Guinea, Liberia, Senegal
Taiyo Fisheries, Japan	Kenya, Ghana, Mauritius
Kellogg's, USA	Somalia

SOFT DRINKS CONCENTRATES:

Beecham, UK	Nigeria
Cadbury Schweppes, UK	Zambia, Zimbabwe
Lonrho (Coca Cola bottling), UK	Zambia
Coca Cola, USA	Kenya
Nestlé, Switzerland	Ghana
Norton Simon, USA	Kenya, Liberia, Zimbabwe
Pepsico, USA	Kenya, Sudan

CONFECTIONERY PRODUCTS:

Cadbury Schweppes, UK	Kenya, Tanzania
Nestle, Switzerland	Ivory Coast
Standard Brands, USA	Zimbabwe
Wrigley, USA	Kenya

BEER:

Allied Breweries, UK	Kenya, Uganda, Zimbabwe
Arthur Guinness, UK	Cameroon, Ghana, Kenya, Liberia, Nigeria, Sierra Leone, Uganda
Heineken, Nld	Burundi, Chad, Congo, Ghana, Nigeria, Rwanda, Sierra Leone, Zaire
Grand Metropolitan, UK	Kenya, Malawi, Tanzania, Zimbabwe
Lonrho	Zambia
Unilever, UK/Nld	Chad, Ghana, Nigeria, Sierra Leone
United Breweries (Carlsberg), Dmk	Malawi
Whitbread, UK	Kenya, Zambia

Sources: Computerised material from the UN Centre for Transnational Corporations, various Annual Reports and company materials.

higher than the cost of importing the finished product or processed foodstuffs.

A report from the UN Centre for Transnational Corporations shows that downstream processing within raw-material producing countries did increase between 1965 and 1976, and the proportion of more highly processed food products sold to developed countries increased from 11 per cent to 23 per cent of total food products shipped. Nevertheless, Third World countries generally failed to increase their sales of more highly processed food products in line with the growth of demand in developed countries.[75] Fisheries and pine kernels were the main exceptions. Historically in the processing sector, as in others, transnational corporations have been privileged over local firms by their ability to attract foreign investors (such as banks) and to obtain favourable terms from governments anxious to increase their foreign exchange earnings. The consequent reliance on big companies has meant that most food processing enterprises (with some exceptions, like coffee roasting and fisheries) have been large scale, technically sophisticated and capital intensive.

A major problem for African countries is the relatively short time in which foreign companies demand a return on their investment. In Kenya, for example, a 1975 study surveyed 21 local subsidiaries of foreign companies (only two of these were in the food or agricultural commodities industry, but the general principle holds true).[76] The general feeling from the companies was that 'one would like to see one's capital back at the end of five years'. Or again: 'In dicey areas, as head office calls this, they want 20-25 per cent return after tax'. Another executive clearly felt restricted by the parent company's policy of repatriating profit and remarked: ". . . head office is scared of expropriation; the major shareholders are anxous to get as much money out as fast as they can". And a German Embassy official remarked of the companies that they "look to get their money back in five to six years. I think that's wrong — they should be prepared to wait eight to ten years". The survey includes another company which decided against building an additional facility locally for processing a by-product, because it "only had a six-year pay-back". Although transnationals are a major source of capital and technology for the establishment of local food processing industries, it is clear that for the companies their own interests are always paramount.

The UN report went further, and concluded that the adverse effects of such large scale foreign investments are likely to offset the benefits, regardless of whether production is for export or for local consumption. First, the companies build very few links with local agriculture and often increase dependence on imports for either raw materials or intermediate products. Second, they frequently use inappropriate and costly technology. As a result it is not always clear whether the net inflow of foreign exchange exceeds the net outflow.

Third, the report points out that breakfast cereals, biscuits, bakery products and some other foodstuffs marketed by transnationals are of doubtful nutritional benefit by comparison with the locally grown staples which they tend to replace. Certainly, when considering staple foods, traditional dishes tend to cost much less per unit of nutritional value than the equivalent processed and branded products.[77] The propensity of big companies to advertise and promote their products means that traditional tastes and nutritional needs are translated into demands for complex manufactured brand name products. Nestlé's Lactogen, for example, has been built up as a prestigious source of baby nourishment, while highly-milled white flour or polished white rice has become popular in place of the less intensively milled maize flour or brown rice. Least appropriate of all, there is a growing demand for manufactured confectonary, such as Lyon's Maid ice-cream or Cadbury's chocolate bars.[78] While there may be no direct local alternative to a particular product being manufactured by a transnational (e.g. chocolate bars or powdered soups), at a more fundamental level local alternatives are available, often in the form of less sophisticated products, perhaps more appropriate to African resources and social priorities. Examples include small-scale posho (maize flour) mills, bakeries or cheese factories.[79]

Finally, the report points out, big foreign companies can have an undesirable effect on local enterprise and may even force out local competition by means of advertising and marketing practices. They can, for example, undermine local competition by cutting prices, only to raise them again after they have established a monopolistic position.

The story of the soap industry in Kenya illustrates some of the problems associated with the intervention of transnationals, in this case including the eclipse of an indigenous industry.

The Soap Industry in Kenya

In 1975, Kenya's 18 soap firms produced annually 28,000 tonnes of laundry, detergent and toilet soap. Of the locally owned factories which were still in business, most were unmechanised, and therefore labour intensive. By contrast, the transnationals, including a Unilever and a Proctor & Gamble subsidiary, were operating factories which were highly mechanised and becoming more so: by 1975, one overseas-owned company had reduced its workforce by 19 per cent every five years.

Many of the raw materials used by the local factories were readily available within Kenya. For example, they used firewood for fuel, which provided work for rural sawmillers and woodcutters, who are spread throughout the country, rather than being clustered in Mombasa or

Nairobi as is most of Kenyan industry. Whereas locally produced soap is made with locally grown coconut oil, the foreign companies import between 75 and 90 per cent of their raw materials, on the basis that coconut oil will not produce a quality appearance soap made to their international standards.

While the indigenous soap manufacturers retain their profits within Kenya, most of the profits of foreign companies are remitted abroad. In 1972 and 1973 the two larger companies transferred around US $1,380,000 to their parent companies overseas and only 13 per cent of their original investment remained in Kenya. Between 1957 and 1972, the cash outflow from Kenya of one soap subsidiary was over six times its inflow.

This account is taken from an article by the Anglican Bishop of Maseno South in Kenya, the Right Rev. Dr. Henry Okullu,[80] who goes on to describe the effects of the greater resources available to the transnationals for advertising, and the way in which this is used to promote a Western lifestyle and to encourage consumers to choose branded rather than traditional soaps:

"The quality of the multinationals' soap is not always better than the local products, but it's publicised and packaged as though the good life depends on it. All part of a 'taste-transfer' process that is turning Kenya into a Western-style consumer society.

"The multinational soap merchants in Kenya run up an annual advertising bill of some $1,500,000. This is over one-and-a-half times the money the government allocated for a five-year programme to build rural health centres."

The transnational soap companies are there on the basis that they are transferring capital, technology and skills from the West, thus boosting 'development', yet the effect is to seriously disadvantage a once-thriving local industry.

In many of the poorer countries, the use of trademarks is important in the marketing of branded foods and other household products made from agricultural raw materials (such as soap). The trademark is the equivalent of a guarantee of a consistent recognisable product and thus is of particular value to underdeveloped countries when the aim is to export processed local products to the West. Access to developed country markets is consequently very limited without the involvement of the transnationals, which own most of the trademarks. The big companies decide whether to process in Africa or the West, and in any event will only process in Africa under their own trademarks. Whereas Kenya has taken almost complete control over coffee growing and marketing, for example, the product is still packaged and distributed by transnationals elsewhere. The well-known 'Kenco Coffee' is not a Kenyan label, but is produced by Cadbury Schweppes in London. In 1980 they opened a new computerised processing plant at a cost of £1 million, one of the most modern in the world: not in Kenya but in the United Kingdom.

There is no technological reason why transnationals should be so dominant in the African market for processed foods. Although they hold the trademarks and own the patents for the more advanced processing equipment, most of the techniques are widely available and are decades, or even centuries old. Canning was invented in the early 1800s and the leading food processing firms therefore have little or no proprietary control of this technology. Nor are there prohibitively expensive capital requirements for canning, especially in fruit and vegetables. But transnationals remain market leaders in all developing country markets,[81] mainly because of effective marketing and promotional activities. In some products, such as packaged oil for cooking and eating (margarine), the branded market in Africa has expanded to the point where it has begun to displace traditional oils and fats.[82]

Where private investment is accepted in order to gain access to industrialised markets, the difficulty then facing governments is how to direct such investment, and to ensure that the outflow of capital is not greater than the inflow. However, there appears much less reason to allow transnationals to continue to enlarge their power as processors of agricultural produce for local use. Involving transnationals in this sector may not only endanger local enterprise, but may increase dependence on *imported* agricultural raw materials for processing. The cheapest, best quality, and most efficiently produced product (in economic terms) may not be that which contributes most overall to local economic activity, employment, use of available resources, diversity, and ability to serve the whole community and countryside, rather than the wealthier urban markets.

Conclusion

This chapter traces the story of how African agriculture became subservient to the needs of industrialised nations, and describes the destabilising effect on African societies, of the slave trade and colonial wars, which paved the way for concession, and later plantation companies. The plantation companies — ancestor's of today's agribusiness combines — dominated the agricultural production of cash crops. Other companies gained control over the buying, marketing and processing of crops grown for colonising nations by peasant farmers. The position of such companies has not yet been successfully challenged by producers, although independent African States now control aspects of local operation and, in many countries, have succeeded in reducing direct ownership of agricultural land by foreign companies.

However, the size, wealth and market dominance of transnational agribusiness remains unchallenged. Many companies have successfully adapted to meet the needs of independent African States by establishing consultancy subsidiaries, and providing management and technical services. Guaranteed fees provide high profit levels, without incurring the element of risk involved in agricultural production. Companies thus influence the direction of African agriculture through their advice and ensure a regular supply of the crops needed for processing. Because agricultural development schemes attract funding on concessional terms from aid agencies, the companies often find that they have developed cheaper sources of supply than are obtainable through direct ownership.

With the growth of affluent urban classes in African countries, companies have expanded into new markets in Africa itself, both selling imported products and establishing local processing plants for branded products. In countries where the most modern and sophisticated processing factories are chosen as an option, and high quality goods are required for the export market, then transnational agribusiness will supply this. However, governments are often insufficiently selective in their policies for building up local processing industries. Frequently transnationals entering the local market are offered unnecessarily advantageous terms, to establish new plant, thus strengthening their already formidable power to compete with local processing industries, as illustrated by the case of the soap industry in Kenya. Transnationals tend to forge few (if any) links with local agriculture and often increase a country's dependence on imports of raw materials, machinery, or intermediate products. At the same time, a major aim of foreign companies is to repatriate capital and they will continue to do so unless governments offer them generous incentives or impose severe restrictions compelling them to re-invest profits locally.

The material in this chapter has been drawn from a wide range of sources and, in the nature of an overview, it covers several different industries. The next two chapters examine more systematically the organisation of the coffee and sugar industries.

CHAPTER 2

Africa and the
International Coffee Trade

Coffee is the most valuable agricultural commodity traded internationally. With an export value of $11,600 million in 1980,[1] it is second only to oil in the primary commodity trade.[2] Many crops are grown on a larger scale and are more important economically, rice and wheat for example, but these staple foods are consumed mainly in the countries where they are grown. Coffee, by contrast, is mostly exported. Only 22 per cent of the world's coffee is consumed in the producing nations, and half of this in Brazil. The producers tend to be poor ex-colonial countries in Latin America, Africa and Asia, whereas most of the consumption occurs in North America, Europe and Japan.[3]

Many coffee producing countries depend heavily on coffee exports. In 1979, the sale of coffee provided over 25 per cent of the total foreign exchange receipts of nine African countries: Ethiopia, Ivory Coast, Kenya, Tanzania, Madagascar, Rwanda, Burundi, Uganda and the Central African Republic;* and six Latin American countries: Brazil, Columbia, Costa Rica, El Salvador, Guatemala and Haiti.[4] In several exporting countries, coffee earns more, or about as much, as all other exports put together. In total, an estimated 20 million people in developing countries work in the world coffee economy.[5]

The marketing of coffee in the industrialised countries is controlled by a handful of transnationals. It is dominated by two companies, General Foods and Nestlé's. The former has subsidiaries in many countries and, after the United States, is the world's largest importer of coffee.[6]

Types of Coffee

Coffee is a tree crop. There are as many as 100 species, but only two are commercially important, *Arabica* and *Coffee Canephora,* of which *Robusta* is much the most common variety. Only two other species are grown commercially, *Coffee Liberica* and *Excelsa,* and together they account for less than 0.5 per cent of world production at present.[7]

Arabica coffees are generally preferred by consumers, having a milder flavour and containing less caffeine than Robusta. They are more delicate than Robustas and, since they require rather lower temperatures, are usually grown either at higher altitudes, or further from the equator.

*See Table I, Introduction.

However, like other species, Arabicas are extremely vulnerable to frost damage, and this imposes strict limits on the area where cultivation is worthwhile commercially. About a quarter of Africa's coffee production is Arabica, and some of it is amongst the world's best. However, its cultivation is limited because of its susceptibility to leaf rust and because the species can only be grown at higher altitudes (in parts of Cameroon,* Eastern Congo,* Rwanda, Burundi, Kenya, Tanzania, Ethiopia, Malawi and Madagascar*).

The hardy and vigorous Robusta forms about three-quarters of Africa's output and is better adapted to lower, humid areas and more resistant to diseases and pests. Growing at lower altitudes it is usually higher yielding and requires less cultivation and care than Arabica. Robusta is, therefore, generally cheaper to grow, and is usually put on world markets at much lower prices than Arabica. Consequently, in almost all European countries, the proportion of Robustas in ordinary coffee blends has gradually increased. This is also true for America, where Robustas are used particularly in the manufacture of 'instant' coffees.

In addition to the two main types of coffee, small amounts of Liberica are grown in West Africa, and a new family, *Arabustas,* is being developed. Arabusta is still an experimental crop, but according to recent reports it is expected to be of some importance by 1990. It is an attempt to combine the best features of the Arabicas and Robustas, and is expected to provide a better return for planters than either of the other two varieties.[8]

The Introduction of Coffee into Africa

Despite the fact that coffee is thought to have originated in the highlands of Ethiopia over a thousand years ago and that it has been consumed in that region ever since, it was not introduced to any other part of Africa until 1885. In that year, coffee was introduced as a crop in Central Africa, a process followed about 1900 in Kenya, where coffee was brought by the British from the French Isle of Reunion. At about the same time it was also planted in Tanganyika (Tanzania) and Madagascar.[9]

In the late 1920s, Britain and France both encouraged more African colonies to grow coffee. This was a response to Brazil's monopoly position, which had enabled the Brazilian government to buy up and store large amounts of its own coffee in order to keep the world price high. Thus, in 1929, coffee was first planted in the Ivory Coast, French

---

* Cameroon, the Congo and Madagascar are classified as Robusta producers in the International Coffee Organisation (ICO) tables.

West Africa, now Africa's biggest producer.

The restricted markets of the war years led to coffee trees being uprooted as land was needed for food crops and other more profitable commodities. After the war, Latin American exports were not allowed access to markets in European countries because of the latter's balance of payments problems. So once again, European powers encouraged production in their African colonies and kept out imports of coffee from 'dollar' areas by high tariffs as well as direct restrictions. When these controls were lifted and Europe began purchasing coffee worldwide, the increase in demand sent prices soaring to reach a peak in 1954. As a result of these high prices, new coffee trees were planted in both Africa and Latin America, resulting in over-production in the late 1950s and 1960s, accompanied by declining prices. These were not to recover until the bad frosts in Brazil in the 1970s. (see Fig. 2.1).

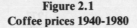

Figure 2.1
Coffee prices 1940-1980

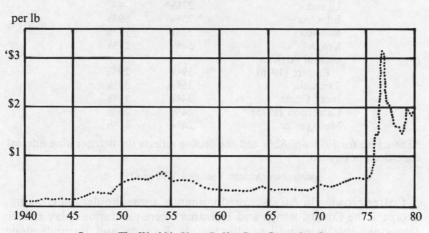

Sources: The World in Your Coffee Cup, Campaign Co-op.
United Nations Statistical Year Book, 1980

Coffee Production and Marketing in Africa

African producers became increasingly important in the world coffee market between the two world wars, and by the late 1930s their production was more than 10 times that of the pre-World War I level, standing at about 2,900,000 bags* a year. By the 1944/5 season output

*1 bag = 60 kilogrammes of green coffee.

reached almost 3,300,000 bags. The post-war expansion resulted in a major rise in output, and by the early 1960s African coffee production represented about 23 per cent of the world's total, i.e. 16 million out of 66 million bags.[10] Production levels were maintained or increased in most African countries throughout the seventies, mainly because of the growing demand for African beans from instant coffee producers. By 1980, the four largest coffee producers in Africa were the Ivory Coast (4,883,000 bags), Ethiopia (3,333,000 bags), Uganda (2,334,000 bags), and Zaire (1,250 bags). Up until 1973/4, Angola was one of the top four, but the war there caused output to fall sharply.[11]

The degree to which many African countries depend on coffee as a source of export earnings can be seen from Table 2.1.

Table 2.1
Percentage of Export Earnings from Coffee

	1977	1978
Burundi	94%	93%
Uganda	27%*	—
Ethiopia	75%	69%
Rwanda	73%	71%
Kenya	54%	27%
Central African Empire (1976)	39%	29%
Tanzania	35%	35%
Ivory Coast	34%	31%
Cameroon (1975)	24%	25%
Madagascar	24%	45%

*The figure for 1976 was 82% and the decline reflects the deteriorating internal conditions in Uganda.

Source: New African Yearbook 1979 and 1981-2

Coffee growing in Africa is predominantly a smallholder undertaking, except in the Congo, Kenya and Tanzania where plantations play a more important role in overall production. In Rwanda and Burundi alone there are more than half a million African coffee farmers owning 50 to 100 trees each.[12] Smallholdings yield on average 300-400 kilograms per hectare, whereas estates generally obtain yields twice this size, with the more exceptional reaching 2,000kg per hectare. On the other hand, smallholders usually grow coffee in addition to other crops and use relatively few inputs, whereas the estates use more intensive methods, employing costly inputs such as fertilisers and pesticides. The trend in Africa as a whole is for estates to produce a declining proportion of total output since new coffee plantings are mainly by smallholders.[13]

Coffee production and marketing in most of the African producing countries involves growers, processors, brokers or other intermediaries, domestic roasters and exporters. The process is nearly always overseen by a government or quasi-government agency called a marketing board, whose purpose it is to implement the country's coffee policies.[14]

Before the Second World War, the movement of coffee from the areas of production to overseas markets was first carried out either by foreign firms acting as agents, or by the processors acquiring the coffee, using capital from foreign sources. Credit therefore flowed from the ports inland via a chain of buyers, each drawing on the resources of the firm that it sold to and to whose agent it often was. The flow of imports was mostly handled by the same firms that shipped the exports.[15]

After the war there was a general distrust of both the foreign firms that previously had been the chief buyers and of the local agents retained by these firms. Although the widely fluctuating and generally falling prices experienced before 1939 originated in the world market, African producers generally blamed their falling incomes upon the foreign firms to which they sold their crops. These firms often had quasi-monopolistic power and frequently extracted unjustified profits from the farmers supplying them. To supercede them new marketing boards were established, usually by colonial government officials who had controlled the disposal of the crop during the war and considered that monopolistic marketing boards were more efficient and presented a greater degree of control[16] than was possible with the imperfect competition arising from foreign firms working through competing local buyers.

Almost all the marketing boards in Africa responsible for exporting cash crops are monopolies. They are owned and/or run by the government, growers or exporter organisations in varying degrees, depending on the country concerned. Marketing boards now generally buy from producers at an average price calculated from world prices. After transport to the ports, and in some cases processing, the crops are sold to foreign buyers for the best price available. Broad purchases are made in advance of sale and are financed either from accumulated reserves or by borrowing from banks, or in some cases by selling the early crop in advance of purchase and thus obtaining funds from foreign buyers for future acquisitions.[17]

The coffee marketing boards are responsible for the well-being of their countries' industries. In times of excess supply and low prices, when buyers willing to meet minimum established prices can't be found, they buy in some of the crop and pay the storage costs. They allocate coffee earnings by setting minimum prices to growers, export tax rates, and minimum registration prices for exports. They use export revenues principally to conduct research, buy and store coffee, subsidise the domestic industry, finance operations, construct facilities and public works, and promote production.[18]

The pricing of coffee

The price paid for coffee is not determined simply by the strength of consumer demand and variations in annual production, it is also affected by such factors as storage in producer countries, the working of the International Coffee Agreement, the futures markets and the operations of the major coffee transnationals.

On the supply side, the world price for coffee is influenced by climatic and domestic conditions inside the producer countries. Thus in 1975, the severe frosts in Brazil dramatically cut production and caused an immediate price rise on the world market. In Africa there were also disruptions in supplies during the 1970s, for example, following the civil war in Angola and the upheavals caused by Amin's rule in Uganda. As coffee can be stored for two or three years without a deterioration in quality, the level of stocks can also be a significant factor determining supply and price. In African countries, however, storage facilities are minimal in comparison with those of richer producer countries like Brazil and so the system of temporarily withholding supplies on a significant scale is less of an option.

A major influence on the price of coffee is the International Coffee Organisation. This was created to negotiate the International Coffee Agreement (ICA) under which the amount that each producing country may sell in the international coffee market is determined annually at negotiations attended by both producing and consuming countries. The first ICA was signed in September 1963, having been preceded by a period of price fluctuation and excess supply. The Agreement was the result of negotiations carried out by a special United Nations' Conference called in July 1962 to study the problems of the world coffee market. The International Coffee Agreement covers about 99 per cent of the world's coffee import needs,[19] and there are now 47 exporting members and 26 importing members of the Agreement.[20] The first Agreement lasted until 1972 when it broke down, the second ICA was signed in 1976 and the latest one was agreed upon in October 1981, giving exporting members the right to export 56 million bags in 1981/2,[21] an amount roughly in line with anticipated import demand from ICA consuming member nations.[22]

The constitution of the ICO was, and is, such that voting strength is determined by the quantity of coffee historically bought or sold by a particular country. This means that the USA and Brazil, as respectively the world's largest consumer and producer, dominate the organisation. The US has 392 votes and Brazil 336. However, an African country like Tanzania, with coffee as its main export, has only 15 votes in the organisation, while Burundi, with coffee providing 93 per cent of its exports, has only 8 votes.[23] Voting strength is important since it determines which countries have the power to affect or change the Agreement and to decide whether or not it should continue.

From the beginning, African governments had mixed feelings about the International Coffee Agreement of 1963. They welcomed the possibility of price stabilisation at an acceptable level, i.e. prices not to fall below those of 1962. Yet the means of achieving this, by a system of annual quotas based on previous production levels, effectively froze their share of the world market. It also failed to take planned production increases into account.[24] This was particularly important since the Agreement was introduced at a time when African producers were in the process of expanding their sales at the expense of Latin American countries.[25] They were in a position to do this mostly because of the suitability of their predominantly Robusta crop for the manufacture of instant coffee, consumption of which rose sharply in the 1950s and early 1960s. Other factors that aided the competitiveness of African coffee were the availability of cheap land, the predominantly smallholder system of coffee growing on the Continent, and the European Economic Community's preference scheme, which increased the export sales of the EEC's African associate members. The Africans had also been helped by Brazil's strategy of withholding supplies from the world market which had effectively held a price umbrella over the market in the early 1960s, thus assisting African producers whose strategy was to sell their coffee at the price needed to move it out of storage rapidly.

However, despite their growing share of the market and the poor terms offered, African governments had little choice but to join the ICA, since without it they were afraid that Brazil would dump its huge accumulated stockpile of coffee onto the market and wipe out the African trade. Such an event was feasible because Brazilian coffee was of a better quality than the African Robustas and, if prices fell low enough, buyers would prefer it. More important than this, however, was the fact that failure to sign the Agreement would have meant that African producers would have been shut out of the United States and other major consumer markets, since the consumer nations were policing the Agreement by refusing to accept coffee from non-signatories.[26]

The price a consumer pays is influenced not just by conditions in the producing countries and by the International Coffee Agreement, but also by prices fixed on the spot market (where the price quoted for coffee is that for immediate delivery). This in turn is influenced by speculation on the futures market, where the price is determined by contracts under which the purchaser agrees to take delivery of coffee at a specified future date for a price fixed at the time of the contract. Consumer prices are also influenced by the purchasing policy and profit margins of the major transnational corporations involved in coffee marketing, particularly the giant United States food company, General Foods.

For most of the post-war period there has been a steady increase in demand for coffee, despite the occasional sharp increase in prices. However, there is considerable uncertainty about the future, not only because of the recession and the availability of cheaper alternatives to coffee, but because consumers are clearly sensitive to major price rises. The dramatic price increases following the Brazilian frosts of 1975 led to a marked drop in consumption in the United States in particular. Overall consumption has now recovered to the pre-frost levels, although the recovery has been slightly less in the United States.[27]

Transnational Corporations and the International Coffee Trade

The coffee marketing chain within developed countries is dominated by two giant transnationals: General Foods and Nestlé (see Boxes 1 and 2). Even if its operations outside the United States are ignored, General Foods is still the world's largest commercial coffee importer, buying up quantities of coffee at a much faster pace than its competitors. The United States may be the world's largest coffee importer, but the second largest is General Foods.[28]

In 1975 General Foods controlled 35.2 per cent of the United States regular coffee market and 50.7 per cent of the instant coffee market. Nestlé has a smaller share of the enormous American market for instant coffee, 29.5 per cent in 1975, but its more dominant position in Japan and Europe (see Table 2.2) makes it the second largest company in the international coffee trade. Another transnational, Coca Cola, entered the coffee trade in 1964, its first departure from the soft beverage business, and the company's coffee division, Tenco, is now playing an increasing role in the United States and European coffee trade.[29]

Table 2.2
Company Shares of European Soluble Coffee Market in 1975

Country	Nestlé	General Foods
United Kingdom	50%	27%
Germany	29%	15%
France	80%	10%
Spain	80%	12%
Netherlands	26%	—
Greece	80%	—
Austria	40%	15%
Norway	66%	16%

Source: Compiled from Report to Congress by the Comptroller General of the United States, Coffee Production and Marketing Systems, 28th October 1977.

Box I

General Foods

General Foods, as its name implies has absorbed a large number of small companies and built itself up as a manufacturer and wholesaler of a variety of food products. It is the largest manufacturer of packaged food in the United States and operates over 60 processing plants and units worldwide, employing a total of 53,000 people. Coffee is its major concern and General Foods buys a total of around one billion pounds of green coffee a year. Its best known coffee product is 'Maxwell House'.

General Foods only began to take an interest in the manufacture of coffee products overseas in the late 1950s and early 1960s. For example, instant coffee was manufactured for the English and German markets in Montreal, Canada until small production plants were built in Birmingham and Elmshorn in 1955 and 1956 respectively. In the late 1950s General Foods acquired the French firm Legal, based near Paris, and began selling its roast ground coffee; by 1960 it was making instant coffee at Legal. Through the sixties, General Foods began processing instant coffee in Australia, Mexico, Sweden, Japan and Korea.

In the period 1964 to 1969, General Foods brought into full commercial production their freeze dried coffee 'Maxim', which by 1972 had captured 13 per cent of the 200 million pound per year instant coffee market in the United States. Nestlé's 'Taster's Choice' achieved similar sales levels in the USA in this period. However, a more serious threat for General Foods was the rapid growth in competition from Brazil, which began to export large quantities of instant coffee to the United States starting in 1966. In 1965, Brazil's soluble coffee exports to the United States were a mere 1 per cent of the United States soluble market. By 1967, however, they had captured 14 per cent of the market, due to the Brazilian government's decision to exempt soluble coffee exports from the taxes that it placed on green coffee exports, thus under-cutting other soluble coffee producers, which were dependent on these highly taxed green beans.

A group of US firms, led by General Foods, enlisted the help of the State Department to crush this trade. It didn't embark on this course, however, until after the collapse of its own negotiations for setting up a plant in Brazil. It then lobbied hard and succeeded in persuading the United States government to refuse to renew the International Coffee Agreement unless Brazil agreed to curb the 'unfair' competition from its own brand new coffee manufacturing plants. Brazil resisted but in the end imposed a tax on its own soluble coffee exports, since the advantatges it obtained from the ICA were too attractive to put at risk. A final settlement was not reached until 1971, and it involved the Brazilian government, under pressure from the State Department, agreeing to export tax-free to the United States a quantity of green coffee (over half a million bags) which was equivalent to the amount of instant coffee exported from Brazil. By escaping the tax on this consignment of green coffee, the US firms using it were able to produce soluble coffee as cheaply as the Brazilian manufacturers. It was a windfall for the United States coffee firms, particlarly General Foods, since the tax-free beans were shared out amongst them in proportion to their share of national production of instant coffee. General Foods thus received over 50 per cent of the $10 million savings enjoyed by the United States companies, money that otherwise would have gone to the Brazilian treasury.

This episode is by no means the only example of General Foods tampering with the world coffee trade. In the early years of the ICA, many African countries produced more coffee than their official quotas allowed them to export. The system was policed by consuming countries, which required certificates of origin for the coffee they imported. It was, however, easy to forge certificates and customs officials were not very strict in insisting that the certificates be authentic ones. Non-member countries such as Liberia and Morocco were also used as export points for dispatching quota busting coffee to consumers. Liberia averaged exports of 57,000 bags of coffee a year from 1963 to 1966/7, but then exported 798,000 bags of green coffee to the United States in the first nine months of 1966. At least 479,121 bags of Liberian coffee went in a block deal to General Foods on false certificates of origin printed in Liberia.

The Ivory Coast also trans-shipped via Morocco, a non-member of the ICO and a non-producer of coffee. Once again, General Foods was the accomplice, enabling it to circumvent ICO enforcement procedures by importing 99,858 bags in 1966 from Morocco. Also in 1966, General Foods avoided high Colombian export taxes by importing 21,082 bags of coffee from Aruba, a windswept island quite without coffee trees but only 45 miles west of the Colombian coast.

This situation came to an end when stamps printed by the International Coffee Organisation were mailed out to each participant in strict ration to its quota, and customs officials were instructed to refuse imports of coffee which did not bear the official stamp. General Foods and other companies involved in these ICA evasions were therefore denied a source of cheap coffee.

The sheer commercial dominance of General Foods can be seen by the fact that in 1975 it controlled 35.2 per cent of the huge American regular coffee market and 50.7 per cent of that for instant coffee.

General Foods Income ($000)

	1976	1977	1978	1979	1980
Gross Revenue	3,978,294	4,904,737	5,376,204	5,472,456	5,959,587
Net Profit	150,428	177,338	169,506	232,149	255,821

Sources:
Coffee, Michael Sevitz, 1977, Chapter 8, page 32;
Moody's Industrial Manual, 1980;
General Foods Annual Reports, 1977, 1979, 1980;
Fisher, B.S., The International Coffee Agreement: A Study in Coffee Diplomacy.

Box 2

Nestlé

Henri Nestlé, who was of German origin, started the company in Switzerland in the 1860s, manufacturing condensed milk in cans for children. Early in the 20th century a spray dried milk product was marketed, and a chocolate milk drink powder was prepared. Milk and chocolate products of this kind were the backbone of Nestlés sales until the early 1930s when the instant coffee beverage, Nescafe was developed. Since World War II, Nestlé has diversified into many other food industries, including Maggi, Crosse & Blackwell, Findus frozen foods, Libby, McNeill & Libby canned foods, mineral waters, wines, cheeses, etc.

After Unilever, Nestlé is the second largest food firm in the world with a 1980 turnover of 13.8 billion dollars. Its headquarters are at Vevey, Switzerland, on the shore of Lake Geneva. It has 300 factories and about 700 offices in 70 countries, with processing plants in 40 countries. Its products all carry the reputation for quality. It has 155,000 employees and around 80,000 stockholders. Until the baby food scandal, the management rarely gave out information to news media and its operations were rather secretive. However, in an effort to improve its international image, it has recently published a lavish public relations booklet, 'Nestlé in the Developing Countries'.*

Nescafe instant coffee had its origins in the early 1930s, when Brazil accumulated extraordinary surpluses of coffee beans, and the Brazilian Institute of Coffee discussed with Nestlé the feasibility of making soluble coffee for export. The key to the production of the new beverage was the fact that every Nestlé milk plant in the world had a spray drier. By simply adding a coffee roaster and set of columnar extractors, it was possible to make a coffee extract which could then be spray dried on the same equipment. Once manufactured, the Nescafe could be packaged in the same tinned metal cans that the milk powder was put into. With this manufacturing concept in mind, the company introduced Nescafe processing facilities into their milk plants in England, France, Argentina, South Africa, Holland, Germany, Italy, Norway, Spain, Australia, Canada, Chile, Columbia, Cuba, Mexico and Peru. The advent of World War II interferred with some of these production facilities, but a major expansion of instant coffee production was made in the USA at the insistence of the US military.

Broad acceptance of Nescafe as a military ration by millions of GI's encouraged Nestlé to expand its post-war production capabilities, so new plants were built in Freehold, New Jersey and Ripon, California in 1948. After the war, other instant coffee manufacturing facilities were revitalised around the world. By 1975 Nestlé controlled 29.5 per cent of the American instant coffee market and was the dominant company in Europe and Japan.

*The activities of Nestlé have been monitored for many years by the 'Nestlé Bulletin', published by the International Union of Food Workers in Geneva.

Nestlé's Income ($000, calculated from Swizz Francs)				
	1976	1977	1978	1979	1980
Gross					
Revenue	7,796,728	9,957,879	12,067,943	13,566,771	13,790,986
Net Profit	356,636	411,298	456,455	511,599	384,789

1976 $1 = 2.445 Sw.Fr; 1977 $1 = 2.018 Sw.Fr; 1978 $1 = 1.619 Sw.Fr; 1979 $1 = 1.595 Sw.Fr; 1980 $1 = 1.775 Sw.Fr.

Some African countries with Nestlé subsidiaries and the products they produce:
   Ghana (Tena): Nescafe packing, shaping of Maggi cubes, evaporated milk, Milo chocolate drink.
   Ivory Coast (Abidjan): Nescafe, Maggi soups, Nesao drinks;
   Kenya (Nairobi): Nespray and Lactogen (baby milks), Milo, Carelac and Nestern (baby foods);
   Madagascar (Tenerive): condensed milk;
   Senegal (Dakar): condensed milk.

Sources:
Coffee, Michael Sevitz, 1977, Chapter 8, page 33.
Moody's Industrial Manual, 1980.
International Union of Food Workers, Nestlé Bulletin No.23 (Geneva, December 1977).
Nestlé, Annual Reports, 1979, 1980.

The transnationals have evolved a basic formula for success in the coffee business which consists of setting up purchasing centres in those countries which offer the most favourable tax incentives, and distributing the product to their branches or subsidiaries spread across the world. Switzerland is a favourite purchasing centre for coffee transnationals because of the numerous fiscal incentives which it offers. The large scale importing firms have also congregated in Switzerland to process the paperwork and direct the distribution of coffee to roasters located in other European countries.[30] Organised in this way, coffee-marketing transnational companies have achieved a dominant position within nearly all industrialised countries.

Competition between Coffee Transnationals

In theory, competition keeps prices to a minimum. In food processing, however, where profit margins are considered slim, the companies have to ensure that the customer buys their product rather than a similar one sold by a rival brand. This means advertising, and the food processing transnationals are by far the biggest spenders on the mass media. General Foods and Nestlé spend millions of dollars every year in trying to capture a larger segment of sales, and this battle has kept other firms on the sidelines, unwilling to enter such a costly melee. Competitors have, however, copied the big companies' successful label and jar design.

Another method of gaining market shares, and possibly forcing competitors out of business, is the relentless pursuit of new and more sophisticated, and usually more expensive, processing techniques. Both General Foods and Nestlé have used this technique over the last few decades in order to gain market shares from each other and from other competitors, some of which have had to retire from the race. Between them, the two companies have pioneered most of the major technical advances in the industry. Nestlé first developed instant coffee production in the 1930s, but in 1950 General Foods then took over the technical lead with the introduction of spray dried coffee. However, the tables were turned again late in the 1960s when Nestlé regained the upper hand with its freeze dried coffee.

The tremendous processing capacity and financial holdings of General Foods have made it possible for the company to pioneer many new and expensive production methods over the years. These have included continuous roaster, large particle spray aromatization, inert gas packaging, freeze drying of frozen coffee extracts, freeze concentration of coffee extracts, etc. The Maxwell House research division spends several million dollars a year solely on coffee development work. Some of the results of these efforts and expenditures are revealed annually in a continuous stream of United States and foreign patent applications on coffee extraction, aroma recovery, freeze drying and packaging. Nestlé is also committed to a huge research and development programme and since the two giants also control most of the patents for the equipment necessary for manufacturing instant coffee it has become very expensive for other firms, or producer countries wishing to develop indigenous soluble coffee industries, to successfully enter this sector of the international coffee market. The degree of control over patents exerted by General Foods, and to a lesser extent Nestlé, is illustrated in Table 2.3.

Table 2.3 Control of Patents

Control of Patents Type of Patent	Years	No. of Patents Held by General Food (per cent in brackets)	No. of Patents Held by Nestlé (per cent in brackets)	Total No. of Patents held
Coffee Agglomeration	1944-73	18 (51%)	4 (11%)	35
Coffee Extraction	1962-72	15 (38%)	3 (8%)	40
Freeze Drying Coffee	1964-73	36 (33%)	8 (7%)	108
Aromatization	1962-73	38 (48%)	7 (9%)	80
Extract Freeze Concentration	1971-72	7 (100%)	—	7

Source: Compiled from Coffee, Michael Sevitz, Chapter 8.

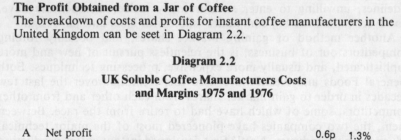

The Profit Obtained from a Jar of Coffee

The breakdown of costs and profits for instant coffee manufacturers in the United Kingdom can be seet in Diagram 2.2.

Diagram 2.2

UK Soluble Coffee Manufacturers Costs and Margins 1975 and 1976

A   Net profit
B   Indirect costs (see below)
C   Direct costs (packaging materials and wages of shop floor workers)
D   Coffee — at the price it is delivered to the factory.

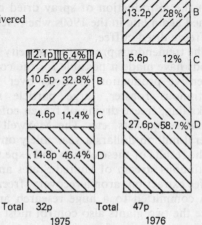

Total 32p
1975

Total 47p
1976

Source: UK Price Commission Report No.29. coffee: Prices Costs and Margins (1977)

Looking at each stage of production, it can be seen that about half the cost of a jar of coffee accrues to the country of origin.

At first glance, the diagram suggests that profits were very meagre in 1976, a mere 1.3 percent of the sale price. However, a further analysis shows that the indirect costs, Section B, are made up of the following constituents:

Royalties	2.4%
Interest	2.2%
Promotion/advertising	10.0%
Factory administration	13.4%

The Price Commission, in its report 'Coffee: Prices, Costs and Margins', made the following comment: "Royalities, which are calculated on the basis of sales, are paid by two of the companies (i.e. Nestlé and General Foods) to their foreign parent companies to cover the use of trademarks, research and development . . . Royalties as a percentage of sales increased in the period 1974-6 from 1.5 per cent to 2.4 per cent or in cash terms from £1.6 million to £4.3 million.[31]

Such cases of what might be termed 'creative accounting' have the official title of 'transfer payments'. Transnationals frequently do use systems of this kind for moving cash from country A to country B in order to record profits where corporation tax rates are lowest and/or the exchange rate works to the company's best advantage. This retention in transnational hands of money that would otherwise go to governments occurs in poor as well as in rich countries.

Coffee Transnationals and Africa

General Foods has no subsidiaries in Africa and compared with Nestlé its interests in the third world are few, being limited to Mexico, Venezuela, Brazil, Puerto Rico and the Philippines. Nestlé by contrast has subsidiaries in Ghana, Ivory Cost, Kenya, Madagascar and Senegal,* as well as Latin America and Asia.

Both General Foods and Nestlé are changing their buying policies so that they are making few direct purchases from producer countries, unless they have subsidaries there. Instead they are moving increasingly towards general purchases on the world market.** It is therefore not possible to produce a breakdown of how much coffee each company buys from different African countries. What is clear is that the companies have a very tight grip on the processing and marketing of coffee internationally.

This makes it particularly difficult for African producers to increase the value of their cash crop by building up a domestic processing industry. Any new processing industry is forced to compete directly with

*A detailed examination of the Nestlé literature reveals discrepancies between the companies public relations claims and its real contribution to the development of African economies. It has been shown that world wide, Nestlé paid out 15.7 per cent of its sales revenue in salaries in 1974, yet salaries represented a mere 1.6 per cent of sales revenue in Africa (and 2.8 per cent in Asia). In the same year, Nestlé exported 84 per cent of the Ivory Coast's coffee, but the producers only receives $393 per tone, while the value of African coffee was $1.290 per tonne at the very least and Nestlé itself claims to have paid $1.625 per tonne on the world market[32].

**This is not to imply that the companies have lost their potential for direct leverage over a producer country. In 1977 for example, General Foods ceased direct purchases of Ugandan coffee as part of a boycott of Amin's regime; the following May the Company halted indirect purchases via its importers and brokers.[33]

the immensely powerful transnationals, with no hope of matching their financial, technical or marketing resources. Tanzania's experience, which is described below, illustrates many of the problems involved in pursuing this course.

Where a transnational has established its own subsidiary in a producing country, as Nestlé have done in the Ivory Coast, processing may take place locally, but the host country remains vulnerable, as it is likely to become increasingly dependent on the company's technology and expertise. It may also find that the company is encouraging a growing domestic consumption of a non-essential food. This is what has happened in the Ivory Coast.

Nestlé and the Ivory Coast[34]

An agreement between the government of the Ivory Coast and Nestlé's French subsidiary, Societe de Produits Alimentaires et Dietetiques, SOPAD, was signed in January 1959, shortly before independence. Nestlé negotiated very favourable terms in return for establishing a factory to produce instant coffee under the 'Nescafé' label in a country where the internal market was small and coffee consumption was not the custom. The Ivory Coast gave Nestlé total exemption from all export duties and taxes on both green beans and instant coffee for agreed tonnages over a period of 12 years. Although exemptions in the first five years were not to exceed the initial investment, by 1970 the Nestlé subsidiary had been exempted from export duties to the tune of Fcs CFA 955,401,428, about 38 times its original investment.

Despite this, the installation of the factory was, initially, only of limited importance to the overall strategy of the group, since its main interest continued to be the purchase and export of raw coffee. By the end of the twelve-year contractual period, however, the picture had changed dramatically, since the habit of consuming coffee had been pushed vigorously in the Ivory Coast, resulting in a very rapid expansion of instant coffee.

The cheapness and convenience of the instant coffee would not in itself have been enough to encourage a dramatic change in the customary drinking habits of the Ivory Coast. A special promotion system had been launched for the purpose with trucks taking the coffee to local markets, equipped with canvassers who offered free samples to people for tasting on the spot. So coffee gradually found its way into the shopping baskets of the urban inhabitants, and, to a lesser extent, spread to the rural population as well.

Thus a growing percentage of the monetary earnings of people in the Ivory Coast, themselves very limited, is being spent on a product with no nutritional value. Significantly, coffee consumption has become part of a new breakfast pattern which is replacing the traditional mid-morning meal of starches seasoned with peppers and sauces. It is now common for breakfasts to consist of foodstuffs made from condensed milk and sugar, and increasingly in urban areas, of bread. These new habits are of course based on imported foodstuffs. More recently, a further addition to the Ivory Coast's import bill has been made because Nestlé is installing more sophisticated processing equipment. This will also serve to increase the Ivory Coast's dependence on the company's technology and expertise.

Tanzania's attempt to process its own coffee[35]

In 1963, soon after independence, the new Tanzanian government set up a factory to process coffee, the country's main export earner. Its short history has been fraught with problems.

From the start, the Tanzanians said that they had 'little choice' but to buy the expertise of multinationals to help set up their small factory in Bukoba. Tanzania is naturally keen to make and sell instant coffee, but it is the Western nations who have the technology and access to markets.

The factory was built by a German company and completed in 1966. The equipment, however, was very old-fashioned. 'Being inexperienced in these matters we would hardly be able to tell', commented one Tanzanian official. From 1966 to 1970 no instant coffee could be produced because the spray drier 'wouldn't work'. another German company had to be called in to make extensive modifications, but because of 'delays', further losses were incurred. 'Operational difficulties' prevented the Tanganyika Instant Coffee Company from making any profits at all until 1972. These profits were immediately absorbed by the losses of the previous 9 years. Once the Tanzianians began producing instant coffee on a regular basis they were unable to find marketing outlets, since their coffee did not have an identifiable brand name. To prevent closure being forced by a lack of orders, they had to call in Nestlé to provide management and marketing skills and training, but this 'assistance' has still not resulted in adequate outlets being found for Tanzania's admittedly more expensive, but high quality, instant coffee. In fact, Nestlé appear to have done their best to limit the plant's production since the factory organisation does not include any marketing department as such, this being left to the Nestlé general manager. Until recently, Africafe, the brand name of the Bukoba coffee, was only marketed in Zambia, Kenya and Tanzania itself. It seems that it may soon be marketed in Mozambique too, partly because the closure of the border with Kenya has cut off that market.

Some Tanzanian officials and most of the factory work-force believe that Nestlé was happy to supply a limited East African market, but did not wish to market aggressively abroad in case Africafe should compete with their own Nescafé. As a result, the factory has only ever produced up to half of its maximum yearly capacity of 500 tonnes (only 198 tonnes were produced in 1978 because of the war with Idi Amin's Uganda).

The cost of Nestle's management was considerable. From 1972 to 1977, the company was paid TShs5,800,000 in fees and commissions, which was 13.8 per cent of total costs and more than the factory's total profit of TShs5,500,000. In 1973, the wages of the two Nestlé employees supervising the factory, a manager and an engineer, exceeded the wage bill of the entire 80-strong Tanzanian work force. The agents' annual fee was 668,469 Tanzanian shillings (£41,000), the worker's wages totalled 628,671 Tanzanian shillings (£32,500). Tanzania's Minister of Agriculture stated, "It's not because we love these management agreements, it's because we have no alternatve".

The Nestlé contract ran out in December 1979, but the Tanzanians are still not in a position to run the factory themselves. The management contract charged Nestlé with providing all relevant training, but effectively left control over the training programme to them as well. The consequence of this appears to be that as yet there is no Tanzanian qualified to take over. It seems that when Tanzanians have received training, it has sometimes been inappropriate, e.g. for processes far more automated than those used at Bukoba, or they have been put in positions where they cannot use the training which they've received to the full. As a result, it has been necessary to renew Nestlé's contract.

Nestlé is not the only company in a position to influence Tanzania's attempt to increase local earnings by producing instant coffee. The packing of 'Africafe' into tins is done by Tanzanian Tea Blenders, which is 60 per cent State owned and 40 per cent owned by Brooke Bond Liebig.

Conclusion.

This look at the world coffee trade and some of its effects on African producers has attempted to show the vulnerability of countries which are dependent on the crop and the extent to which a few large transnationals control the trading, processing and marketing of coffee.

The problem for any developing country which relies on cash crops for earning foreign exchange is that, despite mechanisms such as the International Coffee Agreement, prices fluctuate for year to year, making economic planning difficult, particularly for the poorest countries. A recent World Bank analysis of coffee, tea and cocoa was not optimistic about the future price patterns for these commodities. 'Price movements tend to be cyclical: short periods of boom with attendant over-investment are often followed by long periods of over-supply and low prices. Historically, real prices of the commodities — coffee, tea and cocoa — have tended to decline . . . they may decline rapidly and reach low levels in the mid-1980s.[36]

With real prices for commodities declining and the vast majority of the world's manufactured goods being made in rich countries, the Third World is faced with ever-deteriorating terms of trade. In 1969, a coffee producing country had to sell 66 bags of coffee to buy one 16 tonne truck, but by 1979, it had to sell 123 bags to buy the same truck.[37]

One way to improve the situation would be for coffee producers to process more coffee themselves, rather than allowing the value added to accrue to the transnationals. This chapter has tried to show how difficult it is in practice for African countries to build up their own coffee processing industry. Two giant transnational dominate both trade and processing in the West and Nestlé, which ranks a mere 42nd in the world's 'top 50' companies, has annual sales 21 times greater than Tanzania's total exports. The major transnationals not only have developed firm control over marketing, they have also attained technological dominance by owning the patents of most processing machinery, which makes it very difficult for coffee producing countries to acquire appropriate technology on their own terms, or, if they do, to then break into world markets. Thus Tanzania's attempt to process coffee has been made more difficult by the supply of out of date machinery and the dependence on Nestlé for an expensive management contract that has not resulted in a secure outlet for its instant coffee. On the other hand, when Brazil managed to begin exporting instant coffee to the United States on a large scale in the 1960s, gaining 14 per cent of the market by 1967, General Foods used their domestic power within the United States to claim 'unfair competition'. The result was that the United States threatened to withdraw from the ICA and to cut off aid, forcing Brazil to tax its own exports and hence become less competitive.

Dependence on cash crops such as coffee has one other major hazard, the non-essential nature of the final product. Few consumers in the West regard coffee as a necessity and two things are likely to happen, should producers attempt to raise their prices substantially. First, total consumer demand will almost certainly drop, as occurred during the dramatic price rises of the late 1970s. Second, the transnationals producing the coffee are likely to increase their output of blends, incorporating cheaper products such as chicory. Adding this factor to the others already mentioned, the price outlook for Africa's coffee producers appears somewhat bleak, and it is equally difficult to be optimistic about their having any chance of dislodging the giant transnationals from their position of dominance over the world market.

CHAPTER 3

Sugar

"Sugar in the past was called 'white gold' because it was so profitable. Many colonial rulers, merchants and capitalists amassed great wealth from sugar. In pursuit of power and profits the colonial powers rushed to conquer new territories. Land was taken away from the people and put into growing sugar and other crops for export to the 'mother country'. Native people were forced to become labourers on the sugar plantations. When harsh conditions wiped out native populations, the plantation owners imported black people as slaves from Africa to work on the plantations. When slavery was abolished indentured labourers were brought from India to take the place of the slaves."[1]

Sugar has indeed a long and shameful history. The industry was the cornerstone of a triangular trade, which began with ships leaving England bound for Africa with trade goods, which were bartered for slaves. These in turn were exchanged in the West Indies for sugar and rum to take back to Britain.[2] The economies of some former colonies — British, French and Dutch — were entirely geared to the production of sugar for their ruling countries and it is still of crucial importance to several major producers, including particularly Cuba, the Dominican Republic, Barbados, Fiji, Guyana, Mauritius and, more recently, Thailand.[3] With a few exceptions, such as Brazil, which consumes about two-thirds of its own production, most poor sugar exporting countries have a small domestic market and depend on the crop as a source of foreign exchange.

In Africa, sugar consumption is already significant and is rising rapidly and many countries are now investing in sugar production to ease their imports, with the intention of exporting the surplus. The poorer countries therefore can be conveniently divided into two categories: those producing mainly for export, and those trying to build up their own industries and become less dependent on imports.[4] Among the countries of sub-Saharan Africa in the first category are Mauritius and Swaziland, both with economies heavily dependent on sugar exports, and Mozambique where the crop remains important. Until the mid-1970s Zimbabwe and the Congo were also significant exporters.

The second category is extensive, and includes Kenya, Ivory Coast, Sudan, Tanzania, Malawi, Zambia, Nigeria and Ghana. Furthermore, the numbers of African countries investing in large-scale sugar production is likely to continue expanding, particularly as sugar is promoted as a means of distilling alcohol for extending petrol supplies. The soaring cost of oil, which now accounts for around half the foreign exchange earnings of most African countries, gives an added incentive for such 'gasohol' projects.

This chapter discusses some of the pressures facing African countries: the tight market in which they are competing when exporting sugar, the problems associated with gasohol, the importance of sugar within African economies and the causes of rising demand. The role of the major sugar development companies in building the African sugar industry is examined, and the strands are drawn together by looking at three countries which have put much faith and energy into establishing a sugar industry: Sudan, Ivory Coast and Kenya.

The Market for Sugar

To appreciate the position of African exporters, it is important to understand the precarious nature of the major markets to which they sell their produce — Europe and the United States. In Europe, the tropical sugar cane growing countries face competition from European beet sugar producers, while in the United States they are competing increasingly with new and cheaper maize-based sweeteners.

Traditionally, the price of sugar has been unstable, often fluctuating wildly. In 1974 it reached an all-time high of £665 a tonne, and the idea of white gold caught the imagination of many governments, stimulating investment in sugar in both industralised and underdeveloped countries. For the major sugar-consuming industries there was a new incentive for research into alternatives. In fact, the shortage which had pushed up the price proved short-lived. By 1976 supplies had returned to normal and the price had again dropped. Prices remained low throughout the rest of the 1970s, falling as far as £93 a tonne in both 1978 and 1979. In 1980, a new period of fluctuations began, with prices ranging from £205 a tonne in January to over £400 in October. These higher prices were again short-lived, by May 1981 they were back to a 14-month low of £180, by June 1982 had fallen further to £100.

These price fluctuations indicate the rather limited protection offered to exporters by the International Sugar Agreement (ISA), which has been signed by most major producers, with the notable exception of the EEC.

The ISA is a price-support treaty which came into force in1978, binding its signatories to implement agreed measures to keep the price of sugar within a band of 13-23 US cents a pound. These measures include export quotas, which operate only when the price falls below an agreed level (currently 16 cents a pound) for five consecutive days, thus requiring ISA exporters to build up stocks rather than export. The total world market sales by ISA exporters was limited to 14.3 million tonnes in 1981,[5] a quantity worked out on the basis of annual import demands, excluding special contracts and trading deals between countries (or companies). The total world trade in sugar is about 90 million tonnes a year, so that only about 16 per cent of sugar is traded through the market.

Britain and the United States are the two largest importers of sugar from African countries. Britain alone consumes a total of around 2.5 million tonnes of sugar a year, sold in packeted form directly to households, and in bulk to the food and drinks industries. Before the UK joined the European Common Market, cane sugar accounted for about two-thirds of all sugar refined in Britain, and sugar cane was still imported from former colonies. The rest of the European Community consumed mainly home-produced beet sugar, which grows well in the temperate northern zones. When Britain joined the EEC it was expected to find a way of harmonising with the practices of other EEC countries, by using more beet sugar.

Britain's traditional suppliers (ex-colonies where sugar industries had been established in the days of the Empire) were offered a limited protection for their markets under the Lomé Convention:* they could continue to supply sugar to the EEC up to a specific quota, but only to existing trade channels. Consequently, Britain is virtually the only buyer of cane sugar in Western Europe, and comes under continual pressure from the EEC to switch over to sugar beet.

During the period of record sugar prices in 1974, when supplies were scarce for a short period, the EEC's Council of Ministers encouraged farmers to produce more sugar beet. Price incentives were raised and production increased dramatically. However, in spite of supplies returning to normal by 1976, the incentives remained and EEC beet farmers have been over-producing ever since. Production has consistently exceeded the Community's needs and the surplus is sold on the world market at subsidised prices, making the EEC one of the world's major sugar exporters, second only to Cuba.

In 1980, the EEC *exported* 3.9 million tonnes of sugar, more than was produced in the whole of Africa.[6] This simultaneously depresses the world market price for sugar, and puts pressure on Britain to cut its imports of cane. Recently, Britain has increased its self-sufficiency in sugar and modernised its beet refining capacity , and although it has so far honoured commitments under the EEC's Lomé Agreement to take approximately 1.3 million tonnes of cane sugar a year from the African, Caribbean and Pacific (ACP) countries, there is clearly a shrinking market for it.

Under a special protocol attached to the Lomé Convention, most of Britain's traditional suppliers were allocated a quota for duty-free sugar

---

* The Lomé Convention, signed in 1975, is a multilateral agreement between the EEC and about 46 African, Caribbean and Pacific countries, mostly ex-French or British colonies. The provisions of the Convention cover trade, aid and industrial co-operation.

imports into the EEC and these are shown in Table 3.1.

Table 3.1
UK Sugar Imports from ACP Countries 1978

African Countries	Tonnes p.a.	Other Countries	Tonnes p.a.
Mauritius	487,200	Fiji	163,600
Swaziland	116,400	Guyana	157,700
Malawi	20,000	Jamaica	118,300
Madagascar	10,000	Trinidad	69,000
Congo	10,000	Barbados	49,300
Tanzania	10,000	Belize	39,400
Kenya	5,000	St. Kitts	14,800
Uganda	5,000	Surinam	4,000
		India	25,000
	663,600		641,100
Other countries	641,100		
	1,304,700		

Source: Tate & Lyle, Annual Report 1979.

Virtually all the quota comes to Britain as the traditional purchaser — approximately 1.225 million tonnes a year. And once in the UK the sugar goes almost entirely to Tate & Lyle, the only remaining sugar cane refiner in Britain.* This makes Tate & Lyle and the ACP countries rather unlikely bedfellows, both arguing for the continued imports of cane sugar to Britain. However, Tate & Lyle have found it increasingly uncompetitive to refine cane sugar in the UK and by 1979 had reduced capacity by 650,000 tonnes, shedding over 2,000 jobs in the process.[7] Then in 1981 the company closed its main refinery in Liverpool, with a further cutback in jobs. The company is now on the defensive, sugar consumption has dropped in the UK and export sales of refined cane sugar have been affected by competition from subsidised EEC sugar exports. Tate & Lyle will undoubtedly stop refining altogether if it becomes completely unprofitable, thus removing the only outlet for ACP sugar within the EEC.

This makes for a precarious market and is extremely serious for those African countries, with economies dependent on sugar exports. Sugar exports account for about three-quarters of Mauritius' foreign exchange earnings, and half of Swaziland's, in most years. These countries

* In Britain, beet sugar is entirely refined by the British Sugar Corporation, until recently 24 per cent owned by the government. S. & W. Berisford now hold 40.02 per cent of the shares.

exported a total of 579,044 tonnes and 226,200 tonnes respectively in 1978. The percentage of foreign earnings from sugar for the other countries in 1978 were: Malawi 10 per cent, Madagascar 8 per cent, and smaller, though not insignificant amounts for Kenya, Tanzania and Uganda.

The United States' market on the other hand is supplied largely by domestic production and imports from the Caribbean and Latin American States. However, the US does import from some African countries, as shown in Table 3.2.

Table 3.2

US Sugar Imports (Short Tons) 1977-81

	1977	1978	1980	1981
Mauritius	57,363	112,261	84,876	None
S. Africa	274,227	60,058	164,025	None
Swaziland	61,855	82,456	124,451	192,000
Malawi	38,358	37,028	46,231	88,000
Mozambique	97,311	12,913	29,025	40,000
Zimbabwe	—	—	13,586	92,000

Source: US Department of Agriculture, Sugar & Sweetener Report, SSR Vol.4. March and May 1979.

The largest sugar-using industries in the United States are beverages (51.5 million hundredweights in 1978), then bakery, cereal and allied products (25.6 million hundredweights, 1978), followed by confectionary, ice-cream, dairy and general food uses.[8] Cane sugar markets in the United States are threatened by the development of high fructose corn sugar (HFCS), or isoglucose, produced from refining the starch extracted from maize. It can be made up to twice as sweet as sucrose from conventional sugar and undersells sugar wherever it is made.[9] Production of HFCS leaped from 83 tonnes in 1970 to 2.1 million tonnes in 1980 and it may double again by 1985.[10] Its market share will undoubtedly grow, particularly since it is most suitable for use in the beverage industry and both Coca Cola and Pepsi Cola announced in 1980 that HFCS will be used in the production of *all* their soft drinks.[11] Although HFCS cannot completely replace sugar (at present it is only available in liquid form; must be stored at very high temperatures, and needs processing facilities only available in the industrialised countries), it could lead the United States, the world's biggest importer, to import little more than two million tonnes of sugar by 1985, against more than 4.2 million tonnes in 1979.[12] According to a report from the US State Department, the US may be able to dispense with sugar imports entirely by 1990.

It is not the intention to suggest that the EEC and the United States provide the only outlet for sugar exports. For example, a major buying spree by the USSR was probably responsible for the high sugar price reached in November 1980,[13] while India, which is traditionally a sugar exporter, was forced to import around two million tonnes in the same year. However, the EEC and the US have been the biggest and most stable markets for African exporters and Britain has had particular significance for its traditional suppliers, such as Mauritius. Not only are both these markets now threatened, but the EEC's emergence as a major exporter of subsidised sugar is exacerbating the problem of finding alternative outlets.

Yet, despite the apparently poor prospects for exporters, many developing countries are either establishing new sugar industries or are building up existing ones. In some cases the aim is simply import substitution, but there is growing interest in the use of sugar cane as the raw material for industrial rather than food products. Above all, there is optimism that there will be a big increase in the demand for sugar for processing into petroleum substitutes, such as ethanol or gasohol (which is a mixture of petrol and ethyl alcohol). In 1975, Brazil launched a massive fuels from sugar programme and, if other countries follow this lead, the importance of the crop is likely to grow substantially. Several African countries have decided to invest in sugar conversion plants and the number is likely to grow, with support from governments and transnationals (see below).

Sugar in Africa

Sugar consumption in all Third World countries is rising. F.O. Licht, a leading sugar commodity broker, points out that if current trends continue, worldwide sugar consumption will exceed 100 million tons a year by 1984-5. By 1983-4, consumption in underdeveloped countries is predicted to exceed use in industrialised countries, where sugar consumption is falling.[14] Sugar accounts for a significant proportion of the import bill in some African countries, as shown in Table 3.3, and so, unless its use is actively discouraged, there is a strong incentive for local production. In some years, sugar has been the single largest food import in Chad and Uganda and, in the late 70s, it was the second largest food item imported by Ghana, Nigeria, Senegal, Sierra Leone, Somalia and Sudan. (Despite this, Sudan has been struggling to become a major supplier to the Middle East,[15] and large sugar development schemes are now under construction, as shown below).

Rising demand does not necessarily mean that more sugar is eaten throughout the population, but rather that city dwellers, whose dietary aspirations reflect those of the rich industrialised countries, tend to choose diets with a higher sugar content as their incomes rise. For example, in countries where people have for centuries eaten a breakfast of staple foods, such as maize, yams, cassava, sorghum or millet, the richer city dwellers now eat cereal products which not only have sugar sprinkled over them, but contain it as an ingredient.[16] These breakfast cereals are either imported or developed from an established recipe and sold under their world-famous brand names, having been prepared by a local company under licence. For example, the House of Manji, a large Asian-owned firm in Kenya, sells Alpen and Weetabix (using, incidentally, wheat which has to be imported to Kenya).[17] Generally the biggest sugar users are the African subsidiaries of large food processing companies, and include cake and biscuit manufacturers and food processing companies selling tinned fruits, etc. (see table 1.4). Given the opportunity, several of these industries prefer to import sugar, even when sufficient is produced locally, as the imported product is generally more highly refined and of better quality.[18] A particularly significant user is the soft drinks industry. Several plants now operate under licence in Africa, like the large Lonhro-run Coca Cola factory in Zambia.

Table 3.3

Imports of Sugar by Selected African Countries
(Shown as Percentage of total imports, by value)

	1976	1977
Chad	8	2
Gambia	4	4
Mali	9.6	4.7
Senegal	4	3
Sierra Leone	4.2	3.6
Somalia	7.7	11
Sudan	6.5	3.7
Uganda	—	—

Source: FAO Trade Yearbook 1978.

Increased demand has created pressure to establish local sugar industries, both to save foreign exchange and to cut dependency on imports. Some governments were persuaded to take this step in 1974, when the price of sugar rocketed to £665 a tonne and imports became prohibitively expensive. The high price also made sugar an attractive export crop for those countries wanting to diversify away from one or two cash crops. The rather precarious nature of the sugar market was not always appreciated.

Building a sugar industry rapidly from nothing to a size capable of supplying domestic needs, and perhaps an exportable surplus (as Ivory

Coast has), usually implies dependence on foreign know-how, machinery and, not infrequently, management. Nonetheless, some developing countries have succeeded without creating dependency patterns. India did so by prohibiting imports of equipment for sugar processing. There is a connection between mill size, and the degree of technical sophistication and complexity of the machinery employed, so it is significant that India and Taiwan have concentrated on developing relatively small, widely-dispersed and labour-intensive factories.[19] In the larger mills often found in Africa, it is less easy to achieve appropriate capital labour and labour/output ratios.

Sugar and the Companies

In contrast to the Indian approach, the large transnational sugar corporations offer capital-intensive development through a wide range of services. These include feasibility studies, site surveys, soil advice, pilot projects, studies of existing sugar industries, advice on expansion, and finally the supply of any equipment required for irrigation or for the factory. The companies can oversee the building stage and supply management for the first years of a factory's operations. Two British companies in particular, Tate & Lyle and Booker McConnell, have been swift to take advantage of this developing market and have set up respectively, Tate & Lyle Agribusiness Ltd (formerly Tate & Lyle Engineering Ltd), and Booker Agriculture International Ltd.* During the 1970s, Bookers advised on over 25 sugar projects in 11 African countries, and Tate & Lyle on almost 30 in the same number of countries, as shown in Tables 3.4 and 3.5 below.

An African government has of course the choice between approaching India or Taiwan, or one of the large agribusiness transnationals for advice and assistance in setting up a sugar industry. However, having approached a transnational sugar consultancy, the advice will almost certainly be to adopt the technologies developed for large-scale sugar projects. The trend for African countries to use the services of the companies and opt for large factories and capital-intensive technology is sustained by the fact that it is much cheaper to expand an existing installation to the required capacity than to build an additional one. Old plants not suited for enlargement have been closed down and new factories are built in a way that allows for expansion.[20]

The majority of governments appear to have opted for advice from the transnationals, but even where aid finance is used to develop sugar industries, countries do not have a free choice over consultancies. The World Bank is a major investor in sugar development and prefers advice from transnational consultancies. For example, the Bank has paid for

* See company profiles.

Selected Tate & Lyle Technical Services African Projects
(with Tate & Lyle Engineering)

Country	Commissioning body and Location	Details of Sugar Scheme	Details of Other Schemes	Planning & Feasibility	Implementation	Management
Cameroon	For Redpath Sugars (T&L Canadian subsidiary)	40,000 tonnes per factory 6,000ha irrigated estate		*	*	*
Ghana	For government	Survey, site identification		*[1]	*	*
	For government at: Havi	60,000 tonne pa factory 8,000ha irrigated cane pilot seed cane farm		*[1]	*	*
	For government at: Tono		400ha general irrigated agriculture	*[1]		
	For private client: Aveyime		Irrigating and recommending crops, including relocation of farmers 2,240ha mixed agriculture			
			6,928 acres ag. dev. project maize, rice, soya, vegetables, fish farm			
	Angaw Creek		Identifying project for investment under government's incentive scheme	*		
	Private Client	Sugar Sweetener, pilot project and research				
Guinea-Bassau	For government/FAO sponsored	Sugar appraisal		*	*	*
Ivory Coast	Ferkessedougou, for Société de Developpement de SUCRE	60,000 tonnes pa factory 6,200ha irrigated cane Soil survey		* *	*	*
Kenya	For government/IBRD sponsored	Sugar appraisal		*[2]		
Nigeria	For Sunti Sugar Co.	40,000 tonne pa factory 6,000ha estate		*	*	*
Sierra Leone	For government	Sugar factory & estate		*	*	*
	For government, E Prov. Government/FAO Finance	Sugar factory & estate		*		
	For government		N. Province, onion/groundnut project National rubber survey	*		
Sudan	For government/European Dev. Fund financed	Molasses production, processing & marketing study		*		
Swaziland	For government/Royal Swazi Sugar Co.	90,000 irrigated cane 17,000 tonnes pa factory Factory and estate		* * *	*	*
	For government at Simunye	Factory expansion			*	*
	For Malume Sugar Co. Ltd.	1. Expansion and rehab. of existing estates. 2. Survey potential new areas		*[3]		
Tanzania	National Sugar Survey, For government/IBRD financed	Sugar factory & estates		*[3]	*	*
Zambia	For Zambia Sugar Co.	Technical Assistance		*	*	*
	For Zambia Sugar Co.	Technical Services				
	For Zambia Sugar Co.		Integrated agricultural scheme for oilseeds and cereals			
	For government (INDECO), at Big Concession					
	For government at Luena	8,500ha irrigated estate	6,750 irrigated wheat and rice estate some coffee	*		*
	For Zambia Sugar Co.		Soybeans, banana, other 15,000ha irrigated wheat and soya			
	For Government at Mpongwe	60,000 tonnes pa factory		*	*[4]	

1. With Taylor Woodrow Ltd. 2. With Economist Intelligence Unit. 3. With Booker Agriculture International Ltd. 4. With Landell Mills Associates Ltd and Brian Colquhoun and Partners.

Source: Tate & Lyle Technical Services Ltd., Capabilities and Experience. Ref 1979/3.

Table 3.5

Selected Booker Agriculture International African Projects

Country	Year	Commissioning body and Location	Details of Sugar Scheme	Details of Other Schemes	Planning & Feasibility	Implementation	Management
Angola	1970	Companhia do Acucar de Angola	Advice on Agricultural problems on Tontativa and Dombe Estates		*		
	1972	Agro-Industrial Projects Group	Evaluate soils and land potential at Cahambo		*		
Ethiopia	1976	Government	Study existing sugar industry and markets. Determine location of new factories.		*	*	
Ghana	1971	World Bank	Provide experts in sugar accounting, finance & marketing for sugar factories at Atsutsuare and Komenda.			*	
Kenya	1970	Government, for Muhoroni factory	Expansion, cost and related cane supply needs		*		
	1970	Ministry of Commerce and Industry		Report on production of potable and industrial alcohol, chemicals and food yeasts from molasses	*		
	1974	Government, Nzoia area, in Western province output 100,000 tonnes	Nucleus estate, factory and outgrower scheme. Potential output 100,000 tonnes pa.		*		
	1975	Government. Mumias Sugar Company	Extensions. Increasing collection area from 13 to 21km and expand factory.		*		
	1978	ODM; Kunati and Rubingazi areas of Tana River Basin	Provide agricultural technical, financial and managerial staff (3250ha, plus outgrowers).	Study agricultural development potential	*	*	*
Lesotho	1977	Presumably Government. At Phuthiatsana River Valley, 450sq.m.		Study soil conservation, grazing and livestock management; effect on local population; effect of proposed dam.	*		*
Malawi	1970	National Trading Co, Chombe		Develop tea estate	*		
	1973	UK consulting engineers, UNDP survey; at Lake Malawi Lakeshore Development Project. EEC funded		Define irrigable areas, provide expertise	*		
	1977				*		
Nigeria	1970	Commonwealth Development Corp, with UK consultant at Numan	Preliminary investigation of sugar project	Rice and cassava			
	1971	Federal Ministry of Industries. At Lafiagi.	Soil survey for proposed sugar scheme		*		
	1975	Federal Ministry of Industry & Commonwealth Development Corp	Designing, building, sugar factory, drawing on 12,000ha cane estate.		*	*	

Date	Country / Client	Project
1976	Hadejia-Juma are River Basin Authority, with Nigerian Agricultural Promotions Co (NAPC) and UK Consultants. In Kano river basin.	Major irrigation, agricultural and socio-economic investigation and pilot scheme
1977	NAPC	Potential of aerial crop spraying.
1977	Not stated who commissioned. At Kaduna River Basin.	Potential projects for 7 million ha area, including water control, hydro-power and infrastructure.
1978	NAPC. Chad Basin area. Nigerian Sugar Co.	Technical services, for 4,500ha irrigated cane
—	NAPC. Northern States. Savannah Sugar Co.	New sugar factory, to process 4000 tonnes cane per day and package refined sugar. Study pilot sheep-rearing.
—		Agricultural enterprises: coffee, tea, kenaf.
Senegal	Richard Toll Estate, owned by Compagnie Sucriere Senegalaise.	Agricultural services.
Somalia	Government. Middle Juba Scheme	Develop major project. 6,000ha irrigated cane, factory. Aim to produce 50,000 tonnes of mill white sugar per year.
Swaziland 1972	Commonwealth Development Corp. In north-east.	New sugar factory. 8,000ha of irrigated cane.
Tanzania 1974	Government. Kagera estate.	Redevelopment of estate and planting additional 16,000ha of cane.
1976	Sugar Development Corp, with World Bank.	Comprehensive survey of existing sugar industry, potential development and National sugar plan.
1978	Sugar Development Corp. with World Bank. At Kilombero and Mtibwa estates.	Expansion and new production at Ruipa.
Uganda 1976	Ugandan consultants. At Kinyala.	Monitor commissioning of a new sugar factory. (Monitoring commissioning)
Zambia 1974	Government. At Lake Bangweulu	Feasibility for sugar cane, recommend programme, suggest alternative sugar-producing areas.
1978	Commonwealth Development Corp., Lukulu Estate, Northern Province	Appraise coffee/wheat/soya project. Include other crops in study.

Source: Booker Agriculture International, Company publication 1979.

Bookers and Tate & Lyle jointly to produce a survey preliminary to an overhaul of the Tanzanian sugar industry.

The role played by the companies provide a clear example of how they have adapted to the demands of countries which wish to build up an industry, reduce reliance on imports and at the same time retain ownership within the country. The companies do not own the sugar plantations and factories, but on the other hand they receive fees for feasibility studies, consultancy services, surveys, technical assistance and so on. In the words of sugar expert, G.B. Hagelberg:

> "By setting up this supply of technological, organisational and commercial know-how, the transnational companies have to a certain extent preserved the flow of income they derived from the Third World, although in some cases the services provided may be financed out of grants from industrialised countries. It is possible that under their influence the choice of techniques has been biased in favour of large-scale, sophisticated and capital-intensive methods of production, thus generating or reinforcing forms of dependency not related to ownership."[21]

Both Bookers and Tate & Lyle have UK-based engineering subsidiaries which design and supply complete sugar factories. The consultants can clearly take advantage of their knowledge of a particular scheme to put orders in the way of other subsidiaries in the groups. These two companies also supply management services, and have management agreements to run factories and manage sugar estates in Kenya, Nigeria, Senegal, Somalia (Bookers) and Ghana, Ivory Coast, Swaziland and Zambia (Tate and Lyle).

Another British company with heavy investments in the African sugar industry is Lonrho. Their first sugar venture took place through a sudsidiary, the Sugar Corporation of Malawi, and was part of a plan to develop Malawi into a sugar-exporting country. Lonrho's other sugar interests are in Benin, Ghana, Ivory Coast, Mauritius, Mozambique, South Africa, Sudan and Swaziland. Like Bookers and Tate & Lyle, Lonrho has also built up a large number of consultancies and management agreements. Through the Swaziland subsidiary, Swaziland Sugar Milling Co., Lonrho owns three sugar factories in Mauritius and one each in Malawi, Swaziland and South Africa. The company is principal adviser to one of Ivory Coast's large sugar development projects at Ferkessedougou, and was also involved in the giant Kenana sugar scheme in the Sudan (see below).

Sopex, a Belgian company, won a contract in 1980 to overhaul Angola's sugar industry over a period of 20 years, covering existing plantations, sugar factories and alcohol distillers.[22] The same company is carrying out feasibility studies for the Zaire government, involving three sugar projects, with an eventual aim of setting up a sugar factory in all eight provinces, each with a capacity of 50,000 tonnes, and at a cost of US $67 million. Similarly, in Niger, two French firms are to build a sugar complex with a minimum capacity of 20,000 tonnes a year on irrigated land. The companies, Technip and CFDT, will remain for five years to manage the development and train local staff. This pattern is repeated across the Continent.

Sudan

Sudan is a major sugar-consuming country, where demand has risen from 210,342 tonnes a year in 1969 to 330,678 tonnes in 1979. The first plans for sugar self-sufficiency were mooted as long ago as 1956 and became more urgent as consumption rose. Later plans were aimed at creating a surplus to export to Sudan's richer Arab neighbours. In all, six major schemes have been launched in Sudan, and the two most successful of these, at Geneid and New Halfa, both came on stream in 1966 and were together producing 128,651 tonnes by 1974-5[23] The history of the remaining four sugar schemes has been littered with disasters, including technical and managerial problems, and vast under-estimates of the costs involved.

The largest and most costly project is the Kenana sugar complex, considered the largest sugar scheme in the world, with a capacity to process 310,000 tonnes of sugar a year, and provision to expand to 500,000 tonnes a year. It was designed in 1974 to make the Sudan self-sufficient, and to supply sugar to the Middle East. Although the world sugar price was at an all-time high (£665 per tonne) when the project was launched, it came on stream in 1979, when sugar prices were at a six-year low (£93 a ton). Kenana did not produce *refined* sugar until March 1981, when officially opened by President Numeiri.[24] The aim was to exploit Sudan's soil, sun and water with Arab capital and Western expertise. The brainchild of Dr Khalil Osman Mahmoud, the Sudanese chairman of the Kuwaiti company, Gulf International and his friend 'Tiny' Rowland of Lonrho, Kenana was intended to turn Sudan into a major sugar exporter, and give a return on equity of around 22 per cent.[25] The feasibility study estimated the cost of the project at some $150 million — the final bill was $613 million.[26] The whole project was enormous and involved building a 40-megawatt power station, a network of conduits and canals (the main one 20 miles long), a pumping station to lift the Nile waters 150 feet from the canals to the fields; and a factory to crush 17,000 tonnes of sugar a day. Kenana is 1,000 miles from Port Sudan and roads and transport are also needed to move the sugar.

Lonrho was awarded the management contract for the scheme when it began in 1974, and has a small (3.5 per cent) equity investment in it. Most of the loan capital for the project was raised in the Arab world.[27] The Sudanese government has a 40 per cent interest; the Sudan Development

Corporation has 10 per cent; the Saudi Arabian government holds 17 per cent through the Arab Investment Company; the Kuwaiti government holds 23 per cent. After problems with financing, the Kuwaiti government insisted on choosing a new management company and Lonrho lost its contract in 1977. However, it has been partly reinstated and one of the Lonrho directors, René Leclesio, is back on Kenana's executive committee. The management contract is now with a US company, Arkel International.

The cost of the scheme has been enormous, those benefiting most being the foreign contractors, consultants and managers who had not invested and therefore had no equity to lose. While it is true that Kenana may contribute to sugar self-sufficiency in Sudan, the more modest schemes at Geneid and New Halfa serve the same purpose and can produce sugar at what will probably be a quarter of the cost.[28] At present prices, it seems inevitable that losses will be incurred on sugar exports from Kenana.

Multinational consultants have been involved in all three of Sudan's other major sugar schemes, none of which have run smoothly. The Sennar Sugar Factory, which began production in 1976-77, has produced a negligible amount of sugar, because of technical obstacles (boiler defects and lack of spare parts), irrigational problems and inadequate training, and has cost to date £27.7 million. The second scheme, Hajar Assalaya, built by Fletcher & Stewart, a Booker McConnell subsidiary, ran two years behind schedule, and a legal battle was precipitated when it was found that Fletcher & Stewart had installed secondhand boilers, possibly from the Sennar Sugar Factory. There was an endless list of complaints against Hajar Assalaya, including irrigational defects, pumps out of order, insufficient electricity supply, and poor conditions which made it almost impossible to keep technicians on site. Of the final scheme at Melut little is known, but it is reported to be running into serious problems and the lack of roads to the site is causing extensive delays.[29]

The formidable problems associated with the development of new sugar schemes have meant that, in all probability, Sudan will end up subsidising its own food exports to much richer Arab neighbours. The government has clearly had second thoughts on its role as a major agricultural supplier to the Middle East and has seriously considered growing more wheat for domestic consumption instead of cash crops. But when foreign debt problems forced it to ask for a loan from the International Monetary Fund in 1979, the IMF insisted that Sudan continue to grow cash crops such as sugar, cotton, groundnuts, sesame and gum arabic for export, and pressured the government to drop wheat schemes.[30]

Ivory Coast

Like many other countries, Ivory Coast laid plans for sugar expansion during the brief period of high prices in the early 1970s. The aim was to reduce dependence on sugar imports (around £13 milion in 1974) and to diversify exports. Most of Ivory Coast's investment had gone to the south of the country, and the sugar industry was to be located in the poor northern region.[31] Two large schemes each with production capacities of 60,000 tonnes a year were planned at Ferkessedougou — one managed by Lonrho, the other in the hands of two Tate & Lyle subsidiaries, Tate & Lyle Engineering Ltd and Redpath of Canada. The latter were granted a $172 million contract to construct an agro-industrial sugar complex with supporting infrastructure.[32] The scheme of 14,800 acres included a sugar plantation with irrigation systems, agricultural machinery and equipment, a sugar factory, 850 housing units, roads and a rail spur, and a marine sugar and molasses terminal.[33] Redpath Sugars Ltd also have a five-year management contract, worth several million dollars.

However, the plans for sugar expansion did not stop at Ferkessedougou, and a further eight schemes were proposed. Four of these were dropped and although the others are going ahead, only the one at Borotou-Koro, being built by ADRA, an agribusiness offshoot of Renault, is at an advanced stage.[34] The three remaining schemes are also being developed by European transnational corporations: Technisucre, a French company, is developing a second estate at Borotou; Ateliers Bèlges Réunies (of the Franco-Belgian Empain-Schneider group) and the Dutch Company HVA are building the biggest project at Zuenoula; Krupp's Buckau-Wolff subsidiary is building another at Comeo-Serebou. Ivory Coast was expected to produce a surplus of around 200,000 tonnes a year by 1981, with local demand already being met by the two Ferkessedougou mills.

There is some question about the ease with which Ivory Coast will find a market for its sugar. The size of its schemes provoked a mini-crisis in the EEC in 1978, when the extent of sugar projects in many ACP countries exporting to the EEC received prominence (although Ivory Coast as a late sugar developer is not included among them). The EEC Commission learned that 66 projects were planned to increase sugar capacity, and that 44 were supported financially by banks and firms from the European Community. The EEC would not under any circumstances increase its quota for sugar imports from either ACP or any other Third World countries, and the Community's Development Commissioner, Claude Cheysson, sharply critised European companies, saying they were in the business of "selling boiler plate and it was immaterial to them whether they sold boiler plate for sugar mills or any other kind of factory".[35] While the EEC's own sugar policies are open to severe criticism, it is also clear that the transnational sugar consultancies give priority to their own interests rather than those of Third World producers.

Kenya — the Mumias Sugar Scheme

The Mumias sugar development in Kenya* has been widely praised as a good example of an agribusiness development, particularly when compared to the enormous capital-intensive schemes in the Sudan and Ivory Coast.

Mumias was set up in Western Kenya by the Kenyan government and Booker McConnell, and has been developed around a nucleus estate with over 5,000 outgrowers, who each have an average of four acres of land under cane, but have as much land again available for growing food crops.** The company ploughs, furrows and loads the cane from the smallholders' plots and takes it to the factory. All weeding and cutting is done by the farmers, often organised in teams.[36] The nucleus estate is managed by the company, and contains the sugar factory. But costly labour-saving devices have been avoided and labour-intensive technologies are used in the factory wherever feasible. Although Booker McConnell hold only 5 per cent of the equity (the rest being held by the Kenyan government), they run the factory and estate under a management agreement, and receive a percentage of profit for technical services.

Mumias was planned as one of a series of sugar developments in Western Kenya, and was by far the most successful of the schemes. In other parts of the country, where sugar schemes are less rewarding, farmers have been reported to be uprooting cane and planting other cash crops for sale on local markets.[37] Indeed, Mumias illustrates that African governments can choose alternatives to capital-intensive production, even when using a transnational consultancy, provided that they are clear which objectives they wish to achieve; in this case a labour-intensive factory and smallholder schemes, rather than one large plantation.

In spite of the relative success of the Mumias scheme, it must be recognised that the government has not been able to avoid the food v. cash crops issue. Sugar cane competes directly with food crops for the better land. Kenya is trying to overcome its deficiency in maize, one of the country's staples, at the same time as it is promoting sugar plantations, both for its own processing industries and fuel production. But it is precisely in the traditional breadbasket of Kenya, the Western province,

* For a full description of the Mumias scheme, see Susan George, *How the Other Half Dies,* Penguin 1976, pp.182-185.

** This is large for a smallholder plot. Peasant farmers in Kenya have on average less than 3ha.

that farmers have responded to government incentives and have switched from growing maize to growing sugar, and so contributed to the need to import maize. This competition for land could intensify considerably if Kenya continues to expand its facilities for turning sugar into ethanol and several other countries are likely to experience the same problem.

Although sugar has several attractions as a source of fuel — it is renewable and capable of reducing expensive oil imports — there are dangers in emulating the Brazilian programme in Africa. Some of the drawbacks of the technology are already becoming apparent in Brazil itself.

Fuel from Sugar — An Opportunity for Africa?

The reputed success of the Brazilian Proalcool programme for turning sugar into ethyl alcohol (ethanol) has sparked off excitement among both the sugar companies and sugar-growing countries. Brazil has already moved over to petrol containing up to 20 per cent ethanol, over 400,000 cars have been produced or converted to run on pure ethanol and the number is rising rapidly.* The Proalcool programme aims for an annual production of 10.7 billion litres of alcohol by 1985, by which time over 2 million ethanol-fuelled cars are expected to be on the roads. The motor industry's target is to supply 33 per cent of all new cars with alcohol-burning engines by 1985. On the strength of the success of this scheme, and the advantages offered in terms of savings in fuel imports, Brazil has sold the technology abroad to many other underdeveloped countries, including Kenya. African countries either investing in, or actively contemplating similar schemes, include Zimbabwe, Sudan, Ivory Coast, Malawi, Kenya and Zambia.[38] But already several warning signals are being heard in Brazil, pointing not only to problems with the country's own programme, but suggesting that they might be considerably magnified in poorer, less industrialised African countries.

The scale of the operations required for a major ethanol programme are frequently under-estimated. To achieve its target, Brazil must build one average-sized distillation plant (120,000 litres a day output) every four days between now and 1984, with each distillery requiring the development of a new sugar cane plantation to provide the raw material.[39] The current budget is estimated at about $15 billion and the economic returns are distinctly uncertain.

At present the cost of crude oil falls between $30 and $40 a barrel, while the real production cost of alcohol, which is subsidised, is estimated at between $65 and $70 a barrel. Consequently, ethanol is not yet a commercial proposition and it is only likely to become more

* Without specially built or converted engines, 20 per cent is the maximum replacement ration, as alcohol is much more corrosive than petrol.

attractive if sugar prices remain very low. The Brazilian government was recently forced to cut subsidies to alcohol, and as soon as the price differential was reduced, many converted cars were turned back to run on petrol. Sales of alcohol-run cars dropped to 5,000 in June 1981. compared with 40,000 in January.[40] Subsidies are evidently crucial.

Brazil is not short of agricultural land for growing sugar — indeed some argue that only between 2 and 3 per cent of available agricultural land would suffice to make the country self-sufficient in energy.[41] However, this seems a gross under-estimate. Even the most pro-Proalcool supporters admit that the sugar plantations must compete with food production,[42] and others, like one of Brazil's leading environmentalists, José Lutzenberger, are much more worried. Lutzenberger points out that one alcohol business is growing 1,700 square kilometres of sugar cane to product 1-1.5 million litres of alcohol per day, less than 1 per cent of national fuel needs. The land under cane is not that abandoned by smallhoders, but was previously a unique ecosystem of 'cerrado' forest.[43] Also in the north-east of Brazil, many small farmers are being displaced and their farms taken over by big landowners.

If sugar becomes a more profitable crop, this process may continue and there will be a general trend to grow sugar at the expense of food crops. In Sao Paulo State alone, 500,000 hectares have moved from food to sugar production, and an estimated 2.4 million hectares will have to be incorporated to meet the official target of the Proalcool programme. This involves sacrificing five million tons of food crops.[44]

Another important factor to bear in mind is that alcohol can only substitute for petrol, and not diesel fuel. Yet in Brazil, as in most Third World countries, lorries burning diesel provide the main commercial transport. Without lorries, people living outside the main conurbations would starve. However, vegetable oils have been the subject of experimention for some time and offer a promising source of fuel for lorries. These oils can be blended with diesel and there are several other advantages, for example, it is easier to extract fuel from palm oil than to produce ethanol from sugar; year round production is possible; there are less polluting by-products; there is a good energy return; and water is unnecessary for processing.[45] However, this technique is still in the experimental stage and there is not yet any conclusive evidence of its successful use. African countries interested in biomass programmes (i.e. energy from plant matter) have to date gone for solutions based on petrol substitution, even though Brazil, one of the more wealthy Third World countries, with ample land, is having difficulties with its programme.

Some of the problems which sugar-based technologies have posed for Kenya were reported recently by Gavin Bennett.[46] Three sugar-based chemical plants are under construction at Kisumu, Muhoroni and

Nyanza. Kisumu is expected to come on stream in 1982 and produce 20 million litres of ethanol a year. So far the Kisumu plant has cost 1,000 million Kenyan shillings, which is double the original quote, and more than one hundred times other estimates (e.g. the World Bank's), making the cost of the ethanol produced three times higher than the world price of petrol. The Nyanza scheme has since been abandoned because of poor advice from transnational contractors, which apparently failed to point out that fuel oil was needed to run the plant, at a higher cost than the fuel alcohol produced by the factory.[47]

It is doubtful whether Kenya has sufficiently strong demand for the product, given that diesel fuel shortages are more of a problem that a lack of petrol. Brazil has a thriving car industry, manufacturing over 1 million cars a year, but car ownership in Kenya is minute and all the vehicles ever used in Kenya probably total less than 500,000. It is estimated that crude oil prices would have to reach $100 a barrel before Kenyan ethanol became economically viable.

There is no doubt that the transnational corporations which profit from the development of ethanol technology are actively promoting the use of sugar as fuel, and African countries are greatly interested. An Austrian company, VEW, is providing the know-how, equipment and general contracting work for the Kenyan Kisumu plant, and Tate & Lyle and Anglo-American have been competing for a contract to build a £10 million plant in Zambia.[48] Tate & Lyle are keen to sell their advanced technology rather than exploit energy crops themselves and see turnkey projects, at around £9 million a time as a major new market.[49]

However, it seems extremely questionable whether developments of this kind should receive high priority among the poorer, food-deficit African countries. There is a danger of food crops being displaced, as in Kenya, which is now facing a large food import bill for the first time.[50] The Brazilian experience points to the need for ethanol schemes to be treated with caution, particularly as there are few areas in Africa where the climate permits three crops of cane a year, as it does in Brazil.

Conclusion

If African countries are experiencing a rising demand for sugar and growing conditions are right, there is a good case for them to produce the crop themselves and cut back on costly imports. An exportable surplus may also be justified. However, as European and United States markets for imported sugar cane are contracting, this means building up new outlets in, for example, the Middle East, and African, or other Third World countries, countries where consumption is rising. The question remains whether the large, capital-intensive developments promoted by consultancy companies and other agribusiness subsidaries are compatible with the needs of African countries wishing to develop their sugar industries. Ivory Coast's second Ferkessedougou scheme cost £172 million and created 2,500-3,000 jobs — at $60,000 a job, this is rather expensive for a country with an average per capita income of around $500 a year. But it is precisely schemes of this kind which meet the needs of the large sugar companies since they offer an opportunity to sell machinery, irrigation equipment and sugar factories as well as consultancy and management services.

In general, African governments have opted for the development of the full scale, high-technology industries offered by the transnational corporations, and there is an increasing tendency for this to be reinforced by gasohol schemes. However, sugar factories need not necessarily be on the scale which appears most common in African countries building up their industries. There is a wide range of sugar mills in operation, stretching from the smallest, handling 50 tonnes of cane a day (in Cambodia), to the largest in San Cristobel, Mexico, with a theoretical capacity of 27,000 tonnes a day.[51] (Sudan's Kenana factory has a capacity of 17,000 tonnes a day). Several developing countries, including India and Taiwan, have established their own sugar mill industries, which produce less capital-intensive and more labour-intensive machinery. Taiwan has provided the equipment and technicians to build mills in Rwanda, Gabon and Liberia, capable of grinding 60, 300 and 1,000 tonnes of cane a day respectively.[52]

These schemes seem to offer a greater possibility for self-reliance, and indeed a more dependable form of investment than the grandiose, technically sophisticated schemes promoted by the transnationals and aid donors. However, whatever form of development is adopted, there is no doubt that sugar — either for the food processing industry or for fuel utilisation — competes directly with food production.

CHAPTER 4
Kenya

This chapter looks at some of the direct effects and broader implications of the involvement of agribusiness in the Kenyan economy, especially in the production of cash crops and food, and considers to what extent Kenya has been able to control the activities of the local subsidiaries of large foreign companies.

Both smallholders and agribusiness produce Kenya's two main export crops — coffee and tea. Brooke Bond Liebig Ltd., perhaps the major agribusiness corporation in Kenya, has been closely involved in both tea and coffee for almost sixty years, and has managed to adapt to the demands of independent Kenya, at the same time as remaining profitable and expanding its investments there. Brooke Bond's activities are contrasted with those of another transnational, the US company Del Monte (now owned by R.J. Reynolds), which has turned an industry initially established with smallholders into a plantation-style system of agriculture. There is also a brief examination of the role of agribusiness in Kenya's food processing industries. The chapter ends by asking whether Kenya has been successful in controlling foreign companies and considering the government's record in alleviating poverty and reducing inequality.

Kenya's economy expanded rapidly after independence, with average annual economic growth rates of 6.9 per cent between 1964 and 1970 and 4.6 per cent between 1970 and 1977, but by the late 1970s there were signs of stagnation. Exports had been diversified during this period, but export revenue remained heavily dependent on two cash crops, coffee and tea. Table 4.1 sets out the main exports at 1979. The value of tea and coffee fluctuates considerably: in 1977 the two crops accounted for 77 per cent of total export earnings, but when the commodity boom collapsed in 1979, the figure fell to below 50 per cent.

Kenya's problems have been compounded by the lack of indigenous energy resources, and the rising cost of imported energy has had a major impact on the economy. By 1980 the cost of oil imports alone equalled the price received for the entire coffee crop.

Despite the agricultural base of the economy there is a shortage of fertile agricultural land. Only 7 per cent of the total land area has good soil and adequate rainfall and most of this is monopolised by wealthy farmers. A further 4.5 per cent has adequate soil and the remainder is poor or suitable only for stock raising. Nevertheless, Kenya was traditionally self-sufficient in food, and it was a major setback when maize, the staple food, had to be imported for the first time in 1980 and again in 1981. Food self-sufficiency has now become a priority (see box).

Table 4.1

Kenya's Main Exports 1979, and Changes over Year Earlier

	Value 1979 (£Kmn)	Per Cent	Per cent change over year earlier in: Value	Qty	Price
Coffee, unroasted	110.6	29.0	− 11.3	− 9.6	− 2.0
Tea	62.8	16.0	− 0.5	10.7	− 10.1
Petroleum products*	68.0	17.7	13.0	− 16.0	34.7
Meat & Products	2.7	0.6	− 1.2	− 12.8	13.3
Pyrethrum extract	5.5	1.5	34.8	49.6	− 9.9
Sisal	4.8	1.2	18.8	− 3.4	22.9
Hides & skins, undressed	13.8	4.0	40.2	20.1	16.7
Wattle extract	2.0	0.5	32.2	19.2	10.8
Soda ash	5.6	1.3	50.8	34.4	12.3
Fluorspar	2.0	0.5	− 22.7	− 42.3	34.0
Cement	8.3	2.0	− 7.3	− 16.4	10.8
Beans, peas etc.	1.5	0.4	− 30.3	− 34.1	5.5
Wool	0.7	0.2	− 0.1	− 7.3	7.8
Animal feed	1.0	0.3	− 1.3	− 4.8	3.7
Cotton raw	0.9	0.2	− 33.4	− 10.6	− 25.5
Pineapples, canned	9.3	2.4	− 2.8	− 2.5	− 0.2
Butter and ghee	0.8	0.2	− 10.9	− 23.7	16.7
Wood Carvings	0.7	0.1	8.0	− 2.8	11.1
Metal scrap	0.5	0.1	80.7	109.3	− 13.6
Other	84.0	22.0	23.9		
Total	385.5	100.0	4.2		

*Exported processed products. All petroleum is imported.

Source: The Economist Intelligence Unit Report based on Kenya's Economic Survey 1980. Table 7.10.

About 11 million of Kenya's 14 million populaton are smallholders, owning between them about 1.5 million small farms, which exist alongside 3,200 large holdings. Officially a smallholding consists of any farm of less than 8 hectares, but most are much smaller. About three-quarters are less than three hectares in area and usually no more than half the total is actually cultivated at any one time. The average peasant farmer holds only 0.3 hectares.[1] Government policies to stimulate production of cash crops have benefited only a small proportion of such farmers, and one estimate indicated that as few as 12 per cent of farms are responsible for producing most of the marketable output.[2]   This suggests that about 88 per cent of smallholders are subsistence farmers, growing food for their own family consumption but producing little or no surplus for sale. Cash for the purchase of essentials (matches, tea, sugar, salt or school fees) usually must be raised by selling part of the family's own maize supply, by taking casual employment or by receiving money from relatives working in urban areas.[3] Kenya's colonial history helps to explain how this structure has emerged.

Falling Food Production

While the policy has been to encourage an export-oriented agriculture, and to seek agribusiness advice and investment, Kenya's own food supplies have been hit. Food imports have been rising steadily since 1969,[4] although, like many of the food crops grown for cash sale, imports are mainly used to feed the increasing population in the cities, rather than the majority in the rural areas. However, the situation deteriorated significantly in 1980, when for the first time since Independence, people had to queue to buy maize and large quantities were imported. Maize output had fallen from the 1977-78 record of 2.2 million tons to around 1.4 million tons in 1979-80, and over 300,000 tons were imported to cope with the food shortage. In December 1980 the government was forced to order a further 128,000 tons from abroad.

The reasons for the poor harvest were mixed. The national purchasing bodies could not absorb the heavy crops of previous years; poor or insufficient storage facilities had made it difficult to store the bumper crop; farmers left with a surplus, reduced the area planted in the following year; a drought, shortages of farm inputs (especially fertilisers), and low farm prices compounded the problems.[5] In addition, large quantities of maize were still being exported in 1979, even after the crop failure has been predicted.

In a recent paper examining the issues[6] the government drew some stark conclusions. It believes that shortages of maize, wheat, rice and milk are now endemic, and a return to self-sufficiency in maize by 1989 would mean expanding capacity by 4.9 per cent every year at the very least.

Perhaps even more worrying, given the urgency of the need to increase food production, the report states that agricultural expansion in recent years "has been achieved at the expense of widespread soil erosion, depletion of the nutrient content of the soil, and the destruction of indigenous forests". Any further expansion of agricultural production without controls increases this risk.

Of course, increased food production could come from re-allocation of land now cultivated. There is a clear conflict between the need to grow cash and food crops, and recently production of the former has increased at the expense of the latter as government policies have encouraged export crops. In Western Kenya, for example, the swing to sugar production, partly for export, has undoubtedly replaced food production in the region.

Colonial History and the Growth of Agribusiness Interests

Kenya was originally held under a charter company, the Imperial British East Africa Co (IBEA), with wide-ranging powers that included the ability to recruit its own army.[7] In 1893, this arrangement was replaced by direct British rule and, within ten years, the colony was opened up for European settlement. As in other parts of the continent, Africans were forced to become labourers through the application of hut and poll taxes, which compelled them to earn a money income, thus drawing them away from being purely subsistence farmers and into the cash economy.[8] At the same time, the new settlers took land traditionally used by the pastoral tribes, the Masai, Nandi and Kipsigis. Subsequent land shortages forced the Kikuyu who were a farming community to become squatters on the European farms, where they were allocated small pieces of land to cultivate in return for doing regular or seasonal jobs.[9] Peasant production of the profitable cash crops, coffee, sisal and later tea, was at first discouraged and later made illegal.

By 1924, three million hectares, or some 20 per cent of Kenya's best land, was scheduled exclusively for European settlement and was primarily held by two syndicates and five wealthy individuals. At that time some 1,715 settler farmers employed 87,000 African labourers, and during the 1920s and 1930s a further 2,000-3,000 Europeans settled on the best land. Also in the early 1920s, the first major plantation company, Brooke Bond, arrived to grow tea.[10] The 1940s saw the gradual formation of a movement to claim back land from the settlers and to rid Kenya of European control. After a period of increasing tension the British government declared the 'Emergency' in 1952 and after ten years the Mau Mau were eventually defeated, at a cost of 10,000 Africans dead (compared with 30 Europeans). However, the British government now realised that it could no longer hold the colony, and moved toward independence, which took place in 1963. With co-operation from the Commonwealth Development Corporation and the World Bank, finance was provided for settlement schemes to enable Africans to purchase Europeans farms in the fertile 'white highlands'. By 1969 half a million Africans were settled on farms previously owned by settlers over a total area of 1.5 million acres (0.6 million hectares).

However, the unequal land distribution remained a feature of Kenyan agriculture. During the 1960s, one million acres (0.4 million hectares) were bought by Africans as large farms. More were bought from Europeans throughout the 1970s, with the larger (and generally more fertile) estates passing into the hands of prominent Kenyan capitalists. The former squatters on European farms included in the settlement schemes often ended up crowded onto small sections of inferior land. The 1.6 million hectares estimated to be under plantation agriculture at independence remain virtually intact, though there has been little expansion onto new land.

The land transfers of the 1960s and 1970s gave rise to a class with a vested interest in maintaining large farms,[11] and their estates have remained a prominent feature of Kenyan agricultural development, despite the subsequent growth of smallholder tea and coffee schemes. During Kenyatta's presidency from 1964 onwards, few measures were taken to tackle the basic inequalities in Kenyan society, and economic growth was pursued at the expense of the landless, subsistence farmers and the urban poor. Since coming to power in 1978, President Moi has followed a more populist course, for example while still acting-President he announced that "too many people with too much land are still trying to get more, while most Kenyans have none",[12] and he has taken some steps to regulate land allocation. Moi's main reforms have been aimed at the redistribution of wealth, but there has been little attempt to restructure the economy and it is still the policy to encourage foreign investment in both industry and agriculture. Foreign companies are particularly prominent in the cash crop sector.

Coffee, Tea and Agribusiness

Coffee

Coffee is Kenya's largest foreign exchange earner and agricultural export crop. The coffee boom of 1976-77 proved a great boost to Kenya's balance of payments, but prices dropped rapidly in 1978 and have not recovered. Income from coffee exports in the boom year reached £K204.4 million from sales of 94,344 tonnes.* but fell to £K184.8 million from sales of 85,405 tonnes in 1978.[13] Revenue was even lower in 1979, amounting to only £K110.6 million, although the crop was only 10 per cent down on the previous year.

On 1 October 1980, a new International Coffee Agreement was signed by which producers agreed to reintroduce coffee quotas and attempt to control price movements. This may stabilise Kenya's coffee earnings, but still leaves the country in a vulnerable position. Among exporters, Kenya has the eleventh largest quota, with a maximum export allocation of 1.3 million 60kg bags for 1980-81, with a guaranteed price of between 115 and 155 US cents per pound. Even so, by April 1981 the price had not risen much above the lower end, at around 120 US cents a pound. But Kenya exercises very little leverage within the International Coffee Organisation, and its export quota was reduced in February 1981 from

* The price boom in coffee depressed sales considerably and showed that Western consumers were not prepared to pay the escalating price demanded for coffee. This has important implications for coffee-growing countries since it gives some indication of the limits to the price which they can expect to receive.

78,000 to 70,000 tonnes, although the 1981 crop estimates were for 90,000 tonnes.[14]

The government has established control over coffee production to the extent that all the crop must be sold to the parastatal authority, the Coffee Board of Kenya.[15] The Coffee Board now also warehouses the coffee, having taken over complete control of this from the Express Transport Company, a Lonrho subsidiary in 1978. It also conducts the auctions through which all coffee must be sold in Kenya and thus has a fairly accurate idea of how much of the crop is grown by both smallholders and the estate sector. This control over the market provides a safeguard against a transnational corporation selling coffee to its subsidiaries in other countries at reduced prices, thus depriving Kenya of tax revenue.

Government policy since independence has been to prevent foreign-owned plantations from expanding by purchasing new land, and to extend the number of smallholder coffee growers. The smallholders' coffee co-operatives have expanded and delivered 56.6 per cent of the total crop to the Coffee Marketing Board in 1978. However, the estate sector is still significant. The majority of estates are owned by individuals and in September 1978, 72 per cent of estates were owned by Africans (or 62.3 per cent of total hectarage). Foreign individuals or companies account for approximately 14 per cent of total coffee planted.[16] The yield from plantations has recently been falling, but foreign companies are not running down their estates and the drop in output possibly reflects re-organisation and the replanting of estates with new trees. In general it seems that, since transnational corporations cannot expand their hectarage, they are, following the approach of Brooke Bond Liebig Kenya (BBLK) and 'good husbandry' to increase their yields. This means more intensive farming and more intensive management.[17]

The major foreign companies still in the coffee plantation sector in Kenya are Socfinaf Co Ltd (a French company); Sennah Rubber Co Ltd, a British company which also has a 17.05 per cent holding in Socfinaf; Brooke Bond Liebig Kenya Ltd; and Kakuzi Ltd, a Kenyan public company in which Eastern Produce Holdings Ltd, a UK company, has the largest single shareholding of 23.5 per cent (another UK company, Walter Duncan Goodricke Ltd in turn has a controlling interest of 33.4 per cent in Eastern Produce). Apart from owning plantations, however, foreign companies have subsidiaries in Kenya which are responsible for broking, buying and shipping the coffee. There are four agents servicing the large estate sector: East African Acceptance Ltd, a Brooke Bond subsidiary; Warren Kenya Ltd, a subsidiary of a British company which also manufactures coffee-drying equipment in Kenya; and two companies incorporated in Kenya but run by British expatriates, L.W. Mitchell Ltd and Estate Services Ltd. The estate sector and associated companies have their own trade association, the Mild Coffee Trade

Association of Eastern Africa, and their own employers' union, the Coffee Growers Association, which negotiates with workers over wages and working conditions, and informs the growers of government policies. The Kenya Planters Co-operative Union is the agent for all small coffee growers.

The Kenyan government has succeeded in turning coffee into a predominantly smallholder crop and has prevented foreign companies from expanding onto new land, even though it has no objection to their continued presence. Furthermore, in the Coffee Board of Kenya, an organisation has been built up which, through control of collection, warehousing and auctions, helps to protect Kenya's interests in the coffee trade to the point of export. Yet no matter how successful the State may have been in nationalising or Africanising internal commodity production, processing and marketing, it has no control over the world market and little say in the International Coffee Agreement. Kenya is ultimately dependent on the industrialised world continuing to buy and consume its product.

Similar problems face nearly all countries which rely on agricultural exports, and this is one of the major reasons why underdeveloped countries seek to diversify out of such crops. Richer countries in a similar position can afford to protect their farmers from price fluctuations through subsidies, price supports and so on. But a poor country cannot usually offer such protection and low prices can result in considerable hardship for individual small farmers as well as balance of payments difficulties.

Tea

Tea is Kenya's second largest export, with production and overseas sales reaching record quantities in 1978. In that year 98.3 million kg of tea were processed, of which 84 million kg was exported, to bring in £K63.2 million foreign exchange. Like coffee, tea benefited from the commodity boom in 1977 and exports fetched £K71.8 million. But by 1979 prices declined dramatically and returned to 1976 levels of around £K32 million.[18] The government has adopted the same strategy as with coffee, i.e. restricting the estate sector to land already occupied at independence, concentrating new investment in building up a smallholder section through the Kenya Tea Development Authority (KTDA), and increasing its control over the marketing process. In contrast to the monopoly position held by the Coffee Board of Kenya, not all tea is sold through the KTDA. An international tea auction operates at Mombasa and tea is sold either at the Mombasa or London auctions or by private treaty.

Of the 72 ,068 hectares of planted tea, KTDA smallholders cultivate 46,910 hectares, and this sector has grown rapidly since independence, as shown in Table 4.2. The remaining 25,158 hectares are owned mainly by foreign companies, although there are also non-KTDA co-operatives, and some large independently owned Kenyan estates, such as that owned by the chairman of KTDA.[19] The main foreign companies involved in tea and the approximate estimate of their planted hectarage are shown in Table 4.3. The figures should be regarded as minimum estimates since most estates are held by wholly-owned local subsidiaries and not all of these can be identified.

Table 4.2
Smallholder Tea Production

	Hectares	Growers	Av. size of holding (ha)
1964/5	5,133	22,343	—
1967/8	10,772	37,953	—
1971/2	26,228	66,897	0.04
1973/4	34,384	90,135	0.38
1974/5	36,938	95,244	0.39
1975/6	39,629	103,854	0.38
1976/7	43,636	115,648	0.38
1977/8	46,861	122,348	0.38

Source: Kenya Tea Development Authority, Annual Report 1979

Foreign-owned estates therefore control at least 77 per cent of hectarage outside the KTDA smallholder sector. Many of the estates hold much more land than is planted. Nandi Tea Estates, for example, holds more than double its 1978 planted hectarage, and has a licence to plant 1,560.12 hectares.

Tea is the most popular beverage in Kenya, and all growers put 10 per cent of their production into a central pool which is packaged and marketed locally. Until the end of 1977, Brooke Bond had the sole local marketing licence and teas carried the Brooke Bond label. However, on 1 January 1978 this operation was taken over by the Kenya Tea Packers Association (KETEPA), an organisation set up by the KTDA, and although the packets retain the distinctive green and yellow label they no longer carry Brooke Bond's name, and the Brooke Bond signs are fading on the hundreds of small *dukas* (shops) throughout the country.

All of the companies sell their tea openly through the auctions at either Mombasa or London; none is sold directly from the estates to parent companies in London. The Managing Director of Brooke Bond Liebig Kenya Ltd has said that the company's branches keep 'arms length' operations with each other[20] and this was confirmed by an official in the Ministry of Agriculture,[21] who said that the Ministry had investigated the tea industry in November 1979 and found that all tea grown and processed by the larger estates had been sold openly through the auctions, or through private treaties, at a fair market price. Thus the State has been relatively successful in forcing the tea trade to disclose its transactions, ensuring that duties and taxes are not evaded, and has also built up a smallholder sector to grow a crop once grown only on plantations and estates.

Table 4.3

Tea Production in Kenya by Estates and KTDA Smallholders 1978

	min. h.a.	million kg 1978 prod.
Finlays UK (mainly through its Kenya subsidiary, African Highlands Produce Co. Ltd).	6,640	17
Brooke Bond Liebig Kenya Ltd (UK parent)	6,302	17
George Williamson Ltd (UK)	1,009.5	3
Eastern Produce Holdings Ltd (UK)	2,718	—
Kakuzi Ltd (Eastern Produce Ltd (UK) 23.5% holding)	764	—
Nandi Tea Estates Ltd (Mitchell Cotts (UK) subsidiary)	717.5	—
Warren Kenya Ltd (British parent)	445.5	—
Sasini Tea and Coffee Ltd (ownership not known)	974.5	—
	19,571	35
KTDA	46,910	79
Other tea planters, large co-ops, and probably some foreign companies	5,587	17
	72,068	94

Sources: KTDA Annual Reports; The Tea Board of Kenya Registered Licence Holders at 30.6.79; Economic Survey 1979, Republic of Kenya.

The major disadvantage of the present arrangements from Kenya's point of view is the lack of control over those processes which add value to the product, blending, packing and distribution. These processes are firmly controlled by transnational corporations in the industrialised countries, where the major markets exist. Furthermore, transnational corporations retain some power to influence production at all levels, including within Kenya itself.

Brooke Bond is the largest transnational corporation in the Kenyan tea industry (although Finlays has larger estates, it is a smaller company). Worldwide it is one of the largest transnational corporations in the tea trade and one of the four big tea blenders in Britain, controlling 33 per cent of the market (followed by Allied Breweries' subsidiary, Lyons Tetley, with 23 per cent, Cadbury-Schweppes' subsidiary, Typhoo Tea, with 15 per cent and the Co-operative Wholesale Society with 12 per cent).[22]

Brooke Bond has been in Kenya for about sixty years and as well as developing its own plantations, it has been a prime force in building up the market for tea in East Africa. Since the company is so prominent in Kenya, it is worth examining how it has reacted to the government's demand for increased control over the tea industry, and how it has ensured that the smallholder schemes were developed to suit its marketing needs. Brooke Bond's tea plantations remain important, but not crucial to its interests as a transnational corporation dealing in tea.

Brooke Bond Liebig Kenya Ltd (BBLK)

Brooke Bond established itself in Kenya in the 1920s, concentrating on the development of plantations but also establishing control over the internal marketing of tea. Although seeking to exert control over tea production, and secure regular supplies of good quality, Brooke Bond was — and remains — primarily a processing, marketing and distributing company. After the war, African nationalism in Kenya made it inevitable that independence would be granted, and Africans' demands for the return of their land and participation in the profitable production of cash crops would have to be met. The colonial government initiated an investigation into agricultural practice, resulting in the Swynnerton Plan of 1954, which recommended the development of smallholder tea schemes. Brooke Bond and the other foreign tea producers in Kenya (the larger ones being James Finlay and George Williamson) were initially hostile, but eventually recognised such developments as inevitable and sought to influence the way in which the smallholder tea scheme was established in Kenya.[23]

Tea had been developed as an export crop, and remained so until 1939. However, production fell during the Second World War, at the same time as domestic consumption rose substantially, so that in 1948 Kenya was in the unusual position for an underdeveloped country of consuming 67 per cent of its own tea production — 6.75 million pounds. During this period, the colonial government kept the price of tea in Kenya low, but the world price rose dramatically after the war and the tea companies then wanted to expand quickly and profit from the export market. In the 1950s Brooke Bond expanded, taking over many existing estates as settlers left the country because of the rebellion. The company also planted new areas with higher yielding varieties. Most of their new planting took place between 1947 and 1960, and between 1958 and 1968 yearly production of made tea (i.e. after processing) rose from 4.15

million kg to 7.1 million kg. The company also built four new factories in the 1950s and three in the 1960s.

During this phase of expansion increased productivity of labour was a major goal and Brooke Bond in particular aimed to improve tea quality by refining traditional plucking techniques. From the 1950s onwards labourers were ordered to pluck the tea leaf more finely, i.e. to take only the top three or four leaves and the bud rather than follow the random plucking system previously used. At the same time the company tried to reduce its dependence on labour and introduced improved manufacturing techniques which made this possible, as well as saving production time.

Technological innovations are usually developed at research institutes near the estates, often with company involvement, Brooke Bond Liebig Kenya, for instance, sponsor the locally based Tea Research Institute at Kericho. However, much of the work done at this Institute is of direct benefit to the company, such as the effort devoted to developing new processing techniques, aiming either to improve the quality of tea, to speed up processing, or to save labour costs. Perhaps more important still for the company, given the restrictions on land, is research concerned with improving yields. Success in this direction is illustrated by BBLK's Kapkorech estate which broke a barrier in 1972 by producing 2,000kg of made tea per hectare and then more than doubled this record in 1979, to produce 4,878kg per hectare. The average yield on the company's estates is 2,600kg per hectare.[24] Such research is of little value to smallholders.

What is lacking is a national perspective, an emphasis on gearing the tea industry more closely to the needs of the Kenyan economy. For example, an instant tea factory which opened in 1973 was equipped with highly sophisticated technology developed by the parent company, rather than by Brooke Bond Kenya. It cost £K1 million to construct; is able to process five million kilos of powder per annum; and employs only 76 skilled labourers. Had research on this technology been carried out under Kenyan control, it might have resulted in the development of an instant tea factory more appropriate to Kenya's needs, possibly employing more labour, for example.

BBLK and Smallholder Development

The Swynnerton Plan of 1954 initiated smallholder schemes for the production by Africans of cash crops such as tea, coffee, pineapples and pyrethrum. When the schemes first began, the plucked leaf had to be processed in the factories of the commercial tea companies, as no smallholder factories had been constructed, and tea must be processed within hours of plucking. This gave the commercial firms, such as

Brooke Bond, the right to scrutinise the tea and they insisted on a high standard of plucking. In fact many of the agricultural extension officers who supervised the planting and growing were seconded from Brooke Bond and the other companies to advise smallholders. The Board co-ordinating the scheme was the Special Crops Development Authority (SCDA), which later became the Kenya Tea Development Authority (KTDA). The SCDA was composed of government staff, experts from the tea companies, African representatives from the growing areas, and estate company representatives. When the first smallholder tea factory was constructed (at Ragati in Central Province) the engineer was seconded from Brooke Bond and, until other factories were constructed, the smallholders continued to sell their leaf to the estate company factories of Brooke Bond, George Williamson and James Finlay.

These tea estate firms, which already dominated production in Kenya, played an important role in shaping the conditions under which the smallholder tea schemes developed. Brooke Bond not only acted as advisers on tea growing, but also assisted in linking up British machinery suppliers with the smallholder tea factories. Before Africans were trained to operate the factories, the major tea companies provided management and technical assistance, putting them in a position to directly influence the new scheme from the growing to the processing stage.

While Brooke Bond had at first been reluctant to offer assistance, assuming it would affect its own position as one of the major tea growers, the company gradually realised that it could influence the schemes' development, and that, in any event, it would only be a matter of time before African nationalist demands made such schemes inevitable. Since BBLK was primarily a marketing and distributing company, in a sense it did not matter to it who produced the tea, as long as it was grown to the required standards and a reliable source of supply was established.[25] In return for providing assistance, Brooke Bond could make certain demands and fashion the new scheme to its own advantage. For example the company insisted that the colonial government put an end to competition by banning the widespread growing of 'illegal' tea, which was sun-dried and then sold in up-country markets.[26]

Another area where the company used its influence to its own advantage was the control of plucking standards. The tea firms insisted that the smallholder leaf be of a higher standard than that obtained on the estates, specifying that only two leaves and a bud should be plucked. The standard was to be enforced through a team of leaf officers employed by the SCDA and later the KTDA. Throughout the 1960s, most of the tea companies plucked three or four leaves and a bud.

"This meant that Brooke Bond was able to purchase the highest quality smallholder tea and blend it with their own lower quality tea. The unit costs of production for smallholder factories were obviously higher, a price which was not borne by Brooke Bond but by the parastatal KTDA"[27]

Smallholder tea growing has expanded rapidly since those early days, and has overtaken the estate sector (see Table 4.2) although the plantation sector remains intact. The KTDA now has sufficient administrative and technical expertise to make smallholders independent of the companies in the internal production and marketing of tea in Kenya.

However, Brooke Bond's predominant concern is with the further processing, blending, packaging and marketing of tea and so it remains important for the Company to control the quality of output of the smallholder schemes. Thus the establishment of the schemes created a dual structure which removed political pressure from the company, allowing it to retain plantations, but also meet its needs for a regular supply of high quality tea. The costs of supporting smallholder schemes, in terms of administration, education and quality control, are undertaken by the Kenya government, usually with loans from the international aid agencies,* which are prepared to finance schemes of this kind where they could not, of course, directly fund a transnational corporation.

BBLK's Other Interests

BBLK is probably the foreign company with the largest investments in Kenya. Although it went public in 1972, the UK parent retains 87 per cent of the equity, and the Board of Directors of BBLK is dominated by British employees (two Kenyans, including N.J. Muriuki the Chairman, five British directors and two British/Kenya residents). Brooke Bond has made way for Kenyans in the local tea and coffee industry, but in order to retain its Kenyan subsidiary's high profitability, has been diversifying into other areas.

In the early 1970s the company expanded into new plantations (on land it already held) growing industrial crops, cinchona and tara. Cinchona trees provide quinine, which is used for anti-malarial drugs, and is also an ingredient in mineral waters (e.g. Schweppes tonic water). Tara is a powder obtained from the pods of spinosa trees and is a source of tannic and gallic acids, used in the tanning industry. Neither of these crops have been grown on a commercial plantation basis before, but in spite of this, both are exported as raw materials and all further processing is done in the industrialised countries.[28] Both crops gave their first yield in 1974, and cinchona output has been increasing steadily ever

---

* The World Bank has funded at least two major smallholder tea development schemes and one tea factory since 1964.

since. Tara does not appear to be proving quite so successful, as shown in Table 4.4.

Table 4.4
Cinchona and Tara
Brooke Bond Liebig Output 1974-1979

	Chinchona '000kg	Tara '000kg
1974	406	22
1975	547	83
1976	585	138
1977	508	255
1978	663	236
1979	768	115

Source: Brooke Bond Liebig Kenya Ltd, Annual Report 1979

In January 1979 BBLK took a 75 per cent interest in Sulmac Company Ltd, which grows carnations, ferns, chrysanthemum cuttings, sisal and vegetables on estates. The flowers and vegetables are for export to Europe, express by air freight, to meet the demand for off-season and exotic vegetables and winter flowers. Brooke Bond is here contributing to an established trend among agribusiness investors of using scarce land in African countries to grow food to supply a luxury market overseas. The frivolous nature of such market 'needs' is illustrated by Sulmac's estate at Masongaleni, which has 'the world's biggest production area of asparagus plumosus, a fluffy foliage which is very popular as a green support for bouquets'.[29] Not only is Kenya encouraged to 'develop' its resources to meet the industrialised world's demands for tea and coffee, it is now also encouraged to 'develop' to meet the demand for fluffy foliage for bouquets! Production conditions are strictly controlled to make sure that flowers reach Europe in pristine condition, for example disease control is so strict that workers are not allowed to keep livestock or have their own gardens.[30]

A further natural acquisition for an agribusiness transnational such as Brooke Bond was the purchase of Murphy Chemicals in December 1978. Murphy is a small company, previously a subsidiary of Glaxo, which specialises in pesticides and other agricultural chemicals. The other companies in the BBLK group include: Kenna Coffee — coffee trading; Brooke Bond Mombasa — Kenya's largest tea buyer and exporter; Kabazi Canners — a fruit and vegetable canning plant in which BBLK acquired a 30 per cent interest in 1967. Brooke Bond Liebig itself was formed in May 1968, when the meat processing business came into the group. Until 1974 canned meat products remained with BBLK but were then taken over by the Kenya Meat Commission. The company also owns a factory making flies for fishing and has a part interest, acquired in 1969, in East African Acceptances Ltd, a general banking business and tea agent.

Kenya Canners Ltd

Pineapples are fast becoming a major Kenyan export crop and the government has relied on foreign companies and plantation agriculture to achieve results. Kenya Canners Ltd is a wholly-owned subsidiary of the US company, Del Monte (now owned by the even larger US food and tobacco conglomerate R.J. Reynolds) and grows pineapples almost entirely for export. Only about 2 per cent are used locally and in 1979 the company exported over 60,000 tons of pineapple products.[31] The Kenya government has encouraged the industry as a means of diversifying away from its heavy reliance on tea and coffee as the main providers of its foreign income.

The company was first established by two businessmen in 1949 to supply fresh fruit to Nairobi, but was taken over in 1958 by the Tancot group. The industry had originally been developed as a smallholder scheme, and early newspaper reports indicated that growers responded extremely well. They were offered a good price (about £15 a ton in 1955) and, as more small farmers were attracted to the scheme, there were many complaints about a limit restricting growers to a 25-mile radius around the factory.[32] In 1959, the pineapple growers were being urged to double their acreage within four years:[33] they responded quickly and by 1964 the company was complaining that they were receiving more pineapples than they could deal with? However, the processing plant began running into difficulties, mainly because of a shortage of funds for expansion. In 1964 the government began to look for a company with know-how to manage the industry. They found Del Monte, which was delighted with the opportunity to expand into Kenya, and thus gain access to European markets. Traditionally Del Monte had grown pineapples in Hawaii, but the workforce there had become increasingly restive with the company over low wages, and negotiated large increases in the early 1960s. This, and rising land values, induced the company to expand production in the Philippines and to look for alternative sources of supply — one of which was Kenya.[34]

Del Monte argued that pineapples should be grown on plantations and it put pressure on the government to enforce more stringent control over smallholder production. In response to this, in 1965 the government issued a regulation restricting pineapple plantings to those originally licensed by the Canning Crops Board.[35] Two years later pineapples were designated a 'special crop', giving the Ministry of Agriculture powers to exert special discipline over their growing and marketing.[36]

Under the 1965 agreement by which Del Monte managed Kenya Canners, the government had agreed to purchase an old Anglo-French sisal estate at Thika for leasing in sections to the company at a nominal annual rent. This was apparently on the understanding that Del Monte would at the same time develop its own estate as well as taking supplies from the surrounding smallholders.[37] In 1968, the year Del Monte actually purchased Kenya Canners, they decided that smallholder production would have to be phased out and that pineapples should be grown entirely on estates. The company argued that estate production was more suited to their international standards of production — that it enabled them to control the quality and size of the pineapples, and it also suited their management needs, since it would allow them to bring the fruit into production at a time convenient for the company's schedule.[38] The government had little influence over the actions of the company, and was more concerned with increasing export earnings from pineapples, and developing an industry which would decrease Kenya's reliance on tea and coffee exports, and also establish a processing plant in Kenya.

The strategy adopted by the company has turned pineapple growing into a highly mechanised industry. Although Kenya Canners employ about 6,000 men and women, the 10,000 acres making up one of the world's largest pineapple growing complexes would support a larger number of smallholders. 60,000 tons of canned fruit are produced a year and the growing processing methods used are both complex and capital-intensive. They require:

"gigantic crawler tractors and a series of specialised disc and mouldboard ploughs, rippers and other devices such as fumigation machines, sprayers and harvesting machines, many of them conceived and built in the company's own workshops (in the USA). As fumigation of the soil takes place, long parallel lines of black polyethyline mulching are unwound from behind tractors, into which at pre-marked intervals the slips or crowns are inserted at the start of the two-fruiting, three-and-a-half year cycle. Some 12 to 14 months later a hormone 'forcer' is applied to the pineapple plants, the effect of which is to bring all those plants treated into flower at the same time . . . and ready to harvest some seven-and-a-half to eight months later. Huge tractor-driven conveyor harvesters, behind which lines of workers move cutting the ripe fruit which are conveyed to waiting tippers, dot the fields. Trucked to the canning plant, the fruit is unloaded into channels of clear, running water which carry them on elevators to the upper level of the canning factory. Here they are graded by size, and peeled and de-cored by machines. Conveyors move the fruit onto the next stage, where they are trimmed, sliced, packed into tins and a specially prepared 'syrup' vacuumed into each tin before it is sealed, cooked, cooled and labelled. Packed into cartons which in turn are strapped onto *nationally made wooden pallets* which will carry them to their final destination, fork-lift trucks stack the fruit into containers or in the go-down* to wait consignment by train to Mombasa. Increasingly Kenya Canners is making use of containerisation to move its products in bulk."[39] (our emphasis!)

This description illustrates many of the disadvantages for a developing country of relying on a transnational corporation to develop an agricultural project. Production is geared to the company's international marketing criteria and, for ease of processing, demands sophisticated and complex technology, which can only be provided from industrialised countries — in this case mainly from the company's own subsidiaries. The company places great emphasis on high labour productivity in a country where labour is the most abundant resource, and a scheme which previously provided smallholder pineapple growers with an income (albeit an undependable one), was sacrificed in order to meet the needs of a transnational corporation.

From the Kenyan government's point of view, the scheme was part of a plan to step up and diversify agricultural exports, although it is not clear how successful this has been. Pineapple exports earned £K12 million in 1979,[40] but against this must be offset the foreign exchange required for inputs: heavy machinery, fertilisers, pesticides, herbicides, hormone forcers, even sugar is imported for the canning process. Although Kenya grows sugar it is not of the required quality. The cans are locally manufactured by Metal Box Ltd., but the tin is imported. In addition, foreign companies have the right to remit profits under the Foreign Investments Protection Act, and Del Monte (the US parent) has a management and technical agreement which gives it a commission of 5 per cent of net sales.[41]

Transnationals in Food Processing in Kenya

Foreign agribusiness is not only involved in growing crops in Kenya, it is playing an expanding role in the food processing industry. The pineapple processing industry is one such, but it was established almost purely for the export sector, whereas recently many food companies have invested in Kenya in order to meet local demand. The growth of foreign food processing interests in Africa as a whole has already been discussed in Chapter 1 and it was pointed out that Kenya is one of the most attractive countries for foreign investors. Prior to the dissolution of the East African Community part of this attraction lay in the relatively large market to which companies had access. However, in recent years the wealthier urban markets in Kenya alone have proved large enough to sustain some food processing industries. The disadvantages attached to

* 'Go-down': warehouse or store.

foreign investments in the food processing industry were dealt with in Chapter 1. Briefly, they include the relatively short time in which foreign companies demand a return on their capital (often as little as five years); the tendency of foreign companies to increase dependence on imports rather than develop links with local agriculture; advertising and promotional activities which may replace local food products with commercially processed alternatives; the likelihood of local competitors being forced out of business and a tendency to rely on capital intensive technologies developed for industrialised countries.

One of the principal influences on African governments which invite foreign companies to develop food processing industries seems to be the view that the trademarks owned by the companies are a crucial factor in gaining access to markets in industrialised countries. However, Kenya has encouraged food transnationals to develop products for local consumption, even where local alternatives already exist.

This can be illustrated by a brief look at the Kenyan operations of three well-known companies. The first manufactures cooking oil; the second is establishing a poultry industry; and the third manufactures milk-based products.

East African Industries Ltd

This Unilever subsidiary manufactures fats and cooking oils for local consumption.* As shown earlier, underdeveloped countries are seen as prime growth areas for the oil and fats industries, since consumption has reached saturation levels in industrialised countries. Suitable crops for the extraction of edible oils and fats can be grown in most countries, and Kenya has an ideal climate for growing oil-bearing seeds such as sunflower, rapeseed, colzas and peanuts. However, the company insists on using imported palm oil — a product for which Unilever controls 80 per cent of the world market.[42]

Unilever's policy helps to explain the fact that Kenya imports almost 70 per cent of its edible oils, at a cost of $16 million per annum.[43] Although the company has promised over the years to re-invest locally and build up substitutes for palm oil, they have not done so.[44] Instead, they have argued successfully with the government that as cooking oil is an essential local need and should be available cheaply, palm oil imports should be exempt from duty.[45] This clearly gives the company a considerable advantage over any Kenyan producer preferring to use locally grown oil seeds, which at present are rather scarce and consequently more expensive. These locally available oils will continue to remain expensive without some help in building up the industry.

---

* It also manufactures soap in competition with local manufacturers: See Agribusiness, Chapter 1.

BAT Kenya Developments Ltd

British American Tobacco has a large subsidiary, BAT Kenya Ltd, which operates by setting up smallholder tobacco growing schemes and then buying and processing the crop. It has also expanded into the food processing industry. In 1974 BAT invested in a new poultry business in Kenya using the brand name 'Kenchic'. This involved the establishment of a poultry breeding and marketing organisation, along with a chain of shops selling take-away cooked chicken. (The Kenchic chain is cheaper than its rival, Kentucky Fried Chicken, also in Kenya, but much more expensive than the small old-fashioned corner stalls which previously sold chicken thika, etc, but which have now disappeared).

The company's main aim is to establish a poultry industry in Kenya and build up a local market, and it has so far been very successful. BAT rapidly acquired its own poultry farms, but also started a strictly controlled contract growers scheme in 1976. The company's hatcheries produce over 50,000 chicks a week: of these 15,000 stay on its own farms and the rest go either to the contract growers or are sold to individual farmers. While profitable, the contract scheme is not designed to provide a living for large number of farmers. After three years of operation there were a mere 20 contract farmers, between them taking 10,000 one-day-old chicks a week.[46] At 7-8 weeks, when the birds weigh 2kg each, the company brings them in to its own slaughterhouses, where they are processed, packed, frozen and labelled 'Kenchic'.

It should be stressed that such high technology poultry operations are becoming increasingly popular in many African countries, and are attracting growing attention from agribusiness. Intensive poultry production requires an animal feed industry, as the birds have to be provided with high quality feeds if they are to grow rapidly and reach an economic weight in the shortest possible time. Waste vegetable products suitable as a feed for small flocks have little place in an intensive poultry industry. Indeed, there is a need for grains which might otherwise be available for human consumption. For example, maize is the major cereal ingredient in the Nigerian poultry feed industry.[47]

The Ministry of Agriculture in Kenya has encouraged BAT's Kenchic venture and, as part of an agreement whereby the company has become a catalyst for the new poultry industry, the Ministry has used its influence to set up a suitable marketing system. In some cases this has resulted in a direct clash with the traditional systems for marketing poultry,[48] which are geared to production on small farms, not industrial-scale units.

Food Specialties Ltd

Nestlé first opened this dairy products subsidiary in 1967, although two years previously it had discussed with the government the possibility of signing an agreement to manage a powdered milk plant owned by Kenya Co-operative Creameries (KCC). KCC is a State co-operative which collects and processes fresh milk, and converts some of it into powdered milk for local consumption. In the event, Nestlé did not sign the management contract, but instead set up its own factory in Nairobi to produce Lactogen and Nespray — baby foods based on powdered milk.[49] Nestlés in Kenya has also invested in a plant to manufcture Cerelac and Nestum, cereal-based products for infants. At this factory, which started operating in 1975, it also produces Milo, a chocolate-flavoured drink for mixing with milk.[50]

Nestlé's has been much criticised for its policy of promoting the consumption of baby foods in developing countries. Many of its advertisements are misleading and have suggested that the use of powdered milk is superior to breastfeeding. As well as its conventional advertisements, the company issues free promotional samples through health clinics and employs mothercraft or 'milk nurses' to visit local health institutions — sometimes in uniforms similar to those worn by hospital nurses.[51] In practice, it can be hazardous to use powdered babyfoods in unsuitable conditions, and cases have been documented in which babies have died from diseases related to the use of unsterilised bottles.*

These examples given an indication of the kind of food industry which Kenya is developing, drawing heavily on foreign capital. Although it is clearly difficult in many respects to establish a food processing industry closely tailored to local needs skills and raw materials, Kenya does not appear to have tried this option, but has welcomed foreign investment, even where other resources have been available, or could have been developed.

Conclusion

This section has tried to show some of the complexities and difficulties facing an underdeveloped country when dealing with foreign investors, and to illustrate some of the inequalities perpetuated by a government without policies specifically aimed at breaking down differences in wealth, income and land ownership.

Those who hold power in Kenya have been partly successful in using and directing private foreign investment. The State has insisted that senior positions be Africanised, and has established considerable control

---

* After years of campaigning by groups concerned about the effects of Nestlé's policies in developing countries, in October 1979 Nestlés agreed to conform to World Health Organisation/UNICEF restrictions on formula marketing, and to stop advertising its products. However, by May 1981 the Infant Formula Action Group (INFACT) had found over 1,000 alleged violations of this agreement.[52]

over the agricultural sector, particularly where production is based on plantations, including the crucial crops of coffee and tea. Large estates have been taken over and smallholder agriculture encouraged. Smallholder production of some crops can substantially benefit companies, for which the main source of profitability is in processing, marketing and distribution, because smallholders can deliver good quality crops at a reasonable cost, and attract government and aid funding which would not be available to a foreign firm. While a small proportion of smallholders may benefit from growing export crops, they have no control over the world market price for their produce, and it is difficult for a poor government to subsidise them, should prices fall dramatically.

While there is no doubt that many Kenyans have benefited from the post-independence policies, it is becoming increasingly clear that this has not been the case for the majority. A study carried out in 1973[53] showed that the poorest 30 per cent of Kenya's population earned only 6.4 per cent of total income, while the richest 2 per cent earned 29 per cent. If the distribution of income is taken as a measure of inequality, Kenya is the fifth most unequal country in the world, with only Zimbabwe on the African continent being more unequal.

There has been no radical change in the nature of the Kenyan economy: it remains firmly committed to a capitalist path to development.[54] There is now a powerful class, many of whose interests coincide with those of foreign companies which have brought jobs, directorships and increased earnings for a small minority. It is important to bear in mind this division in Kenyan society, as it helps to explain why certain decisions have been taken by the State which, on closer examination, appear to be contrary to the best interests of the majority of the population.

The distribution of land is a key issue in Kenya, and inequalities appear to be growing. There is a land shortage, characterised by both overcrowding on poor land, and landlessness on a growing scale. Nutritional data indicate that extreme poverty is more common among those who are landless than among smallholders, and more people are estimated to be landless now than at Independence, when the figure was put at half a million men, women and children.[55] The latest Integrated Rural Survey showed that 890,000 people, making up 12 per cent of households, were landless in the six Provinces covered. The problem is increasing as poor people are forced to sell land to finance schooling, repay loans, or just to survive. The figure would be higher still if there were not migration from the fertile but overcrowded areas, such as Central Province, to less crowded areas of low agricultural potential.[56]

In addition, the agricultural population has been subsidising the higher incomes of the urban areas; since 1964 the prices which farmers receive for their produce has risen more slowly than those of manufactured goods and inputs purchased from the towns.[57] Yet 85 per cent of Kenyans live in rural areas and are dependent on agriculture for a living.

Many of Kenya's problems are those faced by any underdeveloped country with an economy heavily reliant on exporting agricultural products. Until recently, Kenya has had an advantage over most African countries in being self-sufficient in the major staple crops, and this is undoubtedly a reflection of the greater concern for and economic support of the agricultural sector relative to many other countries. However, the present need to import food indicates that this has changed, and has created a further dilemma in that there is now direct competition for land and resources between food crops and cash crops for export.

At the same time, Kenya's problems are exacerbated by a path to development which relies on the involvement of foreign transnationals in the food and agricultural sector. The priorities of foreign companies are not those of the majority of the population, though they may coincide with those of a wealthy minority. A recent report from the Economist Intelligence Unit suggests that the Kenyan style of development generates increasing inequality and reproduces poverty, even after reforms instituted under President Moi:

"The problem is that unless a process is initiated whereby the allocation of certain assets, particularly land, housing and effective schooling is completely removed from the market place, the market will work in such a way as to counteract egalitarian reforms. Those allocated low-cost housing will sell it to landlords; beneficiaries of land redistribution will sell to efficient farmers; schools charging higher fees will hire more effective teachers, etc. In other words the intervention necessary to achieve true social harmony may be more thorough-going than a merely populist regime is able to envisage."[58]

Such intervention must include the need to re-examine Kenya's open policy to foreign agribusiness.

The problems faced by Kenya are not unique, and also confront those countries choosing to develop agricultural and food systems without involving agribusiness. In some instances more equitable solutions are achieved, in others more problems arise. The following chapter on Tanzania examines a country which has rejected private foreign investment for a more specifically self-reliant approach.

CHAPTER 5
Tanzania

Tanzania, like most African countries, has an economy based primarily on agriculture. About 80 per cent of the population live and work on the land and primary products, principally coffee, cotton, cashew nuts, sisal and tea, provide about 80 per cent of export earnings. As in many other African countries, there is no powerful land-owning class, although land was annexed for growing coffee, sisal and some other crops during the colonial period.

Shamba (field) sizes are small, with 83 per cent being less than three hectares and only 2.6 per cent more than five hectares. Conditions are such that it is physically difficult for individual peasant farmers to cultivate more than two acres at a time without hired labour or harvesting machines.[1]

Tanzania and Kenya share the problems of poor countries with economies over-dependent on the export of a few cash crops. Kenya has sought to attract foreign capital, as well as aid finance and loans in order to generate development. By contrast, Tanzania has attempted to build a self-reliant economy, but in the process has drawn more heavily on foreign aid and 'soft' loans than Kenya. Tanzania's self-reliance strategy has been based on avoiding private foreign investment, and nationalising or taking an equity share in foreign companies. Development goals are centred on the peasant population to a much greater extent than in Kenya, and reflect a belief that a real improvement in peasant living standards will only be achieved through mobilising their collective strength. This concept of rural development is embodied in Ujamaa (familyhood), living and working together and building on the basis of traditional peasant culture.

Development in Africa is frequently seen as a choice between capitalist and socialist strategies as followed, for example, by Kenya and Tanzania respectively. Since Tanzania has opted for a strategy of self-reliance and has specifically excluded foreign companies from most parts of the agricultural sector, it provides an important example of the kind of challenges and problems likely to be encountered in an attempt to build African socialism. The Tanzanian approach to rural development would not necessarily be appropriate elsewhere; there are different paths to self-reliance though none may be easily achieved. Nonetheless, the Tanzanian experience is worth examining in some detail not only for the contrast it provides with Kenya and other countries which have opted for a more market-based economy, but for the lessons which may be drawn for other African peasant societies.

This chapter outlines Tanzania's colonial experience and landmarks in the development of Ujamaa and villagisation. Three further sections look at Tanzania's experience of collective agriculture, the conflicts between food and cash crops and the role of foreign aid. Has Tanzania achieved its goals? What conflicts exist between the government and peasant farmers?

The past — Tanzania's Colonial Experience

The German administration in Tanzania from the 1880s to 1918 encouraged settlers, but when the British administration took over after the First World War they never lent settlers the same support as in Kenya. Instead, Britain encouraged or forced African peasant producers to grow the crops considered important for the European market: cotton, coffee and pyrethrum. Nevertheless, both settlers and foreign corporations took a considerable stake in Tanzanian agriculture and the major export crop, sisal, was almost exclusively grown on plantations.

Extensive areas of Tanzania were hit by a series of catastrophes at the beginning of the colonial period. The German wars of colonial conquest had destroyed people, crops and cattle, and rinderpest disease, introduced to Africa by the Italian incursions into Ethiopia, reached Tanzania and destroyed most of the livestock.[2] In Uzigaa region, for example, this was followed by a series of famines, exacerbated by loss of livestock, as well as smallpox and jigger epidemics. Old settlements broke up as people fled to the bush to escape the epidemics, to hunt for food, and to avoid the obligation to feed starving relatives. When the German administration imposed taxes and forced farmers to raise cotton, more people retreated into the bush. The bush spread and the people and the remaining stock became prey to tsetse fly and other diseases. The Zigua in Tanga region, for example, had to learn to live as agriculturalists without cattle in an environment only marginally suited to agriculture, and this falling standard of living was by no means unique.

During the first decades of the 20th century, the number of European settlers rose and in many areas Germans were replaced by Britons or Asians, but rarely Africans.[3] By the end of 1957, a total of 2,488,469 acres, comprising 1,618 holdings, were owned by foreign companies and individuals. Even so, Tanzania remained less divided over the land issue than Kenya, and land under settler control amounted to only 1.1 per cent of the total land area, albeit the most fertile areas. Since Independence, plantations have been of shrinking importance to Tanzania. The largest sisal estates were nationalised between 1967 and 1969 and many others were closed as the crop became unprofitable, and declined in importance. Sisal's share of export earnings has fallen from 70 per cent in the 1950s to less than 10 per cent now. There remains a large plantation owned by the Old Tanganyika Wattle Company, a Commonwealth Development Corporation subsidiary, which grows wheat and maize, and also 99 per cent of Tanzanian wattle extract (used in tanning). But Tanzania's main cash crops: coffee, tea, cotton, tobacco, cashew-nuts and cloves from Zanzibar are grown predominantly by peasant farmers. Tea is somewhat of an exception, because of Brooke Bond's vast estates, and this company is the only remaining foreign transnational with plantation holdings in Tanzania.

The colonial approach to agriculture was based on 'improving' peasant farming, initially by a fairly haphazard system of introducing new crops with little attention to their suitability or to soil fertility. Later, the British authorities introduced by-laws and regulations, and backed these with force in attempts to make peasants adopt new agricultural practices.[4] Peasants resented this interference, and many adopted a strategy of passive resistance to any innovation which upset their farm management practices. However, even when the colonial government tried to prevent them, peasants responded readily to cash crops which provided an income without threatening other aspects of self-sufficiency.[5]

The Development of Ujamaa

After independence in 1961, the government, aware of the unpopularity of British agricultural policies, adopted a 'transformation approach' to agriculture on the recommendation of a 1960 World Bank Report. It was hoped that this would lead to rapid progress and greater productivity than the 'improvement' approach. Intensive land use remained a goal, but the report also recommended campaigns in settled areas and the planned and supervised settlement of uninhabited or thinly-inhabited areas. The policy continued to encourage export crops at the expense of food crops and thus met firm resistance from peasants. The new schemes were criticised as over-capitalised and paternalistic since many bureaucrats and administrators tended to discount peasant experience, having a poor understanding of peasant reality.[6] Gradually, it became clear that the strategy had been rejected, with peasants remaining more interested in food than in cash crops, avoiding production targets, and frequently slipping out of government controls.

The Arusha Declaration of 1967, adopted by the only political party on the mainland, the Tanzanian African National Union (TANU), was the first attempt to transform the peasant society, as well as to make peasant agriculture more productive. It proposed a socialised system of agriculture based on peasant traditions of co-operation and sharing, and turned away more firmly from the solutions adopted in most under-developed countries (as for example Kenya) of backing richer farmers at the expense of peasant cultivators. Ujamaa became the central feature of Tanzania's rural development strategy, far wider in scope than previous agricultural policies. Under Ujamaa, scattered rural populations were initially encouraged and later forced to live in villages. Through villagisation the government hoped that it could eventually provide services such as education, health and water supplies to the whole population. In return, each village was expected to farm one shamba (field) communally, on the assumption that agricultural productivity would be increased by a more efficient utilisation of resources, especially labour. Each extended family still retained its own shamba. The major developments and landmarks in Ujamaa since its inception in 1967 are summarised below:

1967-73: Education and Exhortation[7]

January 1967. The Arusha Declaration set out the policy of socialism and self-reliance. In agriculture this called for 'hard work with intelligence', and warned against laziness, especially in rural men. Rural areas were given priority over the towns.

September 1967. Publication of 'Socialism and Rural Development' by Nyerere, in which he set out the three basic assumptions underlying traditional Ujamaa, (a) respect — each member of the family recognising the place and rights of the other members; (b) common property and (c) the obligation to work together. Tanzania would build a classless society based on these principles, working towards a nation of Ujamaa villages. However, although these principles had existed traditionally at the household level, they had not operated at village level.[8]

November 1967. Decentralisation began. Regional Development Funds of 500,000Shs per region were established to finance small village projects. They were later increased to one million Shillings, and then to two Shillings per capita.

October 1968. Publication of 'Freedom and Development' in which Nyerere emphasised the importance of leadership, but, in response to reports of Ujamaa villages being imposed by force and threats, also re-affirmed the democratic intention of Ujamaa. He asserted the need for discipline in achieving the work goals of Ujamaa within villages.

May 1969. The second 5-year plan emphasised the need to mobilise government and political institutions behind Ujamaa. There were only 400 registered Ujamaa villages at this point, and the government felt the pace was too slow.

1970-71. TANU took a more active role in creating Ujamaa villages, and numbers increased so that by the end of 1971 there were 4,484 villages, and a total population of 1,545,240. The rapid increase seems to have been partly the effect of a 'stick and carrot' approach: on the one hand compulsion and on the other distribution of famine relief to Ujamaa villages. It is unlikely that every village had adopted all the requirements of Ujamaa, particularly regarding communal cultivation.

May 1972. Despite the increasing number of Ujamaa villages, agricultural production remained stagnant. In the Iringa Declaration, 'Siasa ni Kilimo' (Politics is Agriculture) TANU stressed the importance of good agricultural practice. The government tried to avoid earlier mistakes of over-capitalisation and premature mechanisation. Ujamaa villages continued to use existing technology. It was hoped that economies of scale would emerge simply from the reorganisation of the labour force.

July 1972. Sweeping decentralisation began, with control, including financial control, devolving to the 20 Regions. Administratively each region was put on the same level as a Ministry. Thus the government hoped to shift the planners closer to the problems of villages.

1973-76 — Villagisation

November 1973. Nyerere proclaimed that "to live in villages is an order".[9] He felt that peasants had been given sufficient time to show the good faith of the government, but had offered nothing in return. Without more militant measures, Nyerere believed there was no possibility of transforming rural agriculture. A series of massive operations followed, in which millions of peasants were moved to new village sites. Force was common, and inevitably there were serious effects on agricultural production. Although the communalisation of agriculture was a clear aim of villagisation, and the government argued that it would make it easier to provide the essential services of education, health clinics, and good water supplies, it is frequently suggested that a major aim was to make people more accessible to administrative and political pressures.

August 1974. Food imports reached high levels following a serious drought and Nyerere called on all families to increase food production. The disastrous harvests in both 1974 and 1975 led to changes in the government's previous policy of de-emphasising prices for food crops. After 1974 all major food crops, and many minor ones (as well as export crops) were guaranteed a price fixed annually by the Economic Committee of the Cabinet.[10]

1975. The marketing co-operatives were abolished. These co-operatives operated as middlemen, and worked on the assumption that they would help incorporate peasant producers into the market economy.[11] The Government believed the co-ops were too numerous and blocked many policy decisions. With their dissolution parastatal companies buying and selling crops could deal directly with peasant producers.

1975. With the dissolution of the co-operatives, the Law on the Registration of Villages was passed, making villages legal entities, able to enter contracts and negotiate. The Village Assembly included all village members and the elected Village Council became the executive arm.

1975. The National Maize Project (NMP) was launched, with the aim of covering 1,000 selected village, providing improved seeds, fertilisers, management and expanded storage facilities. This is a massive project, initially using World Bank funds, but becoming the National Food Credit Programme in 1979, largely funded by a USAID grant.

1973-76. Approximately 10 million Tanzanians were moved: this may be an over-estimate, but indicates the number living in villages at the end of the compulsory villagisation period.

After 1976. Revision exercises were launched to overcome the lack of site planning in the first phase of villagisation, with compensation funds of over 60 million Shillings for peasants whose homes were destroyed.[12]

1977. TANU merged with the Afro-Shirazi Party of Zanzibar and became Chama Cha Mapinduzi (Revolutionary Party). Elections were held and many of those elected to senior leadership positions were younger and more educated people, thought perhaps to be less susceptible to bribes, and more committed to the goals of the party and to getting things done efficiently.[13]

December 1980. Major change in agricultural policy, when the government decided to disband the National Milling Corportion, and re-establish co-operatives this time run by peasants, to collect food and export crops.[14]

January 1981. Elections. Nyerere re-elected for what he emphasises is his final term. But over half of the sitting MPs and several Ministers were swept out.[15]

The aims of Ujamaa remain consistent with those laid down in the Arusha Declaration: a reduction in the influence of the market, and the establishment of a more humane society, where a person's value is not judged by wealth and power. Nevertheless, peasants have shown resistance to any form of organisation which undermines their autonomy from the State and the market. The government found that education and exhortation were insufficient tools to achieve the desired transformation. Faced with the necessity of raising agricultural productivity and extracting a saleable surplus, the State resorted to coercion in reorganising a peasant society into over 8,000 villages containing 14 million of Tanzania's 18 million population — the largest resettlement in African history.

People have now by and large accepted the new locations and have stayed in the villages. However, the question remains of whether this organisation has brought about a collectivised agricultural system which is capable of raising productivity and materially benefiting the peasants.

Africa's most abundant natural resources are land and labour. Until the government can find some way of successfully tapping these resources it cannot build from the ground up, and become self-reliant.[16] However, peasants in Tanzania control the means of subsistence, and have maintained their efforts to be independent of the State, even though this may result in a diminished standard of living. The government believes that by organising around villages it has more access to peasants and that by collectivising agriculture it can better exploit resources. To what extent is this true, and what conflicts and problems have been confronted in this process?

Collective Organisation

The collectivisation of agriculture in Tanzania was not embarked on purely for technical or economic reasons. Michaela von Freyhold makes this clear in her definition of the aims of communal agriculture as "a social and political process in which certain political parties and peasants engage in order to solve certain social and political contradictions".[17] Indeed, Von Freyhold questions whether putting 30 people together to work with their old implements on 75 communal hectares, instead of each working on his or her own, will bring any technical advantages.

Much technology can be used equally effectively by either individual households or collective farms. However, there are exceptions — both labour and expense can be saved by building a single store, water-tank, drying shed, etc., for a group of 30 people rather than one for each household. Communal holdings can also save labour, for example, one person, using a network of strings, can guard a field of 75 hectares against birds, whereas 30 people might have to guard their own fields individually. A single wall built around a large field can protect the communal crop against wild pigs just as effectively as numerous walls built around individual fields. Larger settlements and areas of crop land seem more effective than smaller ones in keeping away tsetse fly and wild animals. Several heavy tasks, such as digging irrigation trenches, laying water pipes and lifting fallen trees are more easily tackled collectively and it is possible to concentrate labour at critical periods, such as planting and harvesting, and to pool knowledge and experience.

However, the communalisation of agriculture was not accompanied by any fundamental technical changes and in general has not been welcomed by peasants, who have yet to experience any widespread benefits from it. There have been some changes, such as the appearance of village fish ponds, but on the whole, peasants have been reluctant to exploit the potential benefits of collectivisation. Increases in food output have been modest (admittedly hampered by severe droughts) and peasant production of export crops declined during the 1970s. These results are disappointing perhaps, but not especially surprising when the difficulties of transforming such a strongly traditional society are looked at more closely.

Investment in Agriculture — to Peasants or State Farms?

The first point to recognise is that villagisation, particularly agriculture, was not accompanied by sufficient financial backing from the government. At present agriculture receives only 12.5 per cent of Tanzania's total investment in development, a proportion which has declined from the 15 per cent allocated under the previous Five-Year Plan. A large slice of this — 80 per cent — goes to large-scale farming projects, apparently in direct contradition to the government's stated policy of encouraging peasant agriculture, and with profound effects of increasing dependency on foreign inputs. Thus, only about 2 per cent of the national development budget is used to support peasant producers, the men and women who form the backbone of the agricultural sector.[18] Additionally, loans from the Tanzanian Rural Development Bank to individuals for small scale domestic food production *shrank* from 6.7 per cent of the total in 1971-72 to 5.1 per cent in 1979-80, and over the same period loans to parastatals and companies *grew* from 6.4 per cent to 70.7 per cent.[19]

Under the second Five-Year Plan, about £4 million was to be used to plant 250,000 acres of various crops on State farms. The Plan indicated that State farms should account for half the proposed area of wheat and that nine new ranches, four partially irrigated farms for rice, and four dairy farms should be added to the State sector.[20] The National Agricultural Food Co (NAFCO) responded by increasing the area planted to wheat from 17,951 hectares in 1979 to 30,193 hectares in 1981, committing TShs260 million of Canadian aid funding over a five-year period.[21] In spite of maize being the major staple food crop, wheat received by far the largest amount of direct State funding.

The government's tendency to emphasise the role of State farms and concentrate its resources on the production of wheat, livestock products and export crops was partly the result of its dependence on foreign aid. Although Tanzania has avoided private investment from abroad as likely to increase inequality and by-pass the peasant sector, it has used foreign aid on a massive scale. Currently around US $430 million a year. Foreign donors, particularly the World Bank and US AID have shown a marked preference for State farms and other specific projects and have channelled relatively little more into more broad-based rural development. The great majority of villages have seen little benefit from projects such as the Canadian wheat scheme, a point which will be returned to later in this chapter.

It appears then that the ideological commitment to genuine peasant control over production has not been backed with the confidence that this sector is able to produce the required agricultural surplus, and that an 'insurance policy' is needed. However, it is precisely because peasants have not received adequate prices for their crops or sufficient financial resources for inputs, that they have been unable, or unwilling, to produce more, either on individual or collective farms. With more government commitment, it may have been possible to introduce new agricultural techniques at the time of villagisation and to extend the Ujamaa process into a wide rural development programmes.

Technical Choices

New techniques are particularly crucial as they provide an opportunity to increase output and accumulate sufficient capital for sustained growth. Appropriate technical choices have been identified, not only abroad, but in Tanzania itself, where the Ruvuma Development Association did valuable work of this kind before being disbanded. The range of possibilities is wide, and includes:[22]

(a) Raising food production by mechanising, using donkeys, oxen, small tractors, etc., varying crop patterns, increasing the use of manure, compost, fertilisers, pesticides, improved seeds etc. New activities such as keeping fish, bees and poultry can also be introduced.

(b) Establishing basic industries, such as brick-making, sheet-metal work and rope-making at the village level.

(c) Extending local processing of agricultural commodities, especially where this would lead to savings in transport costs. Possibilities include corn-milling, tanning, the production of poultry feed, soap, fruit pulp, etc.

(d) Supporting village production of consumer items, such as furniture, clothing and candles.

(e) Supporting small urban factories to produce tools and equipment for agriculture and village industries.

The major advantage of such initiatives is that they offer a path where neither lack of markets nor lack of capital would be the major contraints on development.

However, Tanzania's experience seems to point to the difficulty of achieving such objectives. Introducing animals in areas where people have no experience of them is not easy. Food production cannot be organised purely for local consumption because it is still needed in the cities, although transporting it is expensive. For example, trucking maize 800 miles from one of the more remote fertile areas to Dar-es-Salaam would cost more than shipping it from New Orleans.[23] Starting small-scale operations has not proved straightforward and , to a great extent, Tanzania has continued to import the machines and technology it requires. Even traditional agricultural implements mainly come from abroad. Ox ploughs, sickles and slashers are locally produced but important tools like pangas and hoes are largely imported, as shown in table 5.1.

Table 5.1
Imports & Local Production of Pangas and Hoes, 1976 and 1978

| | 1976 | | 1978 | |
	Import	Local Produce	Import	Local Produce
Panga	750,000	Nil	345,000	Nil
Hoes	1,256,000	346,000	1,661,845	502,403

Source: British Agricultural Export Council, Country Notes, Tanzania.

Tractors, of course, are imported but the high cost of repairs, spare parts and machine replacement limits their usefulness, especially when foreign exchange is scarce.[24]

The biggest manufacturer of agricultural supplies in Tanzania, Ubungo Farm Implement Manufacturing Co. (UFI) is government-owned and operates from a single large factory.* Both UFI and the other large agricultural machinery companies, Manik Engineering Co. and United Engineering Co. of Arusha (the latter two both privately owned) have considerable difficulty in keeping up production because of import restrictions. Thus the original purpose of UFI, to substitute for imports, has been undermined by its own independence on foreign equipment and supplies. Village blacksmiths might have avoided this problem.

Traditionally, many villages have a blacksmith, and Tanzanians have been smelting high grade carbon steel for over 1,500 years. In 1978 rural blacksmiths were producing one-fifth of all hoes, sicklets, knives and spears at a much lower cost than other sources. A hoe in Rukwa region cost $1.75 compared to $3.30 for a hoe from UFI, and the capital investment per worker at UFI was $4,090, compared to $37 for a village blacksmith.[25]

---

* The government's other main venture is the Ministry of Agriculture's Tanzania Agricultural Machinery Testing Unit (TAMTU), which has only one production workshop, but also caters for the Rural Craft Workshops, which produce implements to its designs.

Organising Peasant Farming

Appropriate technological choices and generous government support are important if communal agriculture is to succeed, but more fundamental still is the leadership's ability to mobilise the rural population and secure their active involvement in the process of development. Nyerere and the leadership of CCM have tried to implant such a political will in the peasant communities of Tanzania, initially by education and exhortation and later by forcing people into villages. At first it was assumed that peasants wanted the same reforms as the government and this was the basis of policy up to 1973. However, the reluctance of the majority of the population to share the vision of Ujamaa made it impossible to sustain this assumption. Either the government had failed to find a satisfactory way of expressing and implementing Ujamaa, or Ujamaa did not meet peasant needs.

Unfortunately, this dilemma was not resolved and the government began to apply increased pressure on peasant farmers through villagisation. It was considered essential to raise productivity and also to make peasants more accessible to control and easier to reach with aid projects, but the intention was still to strengthen peasant organisation and encourage self-reliance. In practice, the speed with which villagisation was achieved led to serious agricultural problems. In many of the large new villages people were too far from fertile land, soil was exhausted and over-grazing was common. The greater distance between housing and fields meant that less land was cultivated per person. Some of these problems were purely short-term, but others have been persistent throughout the attempts to reorganise peasant production.

The initial problems were exacerbated by continued reliance on foreign advice and technology, lack of capital, and perhaps most importantly, inability to resolve the reasons for peasant resistance. In the absence of popular demand for reform, the government bureacracy and the party, Chama Cha Mapinduzi, provided the leadership and this reliance on the bureaucracy exposed a central weakness in the Ujamma policy.

Growth of the Bureaucracy

Government bureaucracy is the fastest growing sector of the economy, having almost doubled in size between 1970 and 1976, it now consumes 16 per cent of the national budget.[26] Decisions are made from the top down, without the active involvement of peasant farmers. For example, to encourage production, unrealistic target quotas have been imposed bureaucratically without consultation, and consequently have been ignored by the farmers.

Although many of the new villages have a communal field they are often under-utilised because of poor organisation. Important problems of principle are not always adequately worked out. One basic question, for example, is whether the proceeds from sales should be divided according to work put in (in which case who keeps records?), or according to family size.[27] Without any changes in technology, time spent on a communal shamba usually means time away from individual plots and since under subsistence farming it is difficult to manage more than two acres effectively it is not always clear whether time spent on a commercial shamba represents a net gain in productivity.

The new and relatively inexperienced bureacracy is not well equipped for tackling detailed local issues and finds it difficult to meet its obligations to deliver agricultural equipment, seeds or fertilisers on time and in the correct quantities, and this, coupled with a generally authoritarian approach, generates mistrust and resistance.[28] Among the least popular branches of the bureaucracy are the parastatal organisations which are now responsible for marketing crops.* They are not really accountable for their actions and the only political (and therefore accountable) appointment is the general manager, who may know nothing of the economics of a particular crop. These bureaucracies have been critised as overstaffed, poorly supervised, and liable to run on deficits themselves, while blithely proposing expansion programmes.[29] There seems to be some validity in these criticisms, at least the Cashewnut Authority described below, broadly fits this description.

The government is not unaware of the problems of bureaucratisation. In December 1980, for example, it took a major decision to return responsibility for collecting food and export crops from State enterprises to peasant-run co-operatives[30] and there have been several other attempts to rectify mistakes which have arisen from organising from the top downwards.

Nevertheless, it is difficult to separate those problems which stem from the organisation of the bureaucracy and can, in principle, be rectified, from the more intractable problems arising from Tanzania's poverty and underdevelopment. Like many other African countries, Tanzania suffers from a total shortage of trained expertise in all fields; the Western oriented nature of available training; difficulties in obtaining imports of essential supplies and spare parts; electricity

---

* Marketing is typically organised around parastatal authorities. There is a separate authority which buys each crop, and until recently there was also a separate organisation, the National Milling Corporation, handling all food crops, although this was disbanded by a recent government decision. The authorities do everything from collecting the crop from villages to exporting it in raw or processed form. Processing facilities (normally funded from aid sources) become a wholly-owned subsidiary of the relevant parastatal authorities. Although many crops are processed to some extent before export, this is normally minimal, consisting of whatever is required to preserve a crop. The value thus added is small, especially by comparison with the more sophisticated processing and marketing stages.

breakdowns in processing plants; a shortage of vehicles for transporting crops and a lack of all-weather roads, making collection impossible in bad weather. In addition, the worsening terms of trade between primary and manufactured products offers no short-term relief from these crippling problems.

In conclusion, it must be appreciated that many of the problems described here, including excessive bureaucratisation, are symptomatic of underdevelopment and are not therefore susceptible to simple solutions. The government is undoubtedly aware of most of the failings of the Ujamaa programme, even though it has not responded to all of them. Nonetheless, the difficulties involved in villagisation have become painfully clear over the last decade and other African countries may be reluctant to emulate a policy which has vested so much power in the hands of the bureaucracy rather than the peasants. The original aim of villagisation was to mobilise rural people and involve peasant families in the process of development, but if this goal is to be reached, radical changes in the programme appear unavoidable.

Food versus Cash Crops

In parellel with the Ujamaa programme, the Tanzanian government has tried to establish a more self-reliant agriculture, and to achieve a more satisfactory balance between food and cash crops. The World Bank heavily influenced policy in the 1960s, emphasising intensive land use, new settlements and cash crops. By the end of 1975, the World Bank had invested T.Shs.2015-16 million in Tanzania, 40 per cent of this total was for agriculture, but the Bank had not supported a single project designed to produce basic foodstuffs. Furthermore, only 2 per cent of all State investment in agriculture between 1974 and 1975 was for the production of cereals, peas, beans, etc.[31] Loans from the Tanzanian Rural Development Bank also favour cash crops. For example in 1978-9, of money loaned for inputs, 19 per cent went to maize, and 61 per cent to tobacco.[32]

The bias in investment towards export crops did little to increase food production and indeed tended to push food crops into the more arid parts of the country, while good land was turned over to exports crops. Von Freyhold illustrates this vividly: "Maize and tobacco . . . need about the same amount of rain and maize grows well in places where the more demanding tobacco can be grown. It is therefore remarkable that the drought of 1973/4 reduced the amount of maize marketed by one-third, while the output of tobacco continued to grow.[33]

Disastrous harvests in 1973 and 1974 increased Tanzania's dependence on food imports, but led to a reappraisal of policy, from which emerged a clear priority for food self-sufficiency. For a time this new approach appeared to be succeeding. In 1979 Tanzania was broadly self-reliant in its major subsistence crops: achieved mainly through a system of offering farmers guaranteed and more generous prices for food crops. (Ironically, at the World Bank there was alarm at the threat of peasants returning to food production on too large a scale. In 1976 the Bank provided finance for the National Maize Project, which aimed at limiting the extent of peasant maize expansion by concentrating production on 950 of Tanzania's approximately 8,000 villages).[34]

However, the higher levels of output have not been maintained. A severe drought made the 1980 harvest disappointing, with the National Milling Corporation buying only 94,575 tonnes of maize, compared with about 200,000 tonnes in 1978. Serious food shortages continued in 1982 because of drought and disease, and the government sought 300,000 tonnes of food aid. So there is little evidence of food self-sufficiency.

Without significant stockpiles available from the previous years long-term solutions are impossible. Clearly, stockpiling and storage facilities are an essential element of any strategy for self-reliance, but they represent a costly investment for poorer countries, such as Tanzania, and are likely to be built up only slowly.

Although severe, storage problems were not the greatest threat to the self-reliance strategy. The new incentives to peasants for growing food crops were accompanied by a falling price for cash crops.[35] The combined volume of cash crops exported fell from 404,000 tons in 1973 to 279,000 tons in 1978. While the political choice to back food crops was both desirable and understandable, the effects on an economy so reliant on agricultural exports were serious and illustrate the complexities of the "food v. cash crops" dilemma for countries so dependent on imports. (Indeed the investments in large State farms and costly inputs had increased this import dependency.)

By late 1979 there was a foreign exchange crisis, exacerbated by the rising costs of fuel imports and the cost of ousting Amin from Uganda. Controls have at times been so tight that a shipment of produce must be exported before a licence is granted for one of the many import requests.

The cashewnut industry illustrated some of the problems which arose as a result of output falling and undermining the infrastructure which had been established, with considerable State support, to sustain a viable export crop.[36] As with some other cash crops, financial incentives for growing cashewnuts were neglected after 1973. Cashewnut production declined in the late 1970s as farmers estimated that they needed a minimum 50 per cent price rise to make it worth their while tending the cashewnut trees and harvesting the crop. In fact, the government eventually allowed a price rise of 60 per cent only in December 1980, following an economic assessment of the industry, and reports of peasants burning cashewnut trees to plant food crops.[37]

In the meantime the Cashewnut Authority's bureaucracy expanded greatly and the labour force employed to process cashewnuts grew from 1,200 in 1976 to 1,800 in 1979 without increasing output. Obviously this reduced productivity raised the cost of production. The larger bureaucracy, increased marketing costs, and reduced availablity of cashewnuts resulted in marketing costs per ton rising from around TSh.500 in the mid-1970s to over TSh2,000 in 1980.

During this period the World Bank provided finance for new processing plants to increase Tanzania's income from cashewnuts and the processing capacity has now grown to 113,000 tons of raw nuts a year. But production fell from 145,000 tons in 1973/4 to 57,000 tons in 1978/9, so the plants are operating at less than 50 per cent of capacity, negating the economic rationale of developing processing facilities. The Cashewnut Authority has thus been caught in a vicious circle where it has been unable to pay farmers more because its own costs are so high, yet, until the higher prices were authorised, farmers had no incentive to spend the time and money required to increase yields. The recent price increase involving a government subsidy to cashewnuts may help to solve this dilemma. Similar patterns of falling prices and reduced output can be observed for most major export crops.

Table 5.2 shows how the price of export crops fell in real terms during the late 1970s, while the price of food crops rose as part of the programme of increased self-sufficiency. In theory, Tanzania's system of determining the price to farmers is fair, and is worked out by estimating the export income and subtracting the estimated future marketing costs. However, rising marketing costs without concurrent increases in productivity or subsidies naturally reduce farmers' incomes.

Farmers do respond to the price that they receive for crops, and Table 5.3 shows clearly that marketed output of domestic crops other than oilseeds rose during the period when export crop production fell. However, most peasant farmers have a clear preference for growing food crops, and it may not be easy to establish a satisfactory balance by small adjustments in prices.

Before concluding that higher food prices have led to increased peasant production, it is important to be aware that the new price levels may simply have encouraged more crops to enter the market, rather than be stored in the village as a local reserve against poor harvests.[38] Ellis points out that peasants may have been led to market more sorghum, millet and cassava, previously grown only as subsistence crops, and used as a famine reserve or for local sale. If these crops are now sold to the government, the danger of localised famines may increase. Cassava, millet and sorghum are not as popular as maize and rice and there is no evidence that peasants will voluntarily buy back these foods after they have been milled and treated. In the case of serious food shortages, of course they would have to be subsidised or issued as food aid. Indeed, the National Milling Corporation has sustained enormous losses in storing and disposing of these crops, and would perhaps in future restrict price incentives to marketable crops only.

Table 5.2

Evolution of Producer Prices of Selected Crops between 1973/4 and 1978/9: Current and Real Terms

			% Increase/Decrease	
	1973/74	1978/79	Current	Real[a]
Crop	T.Shs/Kg	T.Shs/Kg	terms	terms
Food Crops				
Maize	0.33	0.85	157.6	34.0
Paddy	0.57	1.20	110.5	9.5
Wheat	0.57	1.25	119.3	14.1
Sorghum/Millet	0.50	1.00	100.0	4.0
Cassava[b]	0.31	0.65	109.7	9.1
Export Crops[c]				
Cashew	0.91	1.64	80.2	− 6.2
Cotton	1.10	2.30	109.1	− 8.8
Pyrethrum	2.75	4.52	64.4	−14.5
Tobacco	5.60	8.34	48.9	−22.5
Coffee	5.60	9.05	61.6	−15.9

Sources: Ellis, Agricultural Pricing Policy in Tanzania 1970-1979: Implications for Agricultural Output, Rural Incomes & Crop Marketing Costs, Economic Research Bureau, University of Dar Es Salaam 1980.

Notes:
(a) Deflated by modified National Consumer Price Index.
(b) Grade Makopa.
(c) Average prices paid for all grades.

Bearing in mind this caution, it seems reasonable to conclude that peasants do respond readily to significant changes in crop prices. Government policies have been insufficiently sensitive to this point in the past, and this has contributed to an unstable balance between food and cash crop production. The difficulty has been to build self-sufficiency in food crops without undermining the balance of payments, while simultaneously trying to resist foreign economic and political pressures without jeopardising the high volume of foreign aid and advice. In the next section we look rather more closely at this second dilemma.

Table 5.3

Trends in the Marketed Output of Export Crops and Domestic Food Crops in the Decade to 1979 (Metric tons)[a]

	Export Crops			Domestic Crops		
3-year average	Estate[b] Pro-duction	Peasant[c] Pro-duction	Total Export	Staple Grains	Domestic Oilseeds	Total Domestic
1969/72	240,003	391,771	631,774	208,284	28,034	236,318
1976/79	161,856	335,805	497,661	261,118	18,127	279,245
% Increase/ Decrease	− 32.6	− 14.3	− 21.2	+ 25.4	− 35.3	+ 18.2

Source: Ellis, as in Table 5.2

Notes:
(a) Measured at point of purchase from producer.
(b) Estate tea and total sisal.
(c) Cashew, cotton, pyrethrum, tobacco, all coffee, smallholder tea.

Foreign Aid, Capital and Technology

Like most other African countries, Tanzania has not been able to draw on sufficient capital from national sources to launch the development projects felt necessary. Foreign aid has been the chief source of finance for these projects, but the growing dependence on aid has had profound implications for self-reliance. It is no longer clear whether the impossibility of achieving self-reliance has driven the government to accepting aid or whether aid has prevented self-reliance from emerging. What is not disputed is that Tanzania is now chronically dependent on aid. As a proportion of the gross domestic product, foreign grants and loans grew from less than one per cent in 1969 to nearly eight per cent in 1979. By the latter date they were the highest in Africa and had reached an annual total of US$580.4 million, or 70 per cent of the development budget.[39] The major donor is the World Bank, followed by Sweden, the Netherlands and West Germany. (Other important sources are Norway, Canada, the EEC, Denmark, the United States and Finland). At the end of 1980, Tanzania's foreign reserves were minimal, and external payment arrears has reached £286 million, half the value of merchandise exports.[40]

After independence, Tanzania at first drew on relatively small sums of foreign capital. In the six years before the Arusha Declaration it received a total of TShs.588 million, but shortage of finance was regarded as a major constraint on important reforms. In the six years that followed, Tanzania was the recipient of loans totalling TShs1,730 million (excluding the Chinese loan for the Tanzanian railway) and from then on the total escalated rapidly, reaching TShs13 billion by March 1978.[41]

The use of credit on this scale inevitably threatens self-reliance. In 1979-80 for example, there was a long feud between Tanzania and the International Monetary Fund, credit from which was badly needed to pay for imports. The IMF laid down conditions for economic reform which were unacceptable to Tanzania and the government held out for ten months, but was eventually forced to negotiate when other donors threatened to withhold aid until the dispute was settled.[42] The IMF did climb down on many of its original demands, partly because it needed some reconcilation with Tanzania in the face of mounting criticism from Third World countries, but although details of the final agreement are not available, it seems that the overall demands of the IMF had to be met. Government expenses were cut back and a ceiling was imposed on borrowing by State-owned institutions and industries, although the government rather than the IMF decided on specific details.

The World Bank is a major investor in Tanzania and has had a considerable influence on the course of both industrial and agricultural development. The Bank has put forward strategies based on the encouragement of import-substituting industries and, in the agricultural sector, an expansion of marketable crops, with increased food production on large farms (the National Maize project). This approach has not led to a marked degree of economic self-reliance and was criticised pointedly in a recent review of the Tanzanian economy.

"The World Bank strategy as a whole — import substitution* and the growing of marketable crops — is in reality no solution for the underdeveloped countries. The nature of the import substitution industrialisation is such as to become a permanent drain on the foreign exchange holdings. The Bank's purpose in encouraging such industrialisation is to encourage export of machinery and intermediate commodities from the advanced West to the Third World countries. The Bank recognises that this creates balance of payments problems. To ease that and at the same time to provide the West with cheap raw materials, it calls on the Third World countries to produce 'marketable crops'."[43]

The World Bank is not noted for its sympathies to communal agriculture. Of the seven main agricultural programmes designed by the World Bank after the Arusha Declaration (cashewnuts, cotton, maize, sugar, tea, tobacco and a project in Kigoma) not a single one was directed primarily at communal farmers, but at block farms** or

* 'Import substitution' here refers to the World Bank's preference for high technology imports, i.e. tractors and the necessary imports for large-scale farming, which will theoretically reduce the need for other imports.
** Block farms are individually owned plots located adjacent to each other so that services can be provided easily.

individual farmers.[44] In addition the Bank is so committed to large-scale agriculture that it has under-estimated the cost, and overlooked the increased cost of inputs over the years. For example, one fertiliser's price (NPK) rose from TShs490 in 1971 to TShs2300 per ton in 1976. The Maize Project has converted an *occasional* purchase of maize from overseas into a *regular* purchase of inputs for production at home.[45]

Although drawing heavily on overseas aid the Tanzanian government has adopted a different course from that of Kenya and has, with the notable exception of Brooke Bond Liebig's tea estates (presumably because of the lack of alternative infrastructure, and marketing difficulties), taken over all foreign-owned estates. The foundations of Tanzania's present policies with regard to private foreign investments were laid down in the Arusha Declaration. Many of the foreign companies then operating in Tanzania were nationalised, and Tanzania paid full compensation to avoid the economic crisis which would probably have followed if the only source of technical and managerial skills had suddenly left the country. By and large, these nationalised companies operate with management on contract from the previous foreign owners. Management is therefore still in a position to transfer money out of the country through under- or over-invoicing, charging for non-existent services, slowing down the training of Tanzanians to replace themselves, and so on. Officers in the Tanzanian Treasury believe that some of these options are taken.[46]

The government has begun to develop methods of separating managerial and technological know-how and, with the increased managerial capacity now available in Tanzania, the country is succeeding in reducing dependence on foreign expertise. However, there remain uncomfortable contradictions in government policy, which recognises that profitability should be a criterion for developing any industry, yet places high emphasis on social goals. There is significant internal criticism of investment strategies, which had led, for example, to the development of industries producing 'luxury' goods such as beer and cigarettes, instead of cheap mass-produced household goods or to centralised and capital-intensive factory production of goods which may threaten established small-scale industries. It is not unusual for industries promoted for their import-substitution value to end up importing more in the form of machinery and management than was previously imported as goods.

Despite efforts to increase self-reliance, a shortage of trained personnel and technical expertise forces Tanzania to draw heavily on foreign advice and consultancies. Foreign transnationals are one source of expertise; for example, the World Bank has recently agreed to pay for a survey of the sugar industry by Tate & Lyle Engineering and Booker Agriculture International. These companies have many consultancies in

Africa and they have an interest in recommending large agricultural developments and capital-intensive projects (see Chapter 3). The dangers of relying too heavily on this kind of advice are vividly illustrated by the case of the automated bread factory, built in Dar-es-Salaam in the mid-1970s under the guidance of a Canadian consultancy (see box).

The Automated Bread Factory
(Based on a Study by Andrew Coulson)[47]

The major grain milling companies in Tanzania were nationalised in 1967 and in 1968 the National Milling Corporation was set up to manage them. In February 1969 the General Manager, a former private businessman, proposed to the NMC Board that it should extend its operations from milling wheat to baking it into bread. A fully automated bakery was proposed, costing around TShs5,000,000, and designed to produce 100,000 loaves a day. The government agreed and touted for aid, receiving a commitment from the Canadian International Development Agency (CIDA) in 1971.

The Canadian consultants, Angus Butler Engineering Co., were appointed, with responsibility for the technical and engineering aspects of design and construction, as well as acting as agents, supervising the building of the plant. Their feasibility study produced a bakery costing TShs11,000,000, over twice the original figure. CIDA authorised a loan for TShs7 million ($1 million) for the foreign exchange costs of the bakery and all internal costs were to be borne by the government, although even this amount proved insufficient to cover the machinery costs and consultants' fees. By 1975 the cost had risen to TShs17 million, over three times the original estimate.

The bakery proved a classic case of an over-ambitious and inappropriate project for an underdeveloped country. Those involved in the design, construction and equipping of the plant seem to have benefited far more than Tanzania, and the new investment was positively detrimental to the local baking industry. Serious criticisms levelled against the bakery include:

1. The huge amount spent on machinery, which even allowing for the provision of a semi-automated factory, could have been obtained from West Germany or Japan for about half the cost of the Canadian supplier, Baker Perkins.
2. The buildings were designed for a cold Canadian climate rather than that of Dar-es-Salaam.
3. The design costs were exhorbitant, particularly given the inappropriateness of the design. The consultants' fees came to 7.5 per cent of the project total.
4. Far more suitable alternatives were available using mechanised rather than semi-automatic equipment, and equally capable of producing

good bread. Ten small factories rather than one large could have been built on this basis, at a total cost of about one-third of the automated factory. This would have provided more employment, less vulnerability to machinery breakdown, and would have avoided dependence on a single supplier of spare parts and maintenance.

5. The above criticisms still *assume that a bakery was necessary*. In fact, the bakeries in Dar-es-Salaam were meeting demand, and had expanded in the past to meet increased demand for bread. There was no reason to assume that they couldn't continue to do so.

6. The government should perhaps have opted in any event to raise the price of bread and limit bread consumption. Tanzania is not self-sufficient in wheat and is unlikely to be in the foreseeable future: indeed, most African wheat is unsuitable for bread-making. Projects which encourage bread consumption — a convenient but nevertheless luxury product — increase dependence on wheat imports.

It is difficult to see who benefited from this project, apart from the Canadian interests: Baker Perkins sold machinery that could have been bought elsewhere for half the price and will no doubt continue to benefit from spare parts and maintenance supplies. The consultancy received a large fee. Canada is one of the world's largest exporters of wheat (particularly bread-making wheat).

The NMC operated on the basis that forward integration into baking from milling was 'good' under any circumstances and an automated factory carried more prestige than mechanised plants. The Boards of the NMC and the Tanzanian Investment Bank, who were responsible for controlling the plant, presumably considered that one large bakery would be easier to control than ten small ones. The conclusion drawn by Coulson is that bureaucracies have "more interest in controlling production than in achieving efficient production; and more interest in attracting foreign aid than in developing grass-roots self-reliance".

Peasant Resistance

If reliance on foreign aid and technologies poses such obvious dangers, it is important to ask whether Tanzania has any real choice. Goren Hyden, for example, argues that until African governments can really mobilise the peasantry, there is no alternative to foreign sources of capital, management and know-how.[48] In his view the failure to increase peasants' productivity should not be seen only in terms of the wrong approach or the wrong technology, but also as peasant resistance to the imposition of outside controls over their lives and work. He does not see how peasants can be reached easily by government policies and he believes that there are profound structural reasons why peasants resist, preferring a subsistence economy that can still survive outside the market system. Although international aid agencies may promote images of peasants as willing collaborators with governments, Hyden believes this is quite misleading and that in peasants' eyes the government has no real legitimacy to act on their behalf; that no reciprocal relationship exists and in the end the government has no real power to impose its policies. In essence, the government needs the peasants more than the peasants need the government.

The history of Tanzania since independence certainly illustrates a government determined to gain such control over the peasant sector. Villagisation is the latest and possibly the most successful attempt to do so, but by itself provides no solutions to problems of top down organisation: bureaucracy, over-dependence on foreign aid and advice, and lack of capital. A writer recently pointed out that no government can afford to become overseer of the whole peasantry.[49] If peasants do not benefit from government policies to any fundamental extent, for example cannot even obtain their very basic needs such as salt, sugar, soap, cooking oil, kerosene, clothing and footwear, then there is little incentive to produce for the market as the government desires. Coercion cannot solve these problems if peasants still have the capacity to withdraw from production for the market.

Conclusion: Lessons from the Tanzanian Experience

In spite of the obvious shortcomings, the Tanzian experience is often held as a model to other African countries. The problems of poverty and over-dependence on exports of a small number of cash crops are widespread in Africa, and Tanzania is not alone in facing worsening terms of trade, mounting foreign debts and high oil imports. Although the country has made only limited progress towards self-reliance and the economy is now under considerable stress, Tanzania's approach should not be dismissed as a failure.

Many of the difficulties encountered are similar to those experienced by other underdeveloped countries and have been exacerbated by external pressures, and uncontrollable elements, such as the drought. Furthermore, there have been some solid achievements. Many aspects of peasants' and workers' lives have undoubtedly improved. Primary education is virtually universal, the adult literacy rate is one of the highest in Africa at 66 per cent (compared to 40 per cent for Kenya) and 39 per cent of the population have access to safe water supplies (compared to 17 per cent in Kenya). There is one nursing person for every 3,080 people, compared to one for every 10,330 at Independence (by comparison the figures for Kenya are 1,090:2,230), there is legislation making discrimination against women illegal and all employed women are entitled to three months paid maternity leave.

Looking at Tanzania's commitment to raising agricultural

productivity, there seems little doubt that favourable pricing policies do encourage peasant farmers to concentrate on food production, although it is important to be clear to what extent this involves an absolute increase in production and to what extent it encourages the sale of previously stored crops. In both Tanzania and Kenya, food production has suffered from a combination of low prices and excessive concentration on cash crops. However, in Tanzania the recent decline in the output of cash crops has had severe economic repercussions, largely because the economy remains heavily dependent on imports. In the short run it is clearly important to sustain a reasonable level of cash crop exports, while continuing to increase self-sufficiency in food. In the longer term it might be appropriate to put greater emphasis on overall self-reliance, rather than self-sufficiency in one particular sector. A careful appraisal of import requirements would be a useful start.

Collectivisation remains a goal, but has yet to achieve widespread success, if measured by increases in agricultural productivity. Among the reasons for this are: (a) The process of collectivisation has not been controlled by peasants — it has always been managed as a top-down exercise, with the development of bureaucracies often taking precedence over local organisation. (b) Peasants have gained relatively little from the reorganisation of labour on collective shambas and have generally preferred the freedom of working their own land. Technological improvements are required to raise productivity, but local community control is important. (c) Peasant agriculture has not received the same degree of investment as large-scale farming projects.

After 1973-74, enforced legislation became the principal means of engineering a more collective agriculture, although fundamental political, social and economic restraints on peasant organisation were not addressed adequately. Bureaucracies have continued to grow and the government has remained heavily dependent on foreign advice, technology and capital. consequently, it has been unable to avoid drawing on the expertise of transnationals and aid agencies which, like the World Bank, remain committed to capitalist development strategies and a closer integration of Tanzania into the world market.

It seems clear that peasants have tried to resist many of the government's strategies but it is difficult to know whether, as Hyden argues, this is inherent in a peasant economy, or whether it is a result of unsatisfactory elements in the policies chosen. Rene Dumont stated in a recent interview that he would try to change underdevelopment by "giving the peasants back their freedom so that they can organise themselves. I would free them of adminstrative constraints and arbitary quotas. I would leave them free to grow what they wish. Of course, technicians have to be sent to them . . . to help them, not to replace them, and to allow them to organise themselves in their own interests."[50]

This degree of autonomy is never likely to become a political reality, and Tanzania is certainly no closer to it than many other countries. In any case, it remains unclear whether, as Dumont believes, farming communities could actually gain control over agricultural production and organise themselves without, initially at least, some form of leadership. Jonathan Barker points out that villagers in Tanzania may now be placed in a position whereby they will have to try to answer some of these questions for themselves: 'Given the heightened economic crisis in Tanzania and the possible receptivity of the newly villagised millions to new forms of social life, the answers that emerge are crucial.[51]

CHAPTER 6

Agribusiness and
Africa's Food Crisis

Agribusiness companies have in the past concentrated on the development of cash crop production for export from Africa. Recently, however, foreign companies have turned to food provision for domestic consumption, as more and more governments have looked to agribusiness to solve Africa's food crisis.

Sub-Saharan Africa is the only region in the world where per capita food production has declined over the last 20 years[1] (see Fig 6.1), dropping in 1980-81 for the 15th time in 20 years.[2] Per capita consumption in 1980 was 15 per cent below per capita consumption at the start of the 1970s and almost 20 per cent below that at the start of the 1960s.[3] This decline shows no sign of abating. In 1980-81 the output of several countries in East Africa and the Sahel dropped by a third or more on the low levels reported in 1979.[4]

In human terms this means that a large proportion of the population has a seriously inadequate diet. In most Sub-Saharan countries per capita calorie intake falls below minimal nutritional standards. Indeed, the authors of one large study contended recently that, even if total food available today were distributed equally and efficiently, there would not be enough to give everyone an adequate diet.[5] In 18 countries where per capita calorie availability is less than 90 per cent of minimal requirements, serious nutritional problems are unavoidable,[6] given present agricultural policies and income distribution.

No government can ignore the social and political disruption caused by food production failures on this scale. Virtually all African governments have intervened in both the production and the marketing of food in order to improve availablity and to control prices. Several governments have resorted to imports on a large scale, (see Apprendix C for details of food imports from 1972-79), a pattern first set in the 1960s when prices were low and food aid was readily available as a result of the accumulation of huge grain surpluses in North America (see Fig.6.2). This made imports appear a cheap and relatively secure method of supplying Africa's growing demand, particularly that generated by the expanding urban population.

These imports have become a regular feature of Africa's food economy. Almost all projections of the continent's food import requirements to 1990 show that, without a sharp increase in domestic food output, the shortfall between production and consumption in

138

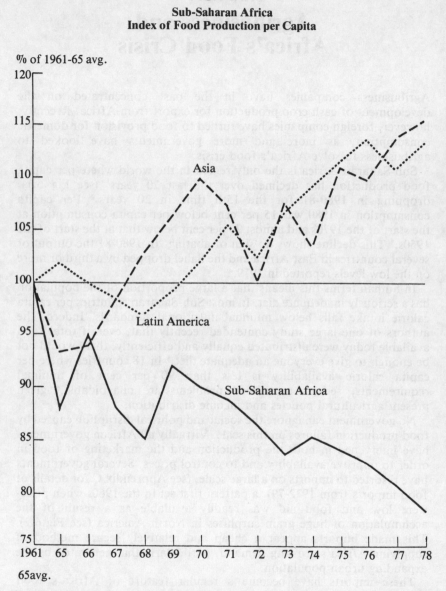

Figure 6.1

**Sub-Saharan Africa
Index of Food Production per Capita**

% of 1961-65 avg.

Source: ESCS Indices of Agricultural Production

Africa will worsen dramatically,[7] resulting in an increase in food imports to as much as two[8] or three[9] times the present level. However, world food trade has changed dramatically since the early 1960s. There is an increasing commercial demand for grain imports from middle income developing countries and from Eastern Europe and the USSR, at a time when the world's major supplier of cereal exports, the USA, is no longer producing the constant surpluses that characteristed the 1960s.[10] The cost of Africa's grain imports has therefore increased sharply. In the 1960s the volume of grain imports doubled, but the total cost rose by only 50 per cent.[11] From 1970 to 1978, however, the cost of Sub-Saharan Africa's cereal imports rose by 100 per cent.[12] Today many of these countries are in no position to pay higher prices. In 1981, Africa was expected to import 18 million tons of food, eight million tons of which could only be purchased if available at concessionary prices.[13]

How did Africa's food situation come to be in such a parlous state? Why has it proved to be so intractable a problem? Why has the temporary resort to food imports become a permanent feature of Africa's food trade? What are the consequences of this dependence? What solutions are being adopted? What prospect do they offer of solving the crisis in domestic food production which faces the continent?

Figure 6.2

Sub-Saharan Africa

Indices of Grain Imports: Volume and Cost

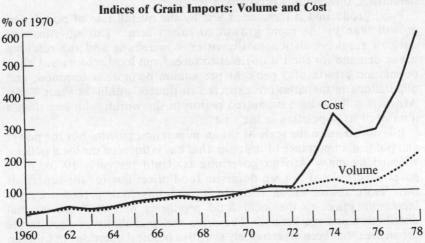

Source: FAO Trade Yearbook

The decline in domestic food production is not a recent development. It began, as was seen in Chapter 1, in the colonial era, when a series of damaging policies were in force. European settlers confiscated the best land; African farmers were excluded from commerical crop production; migrant labour systems broke up stable communities; and cash crops often replaced staple food crops. The result was a general neglect of the domestic food sector, which even after independence remained under-capitalised and underdeveloped,[14] despite the strong growth in demand from an increasingly urbanised population.

Population Growth and Urbanisation

Some analysts have argued that population growth is itself the main contributory factor to Africa's food crisis.[15] It is true that the growth rate of Africa's population has increased steadily over the past 20 years and at 2.7 per cent per annum, it is now the highest in the underdeveloped world.[16] Nevertheless, although some areas face distinct pressures on good agricultural land, only Kenya and Nigeria, with population densities of over 200 per square kilometre, are comparable to such countries as Bangladesh, Indonesia and El Salvador.[17] In fact, many parts of Africa suffer from shortages of labour which limit the amount of food which can be produced. Bottlenecks are created during labour intensive operations such as field preparation, planting, weeding and harvesting, thus limiting production.[18]

Food production is threatened less by the overall rate of population growth than by the rapid growth of urban areas. The movement of Africa's rural population to the cities is increasing and the resulting urban demand for food is difficult to meet from local resources. Urban population growth of 5 per cent per annum or more is common, and populations in the cities are expected to double within 14 years.[19] Yet Africa is still the least urbanised region in the world, with less than a quarter of its population in the cities.[20]

It is not so much the scale of urban population growth, but the power and political importance of the cities that has influenced the local policies adopted by many African governments. Until the early 1970s, most governments aimed to keep domestic food prices low for the benefit of their more restive urban consumers, and this took precedence over increasing prices to the local food producers or improving internal distribution and marketing.[21] The price and availability of food in the urban areas has been an extremely sensitive political question. In Liberia, for example, attempts by the government to increase food prices and impose import controls led to severe 'rice riots' in April 1979, which forced the government to withdraw the increases and paved the way for the coup which later overthrew it.[22] In the Sudan urban demonstrations occurred in mid-1979 and January 1982 in response to withdrawals of subsidies on sugar and wheat.

In the 1960s, cheap food imports appeared an inexpensive and relatively secure method of supplying Africa's growing urban demand, while rural needs were to be met by subsistence agriculture. As urban incomes rose, people were encouraged to develop a preference for convenience foods, often with a high import content, such as bread, rice and the processed products, while little effort was expended on increasing production of local grains and cereals. However, since food import prices have soared in recent years and the size and power of urban populations has continued to grow, food policies of this kind have put Africa even more at the mercy of external forces. Many governments now face a falling foreign exchange income as a result of declining prices for Africa's main exports and the commitment to expensive food imports on an increasing scale has become a major source of weakness.

Agribusiness, Food Imports and Processing

Some African countries have become dependent on the major grain processing and trading corporations for the cereal imports which ensure their political survival. The experience of Zaire provides a dramatic illustration of the weakness of an African country which has seriously neglected local food production only to find itself in conflict with Continental Grain, one of the 'Big Five'* agribusiness companies which control the world grain trade.[23]

Before independence very little wheat was grown in Zaire and only small amounts of flour were imported to satisfy the needs of the Europeans present. After independence from Belgium in 1960, the US shipped flour as food aid under its Public Law 480 programme.** During the 1960s foreign flour and wheat were cheap and exporting governments made credit available. The population of Zaire's capital, Kinshasa, swelled and it became cheaper and considerably easier for the Zairean government to import flour to feed the urban population than to increase agricultural production and improve rural transport and distribution systems. A network of bakeries in cities and towns sprang up in the wake of those imports, and a new system of food distribution and dietary patterns emerged, revolving around imported flour.

* The 'Big Five' are Cargill, Continental, Louis Dreyfus, Bunge and Andre. These transnational giants are owned by seven of the world's richest and most uncommunicative American and European families.[24] Cargill is now one of the world's largest companies. The ability of these five companies to totally dominate the world grain trade stems from their ownership of the facilities for grain transportation, loading, shipping, processing and distribution on all continents.

** PL480 is a permanent US food aid programme designed to promote the foreign policy of the United States, combat hunger and dispose of surplus.[25]

By 1967 bread was displacing the more traditional food of white maize and manioc in Kinshasa. Once bread had become sufficiently established in the capital through subsidised imports, Continental (one of the Big Five) proposed in 1967 that it build a modern flour mill near Kinshasa. The mill was opened in 1973, ensuring Zaire's dependence on imported wheat and US-owned processing technology just when the sharp increases in wheat prices of 1973 and 1974 were imminent.

In 1974 the Zairean government, faced with declining revenue from their copper exports, fell behind in their payments to Continental for the American wheat the grain company was using. By late 1976 the giant company's patience was exhausted and it began to flex its muscles by holding back its monthly wheat shipment to its Zaire facility. The mill was forced to reduce its daily output of flour and queues soon began to form.

The effect of this action was immediate. Zaire officials met with representatives of Continental and agreed to all the company's demands. They not only had to promise that the Central Bank would pay cash for all subsequent wheat shipments and that Zaire would start repaying its old debt at the rate of $1 million a month, but it also had to agree that only American hard wheat would be imported, except in special circumstances; that Continental would have exclusive rights to mill flour in Zaire; and that the company would have the right to approve or disapprove all requests by others to import flour into Zaire. Thus Continental became Zaire's sole importer of wheat, sole manufacturer of flour, and it received authority to control imports of any competing flour, almost as if it were a government agency.

After this capitulation to Continental, American wheat began flowing to Zaire again. In fact US wheat imports increased rapidly and by 1977 they stood at 140,000 tons per annum, three times the amount imported in 1974. Great Plains Wheat, a company that promotes American wheat exports abroad, predicted that Zaire's wheat imports would reach 210,000 tons per annum by 1982, making it the largest US wheat customer in West and Central Africa, after Nigeria.[26]

In recent years American companies have become increasingly attracted to processing food in African countries. The US conglomerate Nabisco has developed a rice soya blend called 'Ricetein', priced higher than rice but less expensive than meat, and is endeavouring to sell processing plants to countries where rice is the staple food. Senegal has signed up for the bulk shipments initially and is interested in the processing plant. The drawback of course is that Senegal grows rice but no soya and so will have to import the latter.[27] The US, on the other hand, is the world's largest exporter of soya. Another American corporation, Seaboard Allied Milling, owns the only flour mill in Sierra Leone, as well as mills in Nigeria and Liberia. Two UK companies,

Spillers and Associated British Foods, have affiliates in Africa, while the French-based Grand Moulin de Paris is active in francophone African countries.[28] Indeed, the grain trade in West Africa is largely controlled by French influence and French companies. Wheat is shipped from France to Cameroon, Senegal and the Ivory Coast, and milling is mostly in the hands of European companies.[29]

Africa of course is not alone in attracting the grain trade. Third World countries have become a major target for market expansion since the rate of growth of consumer flour sales in the developed countries has been among the lowest of all major food product groups. For this reason the pressure on wheat-importing developing countries seems unlikely to diminish.[30]

Agribusiness and Large Scale Food Production

In response to the problems experienced with food imports, African governments are now turning their attention to the question of increasing domestic food production. The most favoured approach for a growing number of countries is a dash for growth in food output, relying on large scale production schemes.[31] The political need for quick results and the deceptive simplicity of a single solution to the complex problems of declining per capita food production have caused many African countries to look to large scale, highly capitalised and mechanised schemes. Among the countries which have done so are Nigeria, Zambia, Kenya, Sudan, Ghana, Ethiopia, Tanzania, Mozambique, Togo and Benin (see Box 1).

The decision to opt for such large scale schemes is often made by bureaucrats who prefer to attribute short-falls in food supplies to inadequacies in peasant production rather than to a more general failure to tackle such underlying causes as low farm prices and poor marketing, storage and distribution systems.[32] There are also strong external arguments and pressures on governments to favour technically advanced, large-scale farms, especially State-owned ones. Firstly there is the apparent success of modern agriculture in the West and the more generalised pressure to adopt the latest technology. Secondly, foreign aid agencies will lend money for such schemes in preference to general policies designed to help peasants in modest unspectacular ways (see Chapter 5). Thirdly, agribusiness is ready, willing and anxious to advise on new schemes, and to provide the inputs required.

At first sight it is by no means obvious how the production of food for local consumption can be a sufficiently lucrative activity for foreign firms. Traditionally they have been involved in cash crop production and their role in food production has been peripheral. Indeed, as the Chairman of General Foods candidly put it: 'It is virtually impossible for a private business establishment to develop, distribute and sell enough of the kinds of food poor people need and still break even, much less look for any profit.[33]

It is the adoption of large-scale schemes by African governments, together with the encouragement and financial guarantees offered by the aid agencies, which is bringing the transnationals into the domestic food sector in Africa. According to the book *Business Guide to World Aid Funds and Projects,* world aid has risen 400 per cent during the 1970s to $20 billion, much of which is spent on goods and expertise from the developed world.[34] Contracts agreed through aid agencies such as the United States Agency for International Development (USAID) or the World Bank also have the advantage of being largely immune from recessions and national cutbacks. Aid agencies effectively guarantee payments and therefore eliminate the financial risks to agribusiness.

Box 1

Methods of Food Production in Sub-Saharan Africa[35]

The most important food crops produced in Africa are maize and the root crops, such as cassava, yams and sweet potatoes. Millet and sorghum are the most important cereals after maize, since the production of wheat, rice and barley is concentrated in only a few areas.

Region	Patterns of Food Production
Sahel and W. Africa	Smallholders responsible for the bulk of food production. The subsistence sector predominates, although a few large-scale mechanised units produce rice and maize, e.g.:
Benin	Government intends to develop a series of highly-mechanised State farms, 1000 hectares or more in size.
Ghana	Large mechanised estates for cash crops but also greater emphasis now being put on smallholder sector, where communal land tenure is widespread.
Guinea	Government policies emphasise collective farming, with village level production brigades equipped to cultivate communal farm units. Yields lower than on smallholdings, which account for 80 per cent of total agricultural production.
Guinea-Bissau	Government stresses the promotion of small-scale family farms, but does not exclude the establishment of State farms.
Nigeria	Government encouraging larger-scale units. The land tenure system differs among States, although it is predominantly communal. In recent years there has been a movement towards freehold tenure, mainly because rapid population growth has exerted pressure on available land and many farmers have ill-defined rights to land.

Sierra Leone	Similar to Guinea-Bissau.
Togo	Agrarian land reform is aimed at facilitating the merging of small fragmented plots and the use of modern agricultural equipment.
Central Africa	The traditional land tenure system whereby the tribal authorities allotted plots has been modified to encourage commercial rather than family subsistence production. Attempts to organise the smallholders to produce food-crops for sale began in the 1950s and have continued until the more recent establishment of co-operative farms in Angola and Congo, and diverse smallholder projects in Zaire.
East Africa	Smallholders produce the bulk of agricultural products and the importance of the subsistence sector varies from country to county. There is little food production for markets in Rwanda and Burundi, but a lot in Kenya and Sudan. In other countries large units are generally limited to some cash crops, with the exception of Ethiopia's expanding State farms and the State farms in Tanzania. Smallholders have been integrated into the market economy more through export crops than food crops, reflecting colonial priorities which have been continued since independence. e.g.:
Kenya	A continuum from small subsistence holdings to large units controlled by individuals, co-operatives and companies.
Sudan	Three distinct sectors: State-controlled, participatory irrigation schemes; large-scale private mechanised farming under rain-fed conditions, and traditional small farmers who grow about 60 per cent of total production.
Southern Africa	The control of land by white farmers and the agricultural investments of private firms has led to a sector composed of larger modern units on one hand and on the other a mainly subsistence sector, e.g.:
Malawi	Small farmers predominate in Malawi with the estate sector producing most of the cash crops.
Mozambique	A broad subsistence sector still exists but the former Portuguese commercial farms, primarily small and medium-sized, have been consolidated into State farms, along with some of the old plantations. Some 4,000 farms cover nearly 50 per cent of the farmland. Some 'communal' villages have been established and are to be expanded.

Swaziland	About 70 per cent of the population live on mainly subsistence farms covering about half the land area. A large proportion of the modern farms are owned by foreigners and private companies.
Zambia	Approximately 500-600 large-scale commercial farms, half of which are European-owned, produce one-half to two-thirds of the marketed output of maize, the staple food, on leasehold land.
Zimbabwe	Just before independence approximately 6,000 white commercial farmers and some plantations controlled almost 50 per cent of the total land area and employed a large amount of wage labour, producing most of the marketed agricultural goods. Over half the population was restricted to Tribal Trust Lands, infertile areas representing about 40 per cent of the total land area. Here farming takes place on small units with little marketed surplus produce. Farms suffer from problems of over-grazing, crowding and lack of infrastructure. Since independence, resettlement from the Trust lands to abandoned white farms has been occurring slowly.[36]

Transnational companies benefit enormously from aid. Roughly 75 per cent of the USAID assistance funds are actually spent in the United States. US-based companies do even better with multilateral development banks, e.g. every dollar that American taxpayers pay into the World Bank generates about $10 in procurement contracts for US companies.[37] These companies have the expertise and capital for large-scale production, providing a wide range of goods and services such as irrigation equipment, fertilisers, seeds and farm implements, food processing technologies, marketing facilities and services and management contracts for technical skills and training. Large-scale schemes depend heavily on these inputs and hence Africa's reliance on transnational agribusiness seems set to increase.

Such schemes, however, are unlikely to solve Africa's food deficiency. They are often inappropriate and expensive and they tend to divert attention and cash from the underlying problems of rural poverty and inadequate infrastructure. A classic example of this process is to be found in Zambia. Since independence all attempts by the goverment to restore and increase food production have failed.[38] The latest policy is to concentrate resources on large-scale agricultural production rather than channel new investment into the peasant sector.

In 1981 Zambia embarked on an intensive ten-year national food production programme costing an estimated US$500 million, largely financed by bilateral aid and international organisations. The programme is intended to make Zambia self-sufficient in food by 1991 by establishing a total of 18 mechanised State farms, two each in the nine provinces, with each farm extending to about 20,000 hectares. These farms will make use of consultants from both foreign companies and aid agencies and all will be managed by foreign personnel.[39] Tate & Lyle, for example, carried out a technical study and then won the contract to develop Mswebe State farm in Central Province as a joint venture with the government. A number of French companies have prepared preliminary information on two farms, one in Western Province and another in Eastern Province. On other farms experts from Bulgaria, Japan, China, East Germany and the European Economic Community are involved.[40]

The inherent assumption made by the Zambian government is that all past failures have been due to projects being too small. This has brought criticism both from inside and outside Zambia. Officials of the Ministry of Agriculture were scarcely consulted, and the response from the Commercial Farmers Bureau and a section of the press was 'lukewarm'.[41] Even the East German consultants, who helped to establish the scheme, believe the proposed farms to be impractical.[42]

The world-renowned agronomist Rene Dumont, with over half a century of experience in Third World agriculture, is highly critical of the Zambian scheme and others like it. President Kaunda asked Dumont to analyse Zambia's agricultural strategy and the ensuing report 'Towards Another Development in Rural Africa' has harsh and depressing words to say about the direction the President has chosen.* Dumont commented that Zambia is 'trying to build State farms. What will these State farms be? Bureaucratic, corrupt and inefficient'. The report claims that the direction of post independence policies has 'accentuated rural underdevelopment, has widened the gap between urban rich and all poor people . . . it has aggravated malnutrition'.[43] Despite these criticisms of Zambia's policy, other African governments are pursuing large-scale food production with the assistance of the United Nations and numerous national aid agencies.

The most ambitious scheme of this kind for improving food production, not just in one country but in a whole region, was launched recently in the Sahel. The drought and famine in this region from 1968-1974 attracted considerable international attention. Since the last drought, the Sahel is no longer an unknown desert fringe, but a region in which hundreds of millions of dollars, major scientific resources and

---

* President Kaunda pushed aside the protests of his bureaucrats and published the study, although, according to one report, only a few copies are circulating in Lusaka, and the version that was printed by the government printer appears to have been withdrawn and is unlikely to be released.[44]

enormous administrative efforts have been concentrated in order to develop what has been called a major new model for development planning. This has culminated in a series of projects and proposals known as 'The Sahel Development Programme'.[45]

The programme covers a gigantic region, several ecological zones, eight national governments (Gambia, Senegal, Mauritania, Mali, Upper Volta, Niger, Chad and Cape Verde Islands), numerous ethnic and linguistic groups and involves several national and international donor organisations. Technical and social science experts, development planners and government officials have together produced an overall plan 'to rid the Sahel of food shortages and ecological deterioration, to overcome dependency, to raise the incomes and quality of life for 26 million people over widely dispersed zones, and to set a potential model for development planning in other regions'.[46] All this to occur by the year 2000.

Inevitably, such a programme relies heavily on large-scale projects. In Niger, for example, the World Bank is supporting pumping and irrigation works for an intensive rice cultivation scheme of up to 90,000 hectares. This could well displace herders onto land that is already over-grazed and thus bring them into conflict with agriculturalists.[47] In Eastern Senegal 80-130,000 hectares of rangeland are to be used in a $2.35 million project to increase the output of calves for beef marketing. The main supporters of the project in the area are 'government officials, foreign experts, and the Soninke cattle-buyers', and it is these people who will doubtless be the main beneficiaries.[48]

A detailed and extensive look at both the history and causes of the Sahel's present situation and the effectiveness of the Sahel Development Programme, including the role of agribusiness, has been published by two American researchers, Richard W. Franke and Barbara H. Chasin, in a book entitled *Seeds of Famine*.[49] During their research for this book they visited three Sahel countries, Senegal, Mali and Niger, and looked at representative projects of every major type, involving a wide range of social and environmental situations and donors including the FAO, France, Holland, Belgium, the US and four non-governmental organisations. The questions they were attempting to address were: how will the project contribute toward restoration and preservation or improvement of the Sahelian ecology, how will the project help overcome drought and famine vulnerability and how will the project benefit the majority of Sahelians, i.e. the poorest farmers and animal herders?

Their findings and conclusions (including the Caramance study described below) were that the Sahel Development Programme is not working and many of the projects are over-ambitious and appear to be producing the opposite of their intended effect. Although the projects have only been going for a few years, the authors feel that they may be contributing to increased rather than decreased dependency on the technologically advanced Western nations, may be leading to increased drought and famine vulnerability, and may be exacerbating differences between wealthy and poor Sahelians.

From their studies Franke and Chasin conclude that 'whatever the intentions of the planners and administrators, and the project directors and technical experts of the donor countries, the Sahel Development Programme is a captive to the overall negative relationships between the Western capitalist nations and the people of the Sahel'. This makes ominous reading in the light of what is perhaps the largest and most comprehensive plan to increase local food production in Africa — the United States Agency for International Development's 'Food Sector Assistance Strategy for the 1980s for Africa'. This is being formulated by AID's African Bureau and, like the Sahel Development Programme, puts much emphasis on increased production, using new seeds and other technological advances, and more educated managers, technicians and administrators, all of which must be funded from the outside.[50]

The strategy is almost entirely production oriented. It assumes that peasants and the urban poor will be earning sufficient income to purchase the food produced. Indeed, the designs of production oriented approaches of this kind rarely consider the effects of such schemes on the vast majority of consumers, and typically little attention is paid to the question of who will benefit from the increased amounts of food grown. In reality, few small farmers or landless peasants will be able to afford the food produced on costly high technology farms and thus are unlikely to benefit from these grandiose plans.

The drawbacks to the high technology approach are not limited to the worsening of social relations, but extend also to adverse enviromental effects. Environmentally large-scale schemes have not enjoyed a good record in Africa. There are many examples of inappropriate crops and technology being imported and applied with predictably dire consequences.[51]

In many parts of Africa the climate and soils are not favourable to intensive agricultural production. Over half of tropical Africa has too little rainfall and even this is erratic and unreliable, thus making farming extremely risky. Isolated areas of fertile volcanic soil exist in the Cameroons, Rwanda, Burundi and the highlands of East Africa, but the majority of African soils are poor in nutrients and extremely fragile.[52] Over centuries peasant farmers have developed a series of techniques to overcome these conditions, including crop rotation, the cultivation of protective ground covering crops and the use of extensive farming methods. These techniques are clearly not compatible with the more intensive methods developed for application in the temperate countries of the industrialised Northern hemisphere. However, because the decline in Africa's food production is seen as primarily a problem of technical skills rather than the culmination of a lengthy historical process in which social and political factors have played a crucial role, the continent is again paying the cost of expensive large-scale experimentation with imported techniques and crops.

In Senegal, a large-scale food production scheme is likely to adversely affect both the rural peasants and the local environment. A large rice growing project involving agribusiness is to be developed in the Caramance region of Senegal. This area has the greatest rainfall in the country and is also endowed with major rivers and tributaries. There is therefore a potential year-round water supply and this, as well as relatively good soils, has made the area appear an attractive proposition for further agricultural development. Among the people already living in the area are the communal and egalitarian Balantas, renowned for their careful soil management techniques and their sound environmental use of animals and crops. However, Senegal's rice shortages of 1975 and the subsequent need to import 124,000 tons, led government planners and development experts to arrange for 30,000 hectares of the eastern Caramance to be turned into a high technology, plantation-like enterprise to grow rice for the urban population.[53]

This scheme was to be paid initially by a loan of $30 million arranged by the US bank Citibank, and now doubled by funds from Saudi Arabia. The Senegalese government will organise production at the local level, but most of the technology and much of the planning and organisation will be carried out by International Control & Systems of Houston, Texas, a farm implement and agri-industrial firm. The Senegalese government's development operation, SODAGRI, will be 50 per cent owned by private American capital and will be the official development agency for the project. The hope is to double the yields in the area, resulting in a total output of 180,000 tons of rice per annum.[54] On a highly mechanised commercial operation of this kind, the usual and most convenient method of operation it to use hired labour. However, a report by the Centre for Research in Economic Development at Michigan University has pointed out, in a delicate under-statement, that the use of hired labour is not in 'complete harmony with the Senegalese goal of communal rural development', although it admits that some individual rice plots could be maintained and low level technical assistance given to farmers.[55]

In reality, however, 'the Caramance rice scheme is to be a profit making venture in which Sengalese farmers will be de-certified from the land under Senegal's "socialist" land reform act of 1964. The land will then be rented or otherwise made available to the SODAGRI corporation, which in turn will hire the farmer-smallholders or village communal farmers as wage labourers for its operation'.[56]

There are also likely to be environmental problems. Much of the Caramance area has already been degraded in past decades by over-ambitious projects designed to increase peasant output for the benefit of French entrepreneurs and the previous colonial administration. Recently fears have been expressed privately by development personnel in Senegal's capital, Dakar, concerning the possible ecological consequences of the dams planned as part of the project. They feel that the possible harmful effects of the dams on water flow, acquatic life and salt content have been inadequately studied.[57]

Even if large-scale schemes were designed to be compatible with the local environent they would still tend to increase the dependence of the host country on its external suppliers and advisors, especially in the case of the poor and smaller countries which are unable to supply their own inputs. Once a scheme is established they are usually compelled to rely on imports on a continuous basis. This dependence is encouraged by agribusiness and aid agencies and is likely to be a problem even when programmes are designed so that small farmers rather than large new projects are (at least in theory) the target.

In Nigeria, for example, a major new food production programme, aimed at small farmers, and backed by aid agencies, is opening the door to agribusiness. Only 34 million of Nigeria's 92 million hectares are arable, but World Bank sources indicate that this area could be expanded to about 72 million hectares with the aid of modern technology.[58] There is considerable enthusiasm for more productive land because both the food and cash crop sectors have performed poorly in the last 20 years, largely because of government concentration on industrialisation and the oil sector, the civil war and the lack of adequate agricultural inputs and price incentives for small farmers.[59]

Nigeria's latest plan to increase food production (which follows two unsuccessful predecessors, 'The National Accelerated Food Production Programme', and 'Operation Feed the Nation') is called the 'Green Revolution' and was conceived by the World Bank and Nigerian experts. It is expected to cost about US$8.24 billion between 1981 and 1985 and is designed to bring an extra 76,000 hectares under cultivation. Using aid funds, the government will provide financial support, including input subsidies and the provision of rural infrastructure. The inputs will be provided by the private sector.[60]

The vast amounts of money involved in this scheme have galvanised the US business community. With a population fast approaching 100 million, one in four Africans is a Nigerian, and the GNP now far exceeds $50 billion. The government policy is to encourage private enterprise and foreign investment, so profit margins are generous. All this makes Nigeria a prime market for agribusiness transnationals, as it is by far their biggest African market.*[61]

Following a visit to Nigeria in July 1980 by the then Vice-President, Walter Mondale, a US-Nigerian Joint Agricultural Consultative Committee was set up. This included representatives from such well-known agribusiness companies as Coca Cola, Ralston Purina Company, the Pillsburg Company and Carnation International, as well as representatives from Ford Motor Co, Chase Manhattan Bank and First National Bank of Chicago. Nigerian members are expected to be drawn from both government and private industry. This committee aims 'to facilitate private sector co-operation in agriculture and agribusiness between the United States and Nigeria'. President Shagari assured the American representatives full support for US private investment in Nigeria, with incentives such as reduced interest rates on loans related to agricultural projects, the liberalisation of capital repatriation controls and consent for companies to retain 100 per cent ownership of investments.[63] The committee will be the principal vehicle for the transfer of US agricultural technology to Nigeria, being involved particularly in the supply of fertilisers, seeds, milling and baking technologies, integrated rice production and processing, and the production of grains and legumes. Also covered are agricultural processing industries, integrated poultry systems and methods for the small-scale production and distribution of fresh produce.[64] Already Texaco's agribusiness arm, Texagri, is involved in a 2,500 hectare scheme to produce cassava flour and Pullman Kellogg is involved in the building of a nitrogeneous fertiliser plant.[65] It has been suggested that US farm exports to Nigeria could reach $1 billion by 1985,[66] although this optimism may be undermined by the recent drop in oil revenues.[67]

In theory, the small farmer is the cornerstone and major beneficiary of Nigeria's Green Revolution and its designers in the World Bank stress integrated rural development as a goal. However, there must be some doubt on this score, since past programmes have led to increasing landlessness and rural poverty (see Box 2) and a rapid increase in the number of individual farms covering thousands of hectares.[68] In the second half of the 1970s, for example, the main area of agricultural investment in Nigeria was large-scale irrigation schemes, which had devastating effects on peasant producers. In Northern Nigeria the Talata-Mafara project involved irrigating 10,000 hectares near the Sokoto River. The work was carried out by Impresit Nigeria Ltd., which is 40 per cent owned by Fiat, and during the three-year construction period 60,000 peasants had to be moved. During this time the peasants were unable to farm, were given no compensation and finally, when they

* Nigeria is America's second largest oil supplier and provides the United States with its largest trade deficit (larger than that of Japan) at over $10 billion a year.[62]

protested, the State used guns against them. For many of them the only way to survive was to mortgage their land to the small bankers, civil servants and businessmen of Kano. The elites in Kano also benefited from a similar irrigation project at Kadawa, which used a Canadian firm for the preliminary study and a Dutch and Yugoslavian consortium for the construction phase. An increasing number of farmers had no choice but to rent their land to local businessmen and civil servants in Kano, since it was they who had the money necessary to invest in irrigation.[69]

A similar pattern has been repeated outside Nigeria, in Northern Senegal, where it was reported that senior civil servants were the main beneficiaries of irrigation schemes. Likewise, in the north of Ghana a rice plantation created by the State as part of a national drive to increase food production has been mainly acquired by civil servants, military officers and businessmen in Accra.[70]

Box 2

Landlessness in Africa

A great deal of evidence exists, especially in Asia and Latin America, documenting the increase in landlessness which results from large-scale food production schemes.[71] Africa, on the other hand, is often thought of as different, as a continent where 'there are few landless labourers, reflecting both the relative availability of land and traditional communal land tenure systems'.[72]

This sanguine view has not gone unchallenged. Although landlessness is difficult to quantify, a recent survey from Cornell University Centre for International Studies estimated that, allowing for substantial variations from country to country, 8-10 per cent of the rural labour force in Africa is now landless and that these numbers and proportions are growing rapidly. A growing proportion of the 5 per cent of Africa's rural population that are pastoralists appear to have no animals, which is the equivalent of landlessness. The result is very low per capita incomes for those involved and the need for large migratory movements, either seasonal or semi-permanent, as wage labourers.

The study found a trend across Africa towards increasing privatisation of communal lands, growing concentration of land ownership, and fragmentation of holdings, all factors further aggravating rural poverty. In some countries lands traditionally available to all tribal members are being appropriated by government officials or foreign firms, usually with the acquiescence of chiefs.[73]

It must be stressed that while large-scale food production using agribusiness and foreign aid may appear to be an attractive option, it can divert necessary resources away from the subsistence sector, where the majority of Africa's population is to be found. The big schemes have a disruptive effect on the social fabric of the rural areas affected and so may only serve to weaken the indigenous subsistence agriculture upon which the majority of the population still depend to avoid famine.

In Gabon, for example, it is planned that almost 60 per cent of the country's investment in the agricultural sector will be devoted to large-scale agro-industrial schemes, whereas a mere 4 per cent is to be allocated to increase small farmers' production. An example of the approach being adopted is the proposal to develop a capital-intensive rice growing scheme. Gabon imports 90 per cent of the rice it consumes, hence the government is very concerned to increase rice production. Not only is the scheme being financed at the expense of investment for small farmers, it is also inappropriate for the conditions to be found in Gabon. Some of these were pointed out in detailed feasibility studies carried out by Nippon Koei Ltd., the Japanese company which is conducting the trials for the planned 500 hectare venture. Low sunlight in the area limits yields, hence large amounts of fertilisers, high yielding seeds, carefully controlled irrigation and large combine harvesters will be necessary. The high humidity in Gabon favours rice blast disease and the paddy will require drying in a fuel fired rice dryer. The initial estimate is that the scheme will cost about $22,600 per hectare; given likely cost escalation the project will be very expensive and its economic viability 'uncertain'.[76]

Conclusion

The long-term decline in Africa's per capita food production, with roots traceable back to the colonial era, has now reduced the continent to dependence on food imports and advanced technology supplied in many areas by the transnational agribusiness corporations. Just as in the earlier era, when land was alienated from peasants in order to grow cash crops, so the reliance on imported food and imported methods has brought little gain for the majority of Africa's peasant producers.

The domestic political pressures from the urban centres in Africa encourage governments to seek quick and what appear to be easily implementable means of overcoming food shortages. In the 1960s this approach, together with the surplus food production in the industrial nations, combined to entrench a reliance on cheap food imports. More recently the increasing cost of these imports and the collapse of Africa's own export earnings has led many African countries to a switch in strategy to the development of large-scale food production schemes. These are frequently grandiose and ambitious in conception, yet expensive and risky in their implementation, being dependent on a high level of overseas aid and imports. Africa will require increasing quantities of foreign exchange to pay for the necessary imported inputs and to repay the loans without which the schemes could not have been established. This could well lock African countries into a further downward spiral whereby they could find themselves forced to maintain or increase their cash crop production, both to pay for these food schemes and to keep pace with the declining terms of trade for agricultural exports. Yet such an emphasis on cash crops, linked to a dependence on large-scale food production schemes, is likely to divert further resources from the subsistence sector, which must ultimately be the major source of Africa's food production.

For the transnational agribusiness corporations the current approach to food supplies in Africa has opened up large new markets, particularly in production orientated schemes financed by aid agencies, which appear likely to dominate the 1980s. If this trend continues, it will doubtless ensure agribusiness an increased role in Africa's food production, thus complementing its historic control of Africa's cash crop production.

Conclusion

In the colonial era, Africa was regarded as a vast reserve of free land, resources and labour. Foreign companies and the colonial powers established patterns of agricultural production to meet the needs of Europe. Peasant-produced crops and plantation agriculture were a source of large profits and capital was drained from Africa. These economic structures were inherited by independent African governments and, although the nature of the exploitation has altered, the essence of the relationship remains. Today the continent's dependence on agricultural exports, and the import of manufactured goods, increases the inequality between the poor nations of Africa and the industrialised world. Independence brought political autonomy, and an increasing awareness of the need to achieve a greater degree of economic independence. But the greatest impediment to change is the poverty imposed on Africa, which limits the governments' chances of development along self-defined paths and allows the governments of industrialised nations and big business to continue to exploit Africa's resources to their own advantage.

The dependence on cash crop production and export is only one aspect of Africa's poverty. Agriculture must provide food for a growing population as well as capital for development, and the level of food shortages in some parts of Africa is now alarming. There is a conflict between the need to grow cash crops for export and the need to grow food crops, and between supplying food for an urban population and ensuring that food supplies in the countryside remain abundant.

Nor is the problem one merely related to increasing agricultural output. Higher production does not in itself contribute to wider goals of establishing economic independence and reducing poverty and inequality. Most African countries have a large peasant population, which has shown itself to be unwilling to adopt the solutions proposed by national governments. Rarely is it in the peasants' interests to do so. Governments lack commitment to, and insight into the structure and economy of peasant societies. They do not pay sufficiently high prices for peasant produced crops; their prime allegiance is to their political base in the towns and the Westernised privileged elite. Peasants will not trade their independence and autonomy for the uncertainties of the market place, particularly when governments are unable to provide industrial goods which peasants want to buy. Finding peasants too difficult to deal with, governments have adopted 'advanced' agricultural schemes, by-passing rural people and further isolating them both politically and economically.

In itself this is a complex set of problems to solve, but it is compounded by other factors. This report has concentrated on one of these, i.e. the activities of agribusiness companies and the way they turn to their advantage Africa's need to generate capital and grow food.

The market for traditional cash crops remains in the hands of a small number of large conglomerates. Yet African governments cannot dismantle the world market and reconstruct it along more favourable lines. Instead they are faced with lengthy and continuous negotiations for international price support agreements and quota systems, which at least reduce some of the unpredictability in their incomes. The nature of perishable agricultural produce means that strategies require the ability to stockpile, and so call for investment to improve storage, and more importantly, to increase the amount of raw material processed before export. Since the marketing and processing are in the hands of big foreign companies such as Nestlé, General Foods, Unilever, Tate & Lyle (see Table 1.2), the freedom to manoeuvre is very limited. Most processing takes place in industrialised centres. Where crops are processed, packaged, labelled and exported from Africa this is usually controlled by the big transnationals and requires foreign inputs. In Kenya, for example, Del Monte imported everything but a few wooden pallets in order to export canned pineapples. The result is not only overdependence on foreign companies, but also a strong probability that more foreign exchange will be expended to pay for these capital-intensive developments than is received from the sale of canned pineapples.

In addition, governments must now deal with the way the companies' role in Africa has changed since the colonial era. Direct investments in plantations have declined, but today the companies provide an abundance of information, advice, persuasion and influence, becoming managers and consultants to the large developments spreading across the continent. In many cases agribusiness both influences and controls the choice of particular cash crops, which now include fresh produce such as flowers, fruits and vegetables for European markets, as well as the more traditional crops. Furthermore, as has been said, the companies dominate the markets into which these crops must be sold. Spanning the world, they control the processing, labelling, marketing and distribution stages through which African exports must pass.

Companies influence the choice of food crops too, both in the introduction of varieties which require inputs supplied by agribusiness, such as fertilizers and agrochemicals, and by encouraging crops which require processing with agribusiness technology, as did Continental Grain by setting up a baking industry in Zaire.

In the drive to expand markets, companies also promote the growth of industries capable of absorbing their own products, expanding the poultry industry to sell animal feed, as seen in this study with British American Tobacco in Kenya, the dairy industry to sell dried skimmed milk, and so on.

In short term, African governments have tried to avoid food crises by importing food for the cities and hoping that peasant communities will look after themselves. However, in the search for long term solutions and the need to increase their wealth, raise the standard of living and, above all, to meet the demands of the growing urban populations, governments have turned to agribusiness and Western solutions.

The companies have available the expertise and technology to profit from Africa's crisis. Just as they have adapted to the demands of independent African governments by relinquishing plantations, so now they are in a strong position to persuade governments to adopt industrialised agricultural systems. Most governments are looking for simple and easily implemented solutions to a politically explosive problem. Yet reliance on agribusiness to develop African agriculture today reinforces the patterns of poverty and inequality inherited from the past.

Agribusiness and Western governments argue that their investment and trading links with Africa are beneficial, and that what is good for them is good for Africa. But this is not so. The companies roots in the industrialised centres are overridingly important. As one businessman summed it up: "It is high time that the US aggressively trades in Africa. Every one billion dollars worth of new business there will create 30,000 to 40,000 jobs in the US, and if we don't get into the development of these countries now, someone else is going to do it."*

The inequality of the relationship means that African governments are in a weak position. In spite of controls to limit capital outflow, profits can be siphoned off effectively through transfer pricing, fees for management and consultancies, royalties on trade names, and the supply and servicing of machinery and equipment. While African governments try to maximise exports and minimise imports, agribusiness aims to increase Africa's dependence on imports by fostering dependence on expensive technology — as illustrated by the big sugar companies' developments. While companies want a quick return on their investments so as to maximise profits, the interests of African economies are better served by low interest loans over a long period. To fill this gap, aid money is frequently available, and so smooths the way for agribusiness to move into projects it might not otherwise touch.

* J. Bruce Llewellyn, the President of the US Overseas Private Investment Corporation, which specialises in easing the path for foreign investment. The statement was published in OPIC's Journal, Topic, in September 1979.

African countries lack the financial resources, the expertise and the technology to develop large-scale agricultural or food processing industries, storage facilities, etc., and so rely either on foreign aid, or on the large agribusiness corporations to lend them the money to build the necessary infrastructure: roads, railways, transport, ports, workers' accommodation. And agribusiness corporations like Tate & Lyle, Unilever and the one hundred-plus companies which formed the United Nations linked Industrial Council for Development, have organised themselves to utilise the benefits of aid and take advantage of Africa's desire to increase its agricultural production.

Large-scale food production schemes, modelled on the production methods of industrialised countries, are a popular means of 'solving' the food crisis, and increasing export-oriented agricultural output. There appears to be an assumption that these large schemes, often backed by aid agencies, will spring Africa from its poverty trap. While it may be unrealistic in the near future to view Africa as a setting for thousands of groups of small self-sufficient producers organised to provide for local needs and an export market, it is doubtful whether these hugely expensive and technologically sophisticated schemes which are springing up across Africa will alter the balance of power and alleviate poverty.

Large schemes displace and pauperise peasant communities, require enormous amounts of foreign exchange, and usually fail to meet production targets. The history of sugar developments in the Sudan, and recent food production schemes in the Sahel each emphasise this point. Many schemes have been totally inappropriate, such as the sugar-for-fuel projects in Kenya — where one factory was abandoned in the end because it used more fuel than it could produce. The main achievement of many such developments has been to provide, at cheap prices, a continuous supply of the raw materials consumed in industrialised countries.

The report's examination of the schemes developed by agribusiness reveals an excessive and unnecessary dependence on foreign sources of supplies, technology, management and expertise. For example, in the food processing industry, some stages of processing for export may benefit by the use of internationally accepted trade names — Heinz, Nestle, etc — but more and more food is being processed for the local market in Africa. Yet the major beneficiary when products processed for local consumption carry internationally recognised labels is the companies. Simpler technology is available, which could process food at a lower cost, and to good and reliable standards. Not only would this lower import costs, it would also encourage local skills repairing machinery and innovations using readily available materials. Self-sufficient industries, or those with low import requirements, have more chance to flourish and may build on local skill and enterprise. In both

Kenya and Tanzania, existing industries were threatened and even extinguished by competition from more capital-intensive schemes: in Kenya the Kenchic chain (British American Tobacco) has been allowed to develop a chicken industry, Unilever a soap and cooking oil industry, and Nestlés a canned and baby food industry. Tanzania encouraged expensive milling industries against the interests of indigenous bakers.

Governments could avoid many of the more wasteful agricultural schemes and the developments of unnecessarily capital-intensive industries which compete with goods already produced locally, by being more active and forceful in their demands and more rigorous in defining their objectives. This implies acquiring a wider knowledge of needs, and more careful assessment of requirements. However difficult this may be, and whatever the shortcomings and gaps, Africans are better able to define their own needs than the multinational aid agencies and transnational corporations. This must be recognised by governments, which too frequently use foreign companies and expertise, without sufficiently clear demands. Too often, African governments have been forced to react in the light of errors, and while the companies have protected themselves under contracts, the governments have had to meet the costs.

There is no straightforward solution to Africa's agricultural poverty. The problems the Tanzania government faced when it tried to de-emphasise cash crops in favour of food crops illustrates the impossibility of quick solutions, and the need for both short-term and long-term strategies. In the short term there seems little alternative to gradually strengthening local production of crops, without ignoring peasant producers, and therefore paying a fair price. At the same time, governments must decrease non-productive imports of technology, reduce food imports, and diversify from their dependence on one or two agricultural exports. The actions of many African governments lead to the conclusion that short-term political objectives frequently over-ride long-term development possibilities, hence the uncritical reliance on foreign corporations and aid agencies, and the faith in capital-intensive agriculture. African governments and civil servants must build up their own knowledge and expertise to assess development, not only on economic grounds, but also on social and political grounds.

Governments have sought and relied on agribusiness to generate capital for development for too long. The evidence suggests that this has only increased economic dependence on industrialised centres. The reluctance to trust peasant-based agriculture suggests that some form of political struggle is essential before any real changes are achieved. Governments have yet to seek radical solutions structured on peasant organisation in an attempt to seek longer term solutions to Africa's agricultural stalemate.

Company Profiles

Unilever Ltd.

Unilever is a massive company. It is an Anglo-Dutch group, with Unilever NV-based in Holland, and Unilever Ltd in the UK. It is the largest food business in the world, and one of the largest companies in the world.[1] Its activities range from plantations growing essential supplies of palm oil, cocoa, coffee or tea, right through to high street retailers in the West. Within this chain the companies trading in the agricultural commodities; shipping lines; warehouses for storage; factories processing primary products into small, houshold-sized packages of branded margarine, cooking oils, detergent, washing powder, etc; marketing organisations to distribute the goods (sometimes back to the countries growing the original commodities); and supermarkets, to complete the sales process.

Unilever has a subsidiary company to handle every imaginable level of production, distribution and marketing — from growing timber to designing and selling wallpaper. And a company to deal with almost every by-product of this process, such as its profitable subsidiary dealing in animal feeds, made from the residues of palm products, groundnuts and soya beans, which are left after the oil extracting process. (Experiments to produce textured vegetable protein for human consumption have been less satisfactory).[2] Its interest in retail outlets has led it not only into supermarkets, but also into selling 'Esquire' clothes for the sophisticated customer in Nigeria and Ghana, through its subsidiary GB Ollivant.[3]

The company's interests embrace almost all aspects of food: margarine, dairy products, ice-cream, frozen food, meat products, fish, retailing and restaurants; not to mention detergents, soaps and toilet preparations, chemicals, paper, plastics, packaging, animal feeds, plantations, etc. It owns transport companies, advertising agencies, import and export companies, and research and development organisations. In 1981 Unilever employed nearly 343,000 people.[4] Of these, 154,000 work in European Community countries, and 193,000 work in Africa. In 1978 Unilever employed 109,000 — it is clearly a policy to increase labour productivity in Africa as well as in Europe.[5] But this is only the tip of the iceberg. Many people depend either directly or indirectly on Unilever for their livelihood and in some African countries the majority of the worforce is dependent on the firm.[6]

Perhaps surprisingly, the vertically integrated Unilever companies do not trade directly with each other. For example, oils from the plantations do not, and never have, been shipped directly to the European factories manufacturing margarine, soap, etc. They are traded on the world market — 80 per cent controlled by Unilever.[7] The trading and broking companies buy and sell to related Unilever subsidiaries in the same way that they sell to all other companies. Exports are over one-tenth of total turnover, and approximately half of these are intra-company, mainly within the EEC. However, about a third involve exports to or from developing countries.[8]

Unilever's African connections have a long history, dating from the first oil plantation in 1911, in the Congo. In 1929 two giant companies, one of which had been operating in Africa for over 250 years, and both of which had become subsidiaries of Unilever, merged to form the United Africa Company. One of the subsidiaries was the Niger Company, which had originally been a charter company, granted rights by the British government to rule an area stretching almost 1,000 miles inland.[9]

The United Africa Company is now UAC International, which is a wholly-owned subsidiary of Unilever, and holds the majority of African investments. As a wholly-owned subsidiary, it is under no obligation to declare its investments in or profits from Africa, which makes it impossible to keep abreast of the full extent of Unilever's African activities. The company publishes a small booklet with a bare outline of UAC activities, and these cover breweries, in partnership with Heinekin and Guinness; technical sales of engineering products, medical supplies, motors, Caterpillar dealerships, merchandise marketing, office equipment, insurance, builders' merchants, textiles, shipping and warehousing. Its timber interests include a large holding in African Timber & Plywood Ltd in Nigeria, one of the world's largest tropical timber extraction and processing concerns, with annual log production exceeding 250,000 tons.[10]

UAC's Food Division in Nigeria manufactures and distributes fresh and frozen meat, English pies and sausage rolls, all baked daily (just the thing for a family returning from a hard days work in the field!). The company brochure, however, gives no details of its palm oil activities, but lists among its activities 'the production of palm oil'.

Plantations

Both the Unilever parent companies own plantations in Africa. Unilever NV is the parent company of the Zaire plantations, and Unilever Ltd is the parent of others. The plantations are accountable to the 'Plantations Group', a committee responsible to the Special Committee of the identical Unilever Boards of the Dutch and UK parents. Before 1955 the plantations were not organised under any particular Unilever department. However, in the mid-1950s, when the company reorganised and divided its administration by function rather than area, the plantation companies were brought under a single central executive to concentrate all the know-how on plantations. This was originally the Plantation Executive, which then became the Plantation Group in 1957, and dealt directly with the Special Committee (the controlling committee which advises the Dutch and UK Boards of the Company) in monthly meetings.[11] In Africa, Unilever's remaining plantations are in Zaire, Nigeria, Cameroon and Gabon.

Mr Lever, one of the dominant figures in the company's history, became anxious to start plantations at the turn of this century, in order to secure supplies of good quality palm oil for his Port Sunlight soap factories. In 1911 he signed a contract with the 'government of the Congo' (i.e. the Belgian colonial authority) to develop plantations there. He established the Societe Anonyme des Huileries du Congo Belge (HCB), which was given the right to choose 74,000 hectares of palm-bearing land, in addition to which, if they treated a minimum of 15,000 tons of fruit after ten years, the company could expand up to 200,000 hectares.[12]

In acquiring these tracts, Lever was alienating land from a population which had been decimated by years of brutal coercion and exploitation. An official survey of the Congo in 1911 revealed a population of 8½ million people — 60 years earlier it had been estimated at 40 million. The company must have been aware of this devastation when they acquired their land rights.[13]

Plantations were a labour-intensive business, and thousands of workers were imported, thus increasing the breakdown of traditional societies, making people totally dependent on the company for food and shelter, and 'turning exploited, but self-sufficient farmers, into dependent labourers'.[14] This frequently involved the destruction of family life, drawing men to work on the plantations, and leaving behind women, now totally responsible for growing the crops, caring for the elderly and bringing up children. Low wages were justified on the basis that subsistence farming supplemented the workers' income, and this still continues today.[15]

At the same time as the expansion into Zaire took place, Lever was trying to open plantations in Nigeria, but the British colonial government there resisted alienation of tribal lands to Europeans, and only changed its policy after the slump in the early 1930s. At that point they invited the United Africa Company to 'show the Nigerians the way to do it'.[16] (The company is still there; one wonders how long it will take them to 'show' Nigerians?) By now the company already owned estates in Cameroon, and Ghana was shortly to be developed. Palm oil was always, and remains, a major preoccupation, but Unilever also has interests in rubber, cocoa, coffee and tea plantations.

Control

". . . as a general rule Overseas Companies should be asked to pay service fees to London for specialist services, particularly in view of the probable extension of local participation."[17]

With the coming of independence to African colonies, Unilever quickly adapted and explored ways of ensuring that profitability was maintained, particularly if the company should lose the majority shareholding in one of its subsidiaries. Service fees, charged for such intangible elements as administrative or technical know-how, have been used for this purpose.

The company has a policy of training nationals of the country in which it operates for management positions. However, at the same time Unilever maintains a policy of retaining expatriate managers in each country, which it justified by saying, "We firmly believe that a degree of internationalisation of management provides opportunities for transferring skills and exchanging experience to the benefit of the countries concerned, the indigenous managers, and our own companies".[18]

Unilever has a strong central management and is organised by product area, a system which has replaced the previous geographical divisions. There are nine co-ordination groups, one for each of: animal feeds, chemicals, detergents, edible fats and dairy, food and drinks, meat products, packaging, printing and plastics, toilet preparations. Each of these reports to the Special Committee, which 'controls overall policy, makes investment decisions, and to whom all the lesser grades of authority are ultimately responsible'.[19] The other divisions which particularly affect Africa are the Overseas Committee, the United Africa Plantations Group.

Almost all of Unilever Ltd shareholders have addresses in the United Kingdom, and a majority of Unilever NV shareholders are in the Netherlands (55 per cent), Switzerland (21 per cent), Germany (7 per cent), United Kingdom (4 per cent), United States (4 per cent), France (4 per cent), Belgium (3 per cent) and 'other countries' (2 per cent). The only control exercised by any African country is over those Unilever 'associate' companies in which they take a majority shareholding. However, even in such cases they are dependent on Unilever's management and technical expertise, and in the case of those associates dealing in commodities, Unilever is far more in command of the relevant commodity market than any African country. Indeed, the yearly gross national product of most African countries is insignificant compared to Unilever's annual turnover. Sales to third parties (i.e. excluding intra-company trade) amounted to a massive £9,842 million in 1978, roughly equivalent to the combined GNP of Angola, Benin, Botswana, Burundi, Central African Empire, Chad, Congo, Gabon, Gambia, Guinea, Guinea-Bassau, Lesotho, Malawi, Mali, Mauritania, Mauritius, Mozambique, Niger, Rwanda, Senegal, Sierra Leone, Somalia, Swaziland, Togo and Upper Volta.

Obviously local subsidaries can make certain decisions about the day-to-day affairs of the company, but as the company itself points out, the major decisions are reserved by the Centre, particularly 'the strategic direction of the business, agreement to forward plans, top appointments, and major investments'.[20]

Unilever Profits 1974-1981

(Combined Accounts of Unilever Ltd and Unilever NV)

	£ million							
	1974	1975	1976	1977	1978	1979	1980	1981
Pre-tax profit	333	328	611	550	609	606	572	709
Profit from Africa	57	91	148	59*	55	57	67	79
Profit from UAC International	39	79	141	65	68	50	43	55
Profit from Plantations, transport and other	25	15**	25	48	34	42	39	26
Profit from margarine, fats, oils and dairy products	81	55	120	109	150	127	139	178
Profit from other foods	57	77	124	111	144	169	138	155
Profit from animal feeds	6	6	14	14	16	16	11	13
Sales to Africa	626	797	1133	834	716	736	761	890
(% total sales)	11%	12%	13%	9%	7%	7%	7%	8%

Employees: 385,000 of which 109,000 were in Africa in 1978.
343,000 of which 93,000 were in Africa in 1981.

*No longer includes Nigerian profit, as this became an associate company.
**Excludes Zaire — prices well down.

Source: Annual reports, Unilever Ltd.

168

Directors: (1981): Sir David Orr (Chairman), H.F. van den Hoven (Vice-Chairman), K. Durham (Vice-Chairman), M.R. Angus, R.W. Archer, W.B. Blaisse, P.V.M. Egan, J.P. Erbe, J.M. Goudswaard, A.H.C. Hill, J. Louden, F.A. Maljers, F.W.L. Mann, H. Meij, Jonkheer IEB, Quarles van Ufford, C.F. Sedcole, A.W.P. Stenham, G.K.G. Stevens, T. Thomas, K.H. Veldhuis, E.J. Verloop.

Advisory Directors (1981): B.W. Biesheuvel, T. Browaldh, Fletcher L. Pyrom, Sir Eric Faulkner, The Rt. Hon Lord Hunt of Tanworth, The Viscount Leverhulme, P.P. Schweitzer, D. Spethmann, E.P. Wellenstein.

Unilever Subsidiaries in Africa
(Italics indicate the company is a subsidiary of UAC International Ltd)

Benin: *Sogerco-Benin S.A, John Walkden et Cie SA.*
Burundi: *Hatton and Cookson Burundi SARL.*
Cameroon: Plantations Pamol du Cameroun Ltd, *R&W King SA, Sogerco Cameroun SA.*
Central African Republic: *SCKN Fonciere de Centrafrique SA.*
Chad: *Brasseries du Logone SA, Nouvelle Societe Commerciale du Kouilou-Njari SA.*
Congo: *Commerciale du Kouilou Niari-Congo SA Ste (SCKN Congo).*
Gabon: *Hatton et Cookson SA.*
Ghana: Benso Oil Palm Plantation Ltd, *Accra Ice Co Ltd, Avenue Motors Ltd, Central Finance Co Ltd, Central Property Co (Ghana) Ltd, GBO Ghana Investments Ltd, Ghana Consolidated Machinery & Trading Co Ltd, Ghana Pan Electric Ltd, Ghana Plant Hire Ltd, Kingsway Chemists of Ghana Ltd, Kingsway Stores of Ghana Ltd, Millers Swanzy (Ghana) Ltd, G.B. Ollivant (Ghana) Ltd, A.J. Seward (Ghana) Ltd, Swiss African Trading Co Ltd, UAC of Ghana Ltd, United Africa Trust Ltd.*
Guinea: *Niger Guinee SA.*
Ivory Coast: *CFCISA, Frageci Sa, SAFRACISA, A.J. Seward Côte d'Ivoire SA.*
Kenya: East African Industries Ltd, Research Bureau (East Africa) Ltd, *Gailey & Roberts Ltd.*
Malawi: Lever Brothers (Malawi) Ltd, Lipton tea (Malawi) Ltd.
Niger: *Foncière du Niger SA, Niger Afrique SA.*
Nigeria: H&S Nigeria Ltd, Hazlehurst & Sons (West Africa) Ltd, Lever Nigeria Plantations Ltd, Linover Nigeria Ltd, Nigerian Electrical Contracting Co Ltd, Norplant Ltd, Pamol (Nigeria) Ltd, Pye (Nigeria) Ltd, *The African Marketing Co Nigeria Ltd, Manufacturers Delivery Services (Nigeria) Ltd, Millers Swanzy (Nigeria) Ltd, Minna Farm Ltd, NAG Ltd, Nigeradio Ltd, Raleigh Industries (Nigeria) (Sales) Ltd, Wall's Nigeria Ltd.*

Rwanda: *Hatton and Cookson Rwanda SARL.*
Senegal: *Nouvelle Societe Commerciale Senegalaise SA (NOSOCO-SENEGAL).*
Sierra Leone: *UAC of Sierra Leone Ltd, Union African Pension Trust Ltd.*
South Africa: Lintas (Pty) Ltd, Media Initiatives Ltd, Melrose Foods (Pty) Ltd, Nairnprop (Pty) Ltd, Port Warehousing (Pty) Ltd, Segnep Investments (Pty) Ltd, Silchem Properties (Pty) Ltd, Silicate & Chemical Industries Natal (Pty) Ltd, Silicate & Chemical Industries Transvaal (Pty) Ltd, Silicate Properties (Pty) Ltd, Unilever South Africa (Pty) Ltd, Aliwal Investments (Pty) Ltd, Van den Berghs & Juergens (Pty) Ltd, Birds Eye Foods (Pty) Ltd, Commercial Chemicals (Pty) Ltd, Duna Foods (Pty) Ltd, Elida-Gibbs (Pty) Ltd, Glenton & Mitchell (Pty) Ltd, Hudson & Knight (Pty) Ltd, Lever Brothers (Pty) Ltd, Lipton (SA) (Pty) Ltd, Octip Properties (Pty) Ltd, Nairn Industries (Pty) Ltd, Natal Oil & Soap Industries (Pty) Ltd, Natal Warehousing Services (Pty) Ltd, E.W. Pearce (Pty) Ltd, A. & F. Pears (Pty) Ltd, The Perfume Design Co (Pty) Ltd, Pitco (Pty) Ltd, Mazawattee Ltd, Pitco Properties (Pty) Ltd, Quality Products (Pty) Ltd, Quelea investments (Pty) Ltd, Research International (Pty) Ltd, Rondi's (Natal) (Pty) Ltd, SA Warehousing Services (Pty) Ltd, Silicate and Chemical Industries (Pty) Ltd, Sodium Chemicals (Pty) Ltd, The Surprise Soap Co (Pty) Ltd, Union Pension Trust (Pty) Ltd, Vinyl Products (Pty) Ltd, T. Wall & Sons (Pty) Ltd.
Tanzania: Dinna Foods Ltd, EAI. (Tanganyika) Ltd, *Gailey & Roberts (Tanzania) Ltd, UAC of Tanzania Ltd, Uniafric Trust (Tanzania) Ltd.*
Togo: *UAC Togo SA.*
Uganda: *Gailey and Roberts (Uganda) Ltd, Uniafric Trust (Uganda) Ltd, The United Africa Co of Uganda Ltd,* Uganda Associated Industries Ltd.
Zaire: *Africaine pour la Promotion des Ventes (SAPRO) SARL, Ste, Lipton Zaire SARL, G.B. Ollivant SARL, Cie, Ollivant Motors and Technical SARL, Sedec SARL, United Agencies SARL.*
Zambia: *K.B. Davies & Co (Zambia) Ltd, ESM Ltd, The United Africa Co Zambia Ltd.*
Zimbabwe: Van den Berghs and Jurgens (Pvt) Ltd, Birds Eye Foods (Pvt) Ltd, Hudson and Knight (Pvt) Ltd, Indprop Investments (Pvt) Ltd, Industrial Processing Co (Pvt) Ltd, Lever Brothers (Pvt) Ltd, Planters & Importers (Rhodesia) (Pvt) Ltd, Unilever Services and Developments (Pvt) Ltd.

Tate and Lyle

Henry Tate started work as an apprentice grocer in Liverpool in 1832, at the age of 13. By 1855 he owned six successful grocery shops, but he sold them in 1861 and the next year opened a small sugar refinery in Love Lane, Liverpool. This was a great age for sugar, with many of the older refining families having already been in the business since the 18th century. Tate's supplies of sugar were drawn from Peru, Mauritius and the East and West Indies, but in these early years there were no overseas investments. Meanwhile, Greenock in the West of Scotland had become a centre of the sugar industry because of its port facilities, and in 1865 Abram Lyle and John Kerr started the Glebe Sugar Refinery. Unlike Henry Tate, Lyle had expanded into the shipping and handling of raw sugar. When John Kerr died seven years after their joint venture began, they already owned eight ships, four of which remained with Lyle's company and eight years later another six had been added.[1]

In 1876 Tate bought and converted a derelict shipyard on the Thames at Silvertown, and five years later Abram Lyle and his sons bought two adjacent sites on the north bank of the Thames at Plaistow. In fact, the move to London marked a separation in the Lyle family. Abram preferred to stay in shipping and remain in Scotland. His sons, of whom there were many, took the name and their interests in sugar refining to London. The move to London was costly for both families, but they survived the crisis and their respective businesses prospered. They tried not to compete directly with each other: Tate produced mainly cube sugar, and Lyle produced as few types of sugar as possible, depending on one specialty, 'Lyle's Golden Syrup', for the main source of earnings.

In spite of the tacit co-operation over product areas, the two families were not friendly (Henry Tate and Abram Lyle never met). Nevertheless, in 1921, they decided to amalgamate so as to strengthen their control of the home market against European competition.

The merger does not appear to have been easy for either family to make, though the Tates were more interested and initiated the move. To this day the Tates and Lyles very much remain evident in the firm, even though it has been a public company from the time of the merger. Only in 1977 did the first non-Tate or Lyle chairman, Lord Jellicoe, join the company. And there is still a significant number of 'family' members (four out of fifteen) on the Board.

By the 1920s Tate & Lyle had no significant overseas investments (the first major acquisitions being in the West Indies in 1936), but it had already begun both to diversify and to integrate vertically, acquiring companies linked to its business as sugar refiners, such as lighterage and transport concerns. However, shipping also remained important. In the 1920s the Company began growing sugar beet in England, and it was only after these interests were taken over by the government, through the British Sugar Corporation, that they invested in the Caribbean.[2] African acquisitions came later still.

The first — and major — African acquisitions were in Zambia and Zimbabwe in 1953 (at that time both countries were part of the Federation of North and South Rhodesia). Tate and Lyle acquired a 50 per cent interest in Rhodesian Sugar Refineries Ltd (RSR) and put capital towards the development of sugar estates at Chirundu on the southern bank of the Zambezi River. RSR already owned two refineries, and Tate & Lyle put up capital for the construction of a third at Ndola, Zambia. Old Tate & Lyle hands took over the running of the estates and others (whites) were hired in from Natal (South Africa) and Mauritius, to help manage it.

There was at that time no question of taking on African senior staff, only African labourers. Since sugar cane was a new venture, the company at first found it difficult to train African labour to reach the same degree of productivity as in the West Indies. By 1960, the estate and factories began to come into their own, with a production of 15,000 tons a year in 1962, and 30,000 by 1965.[3] Rhodesian production was also expanding rapidly, with a growing output from RSR's estates and also from two other estates owned by South African companies, Sir J.L. Hulett Ltd and Anglo American Ltd. Southern Rhodesia was on the way to producing enough sugar to meet not only its own needs and those of Northern Rhodesia (Zambia) and Nyasaland (Malawi), but to have a surplus for export.

The Ndola Sugar Refinery was in operation by 1960, and was capable of refining 20,000 tons a year, while Zambian consumption had by then reached 12,500 tons a year and was rising at 16 per cent per annum. However, within five years the position changed suddenly.

After Rhodesia declared UDI in 1965, Peter Runge, a director of Tate & Lyle and at that time President of the Confederation of British Industry, led a team of businessmen to discuss the situation with Southern Rhodesian authorities. Despite these talks, Tate & Lyle found it impossible to maintain the old integrated pattern of operations with the Chirundu estates supplying raw cane and the refinery at Ndola. They decided to split Rhodesia Sugar Refineries and to operate separately in the two countries. Their major commitment was to Zambia, but they supplied sufficient capital for Rhodesia to erect a new factory, and did not dispose of their Rhodesian estates or factories. The Ndola Sugar Company Ltd opened in June 1965, with the Zambian government's Industrial Development Corporation (Indeco) taking an 11 per cent holding. 6,000 acres of cane were planned for Nakambala, and training for small to medium sized farmers was begun.

In 1966 the Chirundu Estate was closed, and the factory moved across the border to Nakambala. Chirundo had employed 3,500 Africans, and the closing of the estate and factory forced many jobless to return to Tanzania, Angola, Mozambique, Zambia and Malawi, indicating the wide recruitment area. The Ndola Refinery and Nakambala estate eventually became the Zambia Sugar Company Ltd, with the Zambian government taking a majority interest. However, Tate & Lyle retained a 23.58 per cent investment, seats on the Board, and (more significantly) a management contract and responsibility for training.[4]

Tate & Lyle's other major African investments are in Nigeria. They formed Tate & Lyle (Nigeria) Ltd, and took equity shares in a cane-sugar producing company at Bacita — although this is managed by Booker McConnell. Tate & Lyle provided technical help, and also installed a cube-making plant for refining the sugar from Bacita and making cubes for local consumption. Other West African countries — Ghana, Sierra Leone and the Gambia — were important markets for their UK-refined sugar.

In South Africa, Tate & Lyle bought the Illovo Sugar Company in 1969 — the company owned both estates in Natal and refineries. This was not an entirely new connection with South Africa, since one of the Lyles (Leonard, and later, Charles) had been on the Board of Huletts, the SA sugar company, and Hulett's had used TLTS. The Illovo venture was not a complete success and Tate & Lyle were very defensive about their treatment of black employees in South Africa, after the 1972-3 Guardian investigations into British companies paying below the Poverty Datum Line. They pointed out that they were cleared by the House of Commons Sub-committee as being 'good employers',[5] but sold their SA sugar interests in 1977. (According to some reports, the company tried to censor a film about conditions on their estate).[6]

From the late 1960s and early 1970s, sugar refining began to play a smaller part in the overall profits of Tate & Lyle, and the company adjusted to changes in the world economy. Tate & Lyle, and the company adjusted to changes in the world economy. Tate & Lyle Technical Services Ltd (TLTS)* had already been established (now Tate & Lyle Agribusiness), and as African countries became independent, TLTS took on a new role as consultants and advisers to governments; firstly on sugar development projects, and more recently by offering expertise on a wider range of agricultural projects, including the growing of soyabeans, maize, rice, vegetables, cotton, and even fish-farming.

Tate & Lyle were helped in this new orientation by an invitation in the late 1960s to help set up the Industry Co-operative Programme (ICP), originally a group of 16 companies (but later over 100) attached to the UN Food and Agricultural Programme (FAO), with the purpose of

*See Chapter 3, for Selected TLTS African projects.

advising on agricultural developments in under-developed countries. The ICP has been much criticised and was ultimately expelled from the FAO, although they have always protested that any advice and investigations which they provided were completely impartial (see chapter 1). Tate & Lyle were not so sure, however, and a director of T&L suggested that the programme could be effective precisely because "the representatives of the Companies themselves were Chairmen or Chief Executives who could actually commit their Companies"[7]

TLTS has advised on a wide range of sugar and other agricultural developments in Swaziland, Kenya, Sierra Leone, Ghana, Sudan, Guinea-Bissau, Tanzania, Cameroon, Nigeria, Zambia and the Ivory Coast. In Kenya and Tanzania, for example, the company (with Booker Agriculture International Ltd, in the case of Tanzania) appraised the entire sugar industry and recommended expansion and rehabilitation programmes. Here Tate & Lyle made use of its connections with the United Nations, as both these projects were financed by the World Bank. A sugar appraisal mission to Guinea-Bissau in 1977 was financed by the FAO. Many of Tate & Lyle's feasibility studies are treated merely as advice, and do not involve the company further, although Tate & Lyle can also supply and equip sugar factories and supply irrigation engineering (through Tate & Lyle Engineering Ltd) which puts them in a strong position to receive contracts to supply both equipment and services.

In some cases, following a feasibility study, TLTS continues to act as consultants or managers, as with the Simunya estate and sugar factory in Swaziland, where they have an on-going management contract for the Royal Swaziland Sugar Corporation Ltd, and provide senior staff and management training. In 1978 Tate & Lyle confirmed this policy as one of the four major future concentrations of the company, i.e. to:

". . . continue the development of an integrated agricultural engineering projects and service business with the developing world as our prime market, using the technical operational and financial skills which were developed over the years in sugar, and which can also be applied to other crops."[8]

One other relatively new venture for the company has been its expansion into commodity and futures trading. This originally arose out of its interests in the activities of its Raw Sugar Purchasing Department. 'As the refining business grew, so did the opportunities for profitable trading. the chief feature distinguishing Tate & Lyle's dealings in the world sugar market from its businesses in molasses and most other commodities is the use of futures markets'[9] This is because the futures markets provided a kind of insurance against price fluctuations, which in practice means that the level of profit is determined more by the amount of movement in the market than by the absolute level of a commodity price.

In the mid-1970s Tate & Lyle decided to expand its trading activities into other soft commodities, with one firm criterion for choosing an appropriate commodity being the existence of a viable futures market. So in 1976 Tate & Lyle began trading in coffee (and has subsequently taken an interest in a coffee farm in Brazil, as well as 30 per cent of a US company. International Coffee Corporation), and is now beginning to handle cocoa and grains.

The group does trade in commodities with no futures market — in particular molasses, where its subsidiary, United Molasses Ltd, handles around 40 per cent of the world's traded molasses.[10] However, it has declared its intention to concentrate on commodities with a futures market.[11] The company has traded in tea on a small scale, but this may not continue since there is not at present a futures market for the commodity.

Tate & Lyle has managed to remain a family company: the families are minority shareholders, but nevertheless very much in evidence on the Board. There are two committees, the Executive Committee (EXCO) and the Policy Committee (also liberally sprinkled with Tates and Lyles — Saxon Tate is the chairman of EXCO, and the Policy Committee of seven has one member from each family), which are responsible for advising the Board. The majority of directors work for the company in a management capacity. The directors have always exercised tight control over overseas operations, and pay frequent visits to their subsidiaries.[12]

In 1979 they carried out a major reorganisation and simplification of their companies and there are now five principal subsidaries: Tate & Lyle Food & Distribution; Tate & Lyle Agribusiness; Tate & Lyle Trading & Developments; Tate and Lyle Holdings; Tate & Lyle Inc (USA).

Tate & Lyle Profits 1978-1981

£ million

	1978	1979	1980	1981
Turnover	1146.8	1190.4	1420.0	2188.0
Profits				
Trading Profit	36.4	30.1	42.0	44.1
African	5.9 (11%)	n.a.	n.a.	n.a.
Agribusiness	4.5 (10%)	2.3 (6%)	7.6 (16%)	0.2 (1%)
Commodity trading (mainly sugar)	24.3 (56%)	18.0 (52%)	16.8 (34%)	9.6 (18%)
Sugar Refining	1.1 (2%)	6.9 (19%)	5.6 (12%)	9.4 (17%)

Source: Annual Reports

The profits are not shown specifically by region, but by the country where they were declared. This measure shows that 11 per cent of total profit came from Africa in 1978.

Tate & Lyle Ltd: African Subsidaries

South Africa: Subsidaries of Tate & Lyle Holdings Ltd, UK).
African Products Ltd — two subsidiaries, Glucose & Starch Products Ltd and Maize Products Ltd. (Sold controlling interest 1979). Pure Cane Molasses Co (Durban) (Pty) Ltd, a subsidairy of United Molasses Co. Ltd.
Zimbabwe (Subsidaries of Tate & Lyle Holdings Ltd, UK).
Rhodesia Sugar Refineries Ltd, and three subsidiaries, Davies Marketing (Pte) Ltd; T.J. Heyes (Pvt) Ltd; Rhodesia Sugar Distributors (Pte) Ltd.
Nigeria (Subsidiaries of Tate & Lyle Holdings Ltd., UK).
Tate & Lyle (Nigeria) Ltd. (36.69 per cent).
Zambia (Subsidaries of Tate & Lyle Holdings Ltd, UK).
Zambia Sugar Company Ltd (A). (23.58 per cent).
Kenya (Subsidaries of Tate & Lyle Trading & Developments Ltd).
East African Storage Co Ltd (A), (50 per cent), Fraternitas Ltd (A).
Mozambique (Subsidaries of Tate & Lyle Trading & Developments Ltd).
Exportadora de Melacos Ltda Cia.
Mauritius (Subsidaries of Tate & Lyle Trading & Developments Ltd).
Mauritius Molasses Co Ltd.
Tanzania (Subsidaries of Tate & Lyle Trading & Developments Ltd).
Tanzania Liquids Storage Co. Ltd. (A).
Swaziland (8.73 per cent investment in Royal Swaziland Sugar Corp Ltd).
Branded Products: Tate & Lyle sugars; Lyle's Golden Syrup.

Directors: J.O. Lyle (President); The Rt Hon Earl Jellicoe (Chairman); J. Forbes (Vice-Chairman); H.S. Tate (Vice-Chairman); N.M. Shaw (Group Managing Director); *Sir Alex Alexander; M.J.L. Attfield; *Sir Richard Cave; J. Forbes; *R. Haslam; C. Lyle; D.A. Tate; F. Thomlinson.
(*Non-executive directors).

Interlocking Directorships: Sir Alex Alexander is also a director of Imperial Group Ltd, and R. Haslam is also a director of ICI.

The group also operates in: Canada, USA, Guyana, Trinidad, West Germany, Italy, Netherlands, Denmark, France, Belgium, Bermuda, Hong Kong, Belize, Norway, Portugal, Guernsey.

Major Subsidiaries: Redpaths Industries Ltd (Canada); Manbre & Garton Ltd; Hugh Laird & Sons Ltd; Belize Sugar Industries; Talres Development Ltd; Richards (Shipbuilders) Ltd; Tate & Lyle Transport Ltd; United Molasses Ltd; Tate & Lyle Shipping Ltd; Refined Syrups & Sugars Ltd; Tate & Lyle Refineries Ltd; Tate & LYle International Ltd; Unitank Storage Co Ltd; Tate & Lyle Engineering Ltd.

Booker McConnell

Booker McConnell Ltd is a small company compared to giants such as Unilever, but nevertheless its total turnover in 1981 amounted to £932.8 million, and profits were £17 million. Booker is representative of those agribusiness companies building up a large part of their business both by expanding consultancies, management companies and technical services, and also being in a position to provide engineering equipment to back up its areas of expertise. Booker management and technical services contracts in Africa are listed in chapter 3. Booker's principal interests are at present in sugar, shopkeeping, alcohol production, engineering, drugs and travel. the company also owns ships, has international trading subsidiaries, owns the copyrights of well-known authors (including Agatha Christie and Ian Fleming) and operates fish farms in Scotland.

Booker's major agricultural expertise is in sugar. Until recently this was concentrated in Guyana, but is becoming more and more important in Africa, and has begun expanding in Francophone Africa in particular. For example the company is managing Sucrières de Nossi-Bêt et de la Côte Est, in Madagascar, and providing technical services for Compagnie Sucrière Senegalaise (Senegal)[1] Apart from providing a large range of consultancies (see chapter 3), Booker manages or provides advice to sugar estates in Kenya, Nigeria, Senegal and Somalia. It has a small shareholding in the Mumias Sugar Company (4 per cent) and a slightly larger one in the Nigerian Sugar Company (16 per cent). Money from sugar is earned in two ways, firstly from the management and consultancy services, carried out by Booker Agriculture International, a UK subsidiary; and secondly from the engineering company, Fletcher & Stewart, one of Booker's main subsidiaries which designs and supplies complete sugar factories and manufactures sugar machinery and hydraulic presses. Among the company's other engineering subsidiaries is Sigmund Pulsometer Pumps, which designs and supplies 'fluid-handling' systems for irrigation (as well as sewage and fire protection).

Booker's profits from Africa are not high, only £92,000 before tax in 1981. However, this is only profit earned from trade investments and subsidiary companies. It does not include income from sales of sugar machinery (the engineering division is the major profit earner) and consultancy and management fees due to Booker Agriculture Services. Agricultural activities earned £2 million profit for the group in 1981.

1978 was a record year for Fletcher & Stewart (£9.2 million profit), with the main profit contributions coming from contracts for the Mumias factory extension in Kenya and the Juba Project in Somalia. Again, major contributions to Booker Agriculture International (BAI) came from Africa: the Mumias Sugar Company and Chemelil Sugar Company in Kenya (management fees).

BAI is being increasingly used to advise aid-giving organisations; the World Bank has relied on a consortium of BAI and Tate & Lyle Technical Services Ltd in Tanzania and the two companies have also worked for the UK Ministry of Overseas Development, and the EEC.

Booker McConnell has been criticised for conditions on its Malawi tea estates.[2] Without doubt conditions are bad on all estates in the country, and strikes and trade union activity are forbidden by law. The Malawi TUC is an arm of the government, and Liabuya, the head, who is also Mayor of Blantyre, is personnel manager at Booker's (Malawi).

Vertical Integration in Sugar

Apart from investing in sugar production, providing management, consultancy and technical services, and supplying complete sugar factories, Booker's subsidiaries are active in international marketing, export buying and shipping, commodity marketing (Booker Merchants International), sugar marketing and agency services (Bookers Sugar Company), supermarkets and self-service shops (Budgen, Allinsons health foods).

Booker McConnell Profits 1978-81

	£million			
	1978	1979	1980	1981
Turnover	587.7	669.9	833.9	832.8
Profit (before taxation)	24.5	25.0	15.2	17.3

African Subsidaries

Kenya: Mumias Sugar Co (4 per cent), Kenya Molasses Cattle Feeds Ltd (Associate).
Nigeria: Nigerian Sugar Company (16 per cent).
Malawi: Bookers (Malawi) (General retailing, produce processing and packing, tea growing) (80 per cent); Sales Services Ltd.
Zambia: Bookers (Zambia) (Holding Co and management) Eagle Travel (49 per cent); Consumer Buying Corp of Zambia (33 per cent) (department store and retailing); National Drug Co Ltd (49 per cent).

Directors and other interests of Directors in 1981

M.H. Caine (Chairman) (Governor of the Institute of Development Studies, Sussex University and Director, Acklands, a Canadian company).
M.C.W. Wildy (Vice-Chairman) (Director, Norsk Hydro UK).
Sir George Bishop (also Director of Agricultural Mortgage Corporation, Barclays Bank, Barclays Bank International, Ranks Hovis McDougall, and Chairman of the Overseas Development Institute).
M.A. Nicholson (Director, Mersey Docks & Harbour Company).
J.A. Haynes, J.N.W. Hearder, A.K. Stewart, J.F. Taylor, M.H. Fisher.

Lonrho

Lonrho is the 23rd largest company in the UK and its base in Africa makes it particularly significant on the continent.[1] The company was formed in 1909, as the London & Rhodesia Mining & Land Company, and remained a fairly unremarkable company, with most of its assets in Rhodesia, until 1961 when Angus Ogilvy, a director of the company, who was looking for a dynamic personality to put some life into Lonrho, signed up R.W. 'Tiny' Rowland. Rowland was then settled in Rhodesia and had extensive investments, including Nyaschere copper, and his own company, Shepton Estates, which has interests in ranching and mines. When appointed Managing Director, Rowland received 33 per cent of Lonrho shares and Lonrho acquired the assets of Shepton Estates.[2]

The individualistic and flamboyant style of management which Rowland brought to the company has aroused the attention — and criticism — of the press, though it is sometimes difficult to see why this company in particular is regarded as 'the unacceptable face of capitalism' (Heath's famous statement about Lonrho). The operation of its investments and their effects on underdeveloped countries are fundamentally little different from other transnationals, and one suspects that other big companies are quite happy for Lonhro to take criticism, which diverts attention from their own activities.

Nevertheless, there is no doubt that Rowland manages Lohrho in a style somewhat akin to that adopted by the old-style entrepreneurial capitalists of the last century. He has frequently been likened to Cecil Rhodes by his admirers, and indeed what they share in common is a 'vision of Africa'. Rhodes' vision centred on white settlers, vast mineral wealth and the Cape to Cairo railway; while Rowland's grand designs have included the oil pipeline from Mozambique to Zimbabwe, and the energy plan for Africa, designed to harness Arab oil money to African resources and forge a less-dependent energy strategy for Africa. It was this latter project which split the Organisation of African Unity (OAU) and forced Ekangaki's resignation in 1973, when he appointed Lonrho as consultants to the OAU.

Lonrho has expanded by taking over companies which already have investments in Africa. In general these have not been reorganised once taken over, but incorporated into one of Lonrho's major investment companies, either ACGE Investments Ltd, or African Industrial & Finance Corp. Other African subsidiaries are owned directly by the parent company, Lonrho Ltd. The arrangement still appears quite chaotic, although in 1972 a re-arrangement of accounting methods was undertaken, after publication of a report by Peat Marwick Mitchell & Co, the auditors,[3] which criticised the idiosyncratic accounting methods used by the company. The effect of this is that Rowland's intimate knowledge of the companies in the group gives him more personal control than that of the chairmen of other agribusiness companies in which decision-making tends to be centralised around the whole Board of Directors.

Most of the African takeovers occurred during the late 60s. Among the first, in 1967, was Consolidated Holdings Ltd, with investments in Kenya, Uganda and Tanzania, including interests in printing, transport and distribution. One subsidiary, ETCO Ltd, handled the entire warehousing and distribution of Kenya's coffee crop at the time. In 1968 the company bought David Whitehead, a UK textile firm with mills in Malawi, Rhodesia, South Africa and Nigeria. In March 1969, Lonrho acquired John Holt, a Nigerian-based colonial company, dealing in produce and general merchandise, drugs, tanneries, agricultural engineering, motor distributors and river fleets. Also in 1969 the company bought Slater Walker Securities' interests in East and Central Africa, which included Motor Mart Ltd. Motor Mart was based in Kenya, Tanzania and Uganda and had wide-ranging interests as distributors of motor vehicles and agricultural equipment, being sole distributors of Massey Ferguson, and owning tea estates, cotton factories, and neon sign agencies. The purchase of EA Tanning Extract Co., another Slater Walker subsidiary, brought Lonrho into the wattle industry in both East Africa and Rhodesia, through the Rhodesian Wattle Co. Ltd. The latter company owned both plantations and tanning extract factories. Again in 1969, Lonrho bought the profitable Ashanti Goldfields in Ghana.[4]

Until 1967 most of the companies were purchased for cash, but the burst of acquisitions after this was made mainly in exchange for the issue of Lonrho shares and convertible loan stock.[5] This is an unusual way of financing a takeover, and with less need to raise money, facilitated the rapid expansion. This, coupled with the informal management style, meant that the Board's control of the company weakened and Rowland's knowledge and management skills put him in a strong position.[6]

Lonrho's larger agricultural developments are in sugar, and like Tate & Lyle and Booker McConnell, the company has management contracts to operate sugar estates, as well as direct subsidiaries. Its most well-known involvement in sugar is in the giant Kenana scheme in the Sudan, 130,000 acres on fertile soil designed to turn the Sudan into the sugar bowl of North Africa, and to supply all of Arab Africa with sugar. Unfortunately the scheme has seen disaster follow disaster, costs rose dramatically and the whole project was well behind the schedule before coming on stream in 1979. Lonrho had the original management agreement, but because of disagreements with the financiers, the Kuwaiti government, Lonrho was forced to leave and for a time an American firm was brought in to manage the investment.[7] Lonrho retains its small equity investment in the Kenana Sugar Co Ltd* (3.5 per cent), and the dispute was eventually settled amicably.[8]

The major sugar subsidiary is the Lonrho Sugar Corporation Ltd, incorporated in Swaziland but operating from South Africa, which grows and processes sugar in Mauritius, Malawi, South Africa and Swaziland. Other major sugar interests are in the Dwangwa sugar project in Malawi, and the Save Sugar venture in Benin (5 per cent stake). The company also has interests in sugar in Kenya.

In tea, Lonrho has interests in Malawi and East Africa, though its largest investments in tea were in Tanzania, where it owned estates, a factory and warehouses, all of which were taken over by the government in 1978.[9] In Zambia, Lonrho manages two large schemes in the copperbelt, growing wheat, cotton and soyabeans. The company has subsidiaries importing and distributing Massey Ferguson agricultural equipment in Malawi, Zambia and Kenya. Its other main agricultural subsidiaries in agriculture in Africa are:

Central Africa Co (100 per cent), with tea estates in Malawi;
East African Tanning Extract Co Ltd (100 per cent), crop and livestock farming and wattle processing in Kenya (Wattle bark extract is used in tanning):
Holts Nigerian Tanneries Ltd (53 per cent), leather tanning and finishing in Nigeria;
Kalangwa Estates Ltd (80 per cent), mixed livestock and crop farming in Zambia;
Lonrho Sugar Corporation Ltd (99 per cent), sugar growing and processing in Mauritius, Malawi, South Africa and Swaziland;
P.S. Mandrides & Co, Ltd (88 per cent), oilseed crushing in Nigeria.

Lonrho's unique style of operating in Africa has involved a strong commitment to black leaders, and Rowland has close contact with many political leaders, such as Banda in Malawi, and with the economically powerful, such as the Sudanese millionaire, Khalil Osman.[10] He has an inflexible rule that it is absolutely essential for the company in Africa to work in harmony with the governnment of the day, and has been quoted as saying: "Even if your man out there is doing a first-class job and he falls foul of the government, then he must go".[11] This was illustrated in 1979 with the fall from grace in Kenya of Udi Gecaga, the late President Kenyatta's son-in-law, and head of Lonrho's East African empire (which earned 38 per cent of Lonrho's profits in 1978). Gecaga's posts in Kenya included a directorship on the board of *The Standard* newspaper in Nairobi, and the Moi government maintain that Gecaga was part of a group campaigning to secure constitutional changes which would have excluded Moi from automatically succeeding to the presidency on

*For a fuller account of Kenana see chapter 3, Sugar.

Kenyatta's death, and that he exploited his position as chairman of *The Standard* to promote this campaign.[12] Rowland made sure that Gecaga was forced to resign from *The Standard*. Udi Gecaga was on the Board of Lonrho in the UK, which made Lonrho quite unique in taking an African director on to the company's main Board, but, in line with Rowland's rule, he was soon dropped.

Lonrho has begun to reduce its dependence on its African interests for profits, and has in recent years invested more heavily in the UK, taking over a host of UK companies, including Volkswagen GB, Balfour Williamson, Dunform & Elliott and AVP Industries.[13] However, the African interests remain substantial.

Lonrho — Profit by Region and Product
1977-1980

	£ million			
	1977	*1978*	*1979*	*1980*
Turnover	1257	1491	1565.5	2100.7
Profit before tax	90.2	93.6	78.2	119.1
Profit by Region	*%*	*%*	*%*	*%*
East & Central Africa	30.62 (33)	35.03 (38)	30.40 (32.5)	46.05 (33.4)
West Africa	20.44 (23)	7.42 (6.5)	6.00 (6.5)	20.74 (15.1)
Southern Africa	15.13 (17)	22.84 (24.5)	23.07 (24.5)	38.06 (27.6)
UK	21.25 (23)	25.04 (27)	34.87 (37)	32.62 (23.7)
Europe & Other	2.75 (3)	3.31 (3.5)	.29 (0.3)	.23 (0.2)
	90.19	93.64	94.05	137.7

Profit by Activities				
Agricultural equipment, machinery & motors	21.63 (23.6)	17.48 (19)	18.58 (19.6)	20.01 (13.02)
Agriculture	14.06 (15.6)	20.79 (22)	10.46 (11)	12.95 (8.5)
Export confirming, finance, property & insurance	27.47 (30.5)	18.48 (20)	7.89 (8.3)	10.02 (6.6)
General Trade	5.91 (6.5)	12.28 (13)	9.47 (10.0)	14.79 (9.8)
Mining & Refining	10.96 (12.0)	9.59 (10)	26.11 (27.5)	63.34 (41.8)
Other	17.7 (19.6)	23.97 (26)	22.42 (23.6)	30.58 (20.2)

Source: Annual reports

Directors in 1980: Rt Hon Lord Duncan-Sandys C.H. (Chairman), Sir George

LF. Bolton, KCMG (Deputy Chairman), R.W. Rowland (Managing Director & Chief Executive), A.H. Ball, F.A. Butcher, Rt Hon Edward du Cann, MP, P.F. Doye, R.F. Dunlop, M.J.J.R. Leclezio, T.R. Prentice, P.G.B. Spicer, P.M. Tarsh, Sir Peter W. Yoeuns, CMG, OBE.

Lonrho Limited: African Subsidiaries*

Benin: John Holt (Benin) Ltd (Subsidiaries of Bartholomew (London) Group and John Holt & Co, Liverpool); Save Sugar Project (5 per cent equity plus management).

Botswana: Delkins BP Ltd (Subsidiary of African Industrial & Finance Corporation); Bechuanaland Airways Pty Ltd (Subsidary of National Airways & Finance Corporation, South Africa).

Ghana: The Ghanian companies are mostly subsidiaries of Bartholomew (London) Group, John Holt & Co. Liverpool, and ACGE Investments Ltd: Supreme Motors Ltd; Continental Cars Ltd; Ghana Properties Ltd; John Holt Bartholomew Ltd; John Holt Industries (Ghana) Ltd; Pito Industries (Ghana) Ltd; Ashanti Goldfields (Ghana) Ltd (Associate).

Kenya: The parent company is African Industrial & Finance Corporation Ltd, UK. Consolidated Holdings Ltd — printers and publishers of the *Standard* newspaper and general printers — and its subsidiaries: Baraza Ltd, ETCO Ltd, Chancery Investments Ltd, ETCO East African Services Ltd, Express Kenya Ltd (A), East African Standard (Newspapers) Ltd, D.A. Hawkins Ltd; Kenya Paper Mill Ltd, Printing & Packaging Corp Ltd, Publishers & Distribution Services Ltd, Standard Properties Ltd, Stationery and Office Supplies Ltd.

East African Tanning Extract Co Ltd — crop and livestock farming, together with wattle processing — and its subsidiaries: EATE Provident Trust, Kenya Agricultural Consultancy and Engineering Services Ltd, Kenya Tanning Extract Co Ltd (A), Nairobi Wattle Co Ltd, Nanyuki Textile Mills Ltd (A), Western Kenya Air Charter Co Ltd.

Kenya Motor Holdings Ltd and its subsidiaries: Motormart & Exchange Ltd (67 per cent), sole distributor of Renault, Vauxhall and Bedford in Kenya and Tanzania, and distributor of Massey Ferguson agricultural equipment in Kenya, Tanzania and Uganda, Automotive Components and Equipment Ltd, Bruce Ltd, East African Motor Holding Co Ltd, Kenya Motor Corporation Ltd, Farm & Industrial Machinery Distributors ltd, Multispares Co Ltd, Lea Securities Ltd, Motormart and Exchange (Finance) Ltd, Motor Mart Investment Corporation Ltd, Press Limited, Motor Mart Management Services Limited, The Motor Service Co Ltd, Pilion Estates Ltd, Tancot Ltd,

*Excluding South Africa where there are numerous subsidiaries.
(A) — Associate   (d) dormant.

Burns & Blaine Ltd, Burns & Blaine (Kenya) Ltd, Neon & General Signs Ltd, Westland Motors Ltd — agents for Toyota vehicles and spares.

Lonrho East Africa Limited, Teal Holdings Ltd, AIT Records (Kenya) Ltd (A), East African Investment Trust Ltd (subsidiary of African Investment Trust Ltd, UK; Balfour Williamson & Co (East Africa) Ltd (subsidiary of Balfour Wiliamson & Co Ltd, UK).

Liberia: International Ship Management Ltd.

Malawi: (Subsidiaries of ACGE Investments Ltd): David Whitehead (Technical Services) Ltd, David Whitehead & Sons (Malawi) Ltd (textiles factory).

(Subsidiaries of African Industrial & Finance Corporation Ltd): The Sugar Corporation of Malawi Ltd, General Construction Co Ltd, Leopard Developments Ltd, Lonrho (Malawi) Ltd — imports and distributes British Leyland motor vehicles and Massey Ferguson and Perkins agricultural equipment — Alumina Corporation of Malawi Ltd (d), The Central African Transport Co Ltd, Chibuku Properties Ltd, Consolidated Properties Ltd, Corundum Mining Ltd, General Distributors Ltd, Halls Holdings Ltd, Consolidated Motors (Lilongwe) Ltd, FES Electrical Contractors Ltd, Farming and Electrical Services Ltd, Halls Garage Ltd, Motor Supplies Ltd, Mobile Motors Ltd (A), Central Africa Co Ltd, UK (Tea Estates), Dwangwa Sugar project (Lonrho has a 'substantial equity interest' and a management contract), Mindali Tea Factory.

Mauritius: Merville Ltd (55 per cent) (luxury hotel), Benares Sugar Co Ltd, Exotic Exports Ltd, Mon Tresor & Mon Desert Ltd, Mon Tresor Holiday and Leisure Ltd, Tourism Development Co Ltd, Rogion Ltd, David Whitehead & Sons (Mauritius) Ltd, Lonrho Mauritius Ltd (The last two companies are subsidiaries of ACGE Investments Ltd).

Mozambique Discos de Mocambique Ltda, cia de, Teal Discos Ltda, CPMP (Cia do Pipeline Mocambique-Rhodesia SARL).

Nigeria: (Mainly subsidaries of Bartholomew (London) group and John Holt & Co, Liverpool): John Holt Properties (Nigeria) Ltd, John Holt Agricultural Engineers Ltd (60 per cent) (ploughs and other agricultural equipment), John Holt Ltd (40 per cent) (general merchandising & trading), John Holt Rubber Co Ltd, Holts Transport Ltd, Niger Traders Ltd, P.S. Mandrides & Co Ltd (oilseed crushing); Maiduguri Oil Mills Ltd, Nigerian Net & Twine Co Ltd, Nigerian Securities Ltd, John Holt Investment Co Ltd (A), Holts Nigerian Tanneries Ltd, Nigerian Enamelware Co Ltd, Phoenix Motors Ltd, distributors of Chrysler, Daf and Mitsubishi, Pito Industries Ltd, The Plateau Confectionery Co (Nigeria) Ltd (A), Star Motors Ltd, David Whitehead & Sons (Nigeria) Ltd, Kaduna Textiles Ltd, David Whitehead & Sons (Pensions) Ltd (d), J. Allen & Co Ltd (40 per cent), distributors in Nigeria of Ford, VW, Scania, Yamaha, Clarke & Petbow Products, Holts Nigerian Tanneries

Ltd (53 per cent), leather tanning and finishing.

Sudan: Lonrho Sudan Ltd, Kenana Sugar Co Ltd (3.5 per cent).

Swaziland: (Subsidiaries of African Industrial & Finance Corporation): Lonrho Sugar Corporation Ltd — sugar growing and processing in Mauritius, Malawi, South Africa and Swaziland, including the Ubombo Sugar Mill — Talbot Syrups Ltd, Ubombo Ranches Ltd, Bar Circle Ranch Ltd, Moyeni Ranch Ltd, Poorzicht (Pty) Ltd, Harmony Estates Ltd, The Aqua Cane Co Ltd, Umfula Planters Ltd, Uoufu Planters Ltd, Swaziland Aero Sales (Pty) Ltd (d), Lonrho Swaziland Ltd.

Togo: John Holt (Togo) SA.

Uganda: (Subsidiaries of African Industrial & Finance Corporation): Stationery & Office supplies (Uganda) Ltd, Neon & General Signs (Uganda) Ltd, Uganda Motor Corporation Ltd, Bruce (Uganda) Ltd, Farm Machinery Distributors (Uganda) Ltd, Motor Mart (Uganda) Ltd, Motor Service Co (U) Ltd, Uganda Vehicle Finance Ltd.

Zaire: (Subsidiaries of ACGE Investments Ltd): Afrimba SZRL, Immoaf SZRL (Societe Immobiliere et Hypothecaire D'Afrique), Immobiliere du Maycumbe SZRL, Lonrho Zaire Ltd.

Zambia: (Subsidiaries of African Industrial & Finance Corp): African Commercial Holdings Ltd (retailers of electrical goods, wholesalers cosmetics and Coca Cola), Consolidated Motors Zambia Ltd, Copperbelt Bottling Co Ltd (Coca Cola bottling), Hoozam Ltd, Marketing Distributors Ltd, Northern Theatres Ltd, Plaza Theatres Ltd, Zambia Cinemas Ltd, Radio Ltd, Heinrichs Syndicate Ltd (Edinburgh and Lusaka Hotels), Consolidated Properties Ltd, Heinrichs Hotels Ltd, Lusaka Hotels Ltd, Maxcon Ltd, Mulungushi Hotels Ltd, National Breweries Ltd (49 per cent); Industrial Credit Co Ltd (A), Lonrho Zambia Ltd (distributors of Toyota, Fiat, Land Rover, Mercedes and of Massey Ferguson agricultural equipment), African Paint Co Ltd, Lonrho Construction Co Ltd, Delkins Ltd, Burroughs Joinery Ltd, Flowers Contractors Ltd, A.E. Delkins Ltd, Premier Soils Laboratory Ltd, Eastern Construction Co Ltd, Pan Africa Construction Co Ltd, Construction & Investment Holdings Ltd, Medlab Ltd, Motor Holdings Zambia Ltd, Canberra Motors Ltd, Central African African Motors Ltd, Central African Motors (Midlands) Ltd, Commercial Motors Ltd, Louden Investments Ltd, Consolidated. Welding Ltd, Metro Zambia Ltd, Mobile Motors Zambia Ltd (A), Motor Delivery Services Ltd, Nippon Motor Sales Zambia Ltd, Star Motors (Commercial) Ltd, Star Motors Ltd, Power Equipment Ltd, Power Properties Ltd, Printpak Zambia Ltd, Times Newspapers Zambia Ltd, Teal Record Co (Zambia Ltd), Emerald Appliances Ltd, Musical Producers & Manufacturers Ltd, Selected Investments Ltd, Turnpan Zambia Ltd, Kalangwa Estates Ltd (80 per cent) (mixed livestock and crop farming, including wheat), Northern Minerals (Zambia) Ltd, Zambia Gemstones Ltd, Vitretex

Paints Ltd.
Zimbabwe: (Subsidaries mainly of ACGE Investments Ltd): Rhodesian Spinners Ltd, Corsyn Consolidated Mines Ltd, Nyaschere Copper (Pvt) Ltd (A), Lonrho Investment Co Ltd, Lonrho Finance Co Ltd, Northchart Investments Ltd, Rhodesian Wattle Co Ltd, Zambesi Coachworks Ltd.

Source: Who Owns Whom, Europe, 1979, and Lonrho Annual Reports.

APPENDIX A

The Importance of
Cash Crops in Africa

Between 1977 and 1979, 27 of the 43 countries considered in this report depended on agricultural exports for over half of their foreign earnings. Many depend on just one main crop, and even though agriculture in other countries is more diversified, one crop is generally significant, such as coffee in Tanzania or cashewnuts in Mozambique. As shows in Table 1, twelve of these are dependent on just one main crop for over 70 per cent of their income, and a further eleven countries depend on only two crops for well over half their income. Although agriculture in the third group of countries is more diversified, one crop is generally quite significant, such as coffee in Tanzania or cashewnuts in Mozambique.

While historically Africa was used to grow the crops needed for Europe, production of export cash crops increased quite impressively after the second world war. Coffee output increased four times in 20 years, tea six-fold, sugar three-fold, cocoa and cotton doubled, and tobacco increased by 60 per cent.[1] With some exceptions, the increase came from an expansion in the area under cash crops rather than from higher yields. Some new land came into production, and some land previously used to grow food was turned over to cash crops. There were, of course, variations between countries but the large increases in production appear to have levelled off through the 1970's. A brief look at the major crash crops follows.

Table A1

African Dependence on Cash Crops —
by Country, 1977 and 1979

A. Countries heavily reliant on one crop (over 50 per cent of export earnings)

Country	Crop	Per cent export earnings 1977	1979	Per cent arable land in crop
Burundi	coffee	94	93	3(1975)
Mauritius	sugar	94	68	90(1977)
Gambia	groundnuts	90[1]	na	73(1976)
Uganda	coffee	82[1]	27	—
Chad	cotton	80[1]	na	4(1976)
Ethiopia	coffee	75	69	5(1977)
Rwanda	coffee	73	71[4]	2(1977)
Equatorial Guinea	cocoa	66[3]	na	—
Somalia	live animals	61[1]	71	—
Guinea Bissau	groundnuts	60	na	31(1977)
Sudan	cotton	60	65	9(1977)
Ghana	cocoa	61	na	35(1976)
Kenya	coffee	54	27	5(1976)
Swaziland	sugar	54[2]	na	10(1976)
Lesotho	wool & mohair	50	na	—
Mali	cotton	50[1]	47[4]	1(1976)
Senegal	groundnuts	50[1]	37[5]	55(1976)

B. Countries heavily dependent on two crops[7]

		1977	1979	
Benin	cotton & cotton seed (48),[5] palm product/cocoa significant	77	43[8]	—
Malawi	tobacco (47),[5] tea	66	71	3(1976)
Upper Volta	cotton 46,[5] karite nuts/live animals	62	41[8]	4(1977)

C. Countries dependent on a number of cash crops, together accounting for over 70 per cent of Export Earnings

Country	1st Crop & per cent	Other Significant Crops	1977	1979	
Central African Republic	coffee 39[1]	cotton, timber	79[1]	51[4]	3(1975)[6]
Tanzania	coffee 35[4]	cotton, tobacco, sisal, tea	73[4]	na	—
Cameroon	cocoa 34[2]	coffee, timber, palm, rubber	70[2]	49[8]	4(1976)
Ivory Coast	coffee 24[1]	cocoa, timber, cotton, bananas, palm oils	83[1]	74	—
Madagascar	coffee 24[2]	cloves, sugar, vanilla, sisal	86[2]	67[8]	—
Mozambique	cashew-nuts[24]	sugar, shrimps, tea, cotton, sisal, coconuts	80	na	—

Notes
1. 1976; 2 1975; 3 1970; 4 1978; 5 1977.
6. Coffee and cotton only.
7. Because of the nature of African agriculture, the importance of the particular second crop may vary from year to year.
8. Estimated.

Sources: US AID Congressional Report 1980, New African Yearbook 1979 and 1981-2.

Coffee *

Coffee is grown in about 50 countries throughout the world. There are two basic types of coffee, robusta and arabica. The former is more common and is grown widely in Africa, although most of Kenya's coffee is arabica. Robusta is the stronger flavour used for making instant coffee; the more delicate arabica fetches higher prices. Africa's share of world production grew in the 1950s and 1960s, but between 1968 and 1979 fluctuated between 34 per cent and 23 per cent. East Africa is the major producing region in the Continent and grew, for example, 48.2 per cent of Africa's total in 1977, while West Africa produced 27.6 per cent. The major exporting countries are Ivory Coast, previously followed by Uganda and Angola, but now by Cameroon, Zaire, Kenya, Madagascar and Ethiopia.[2] Coffee is largely a smallholder crop in Africa and is frequently inter-cropped

*See Chapter 2, Africa and the International Coffee Trade.

with bananas or plaintain, a banana-like crop which is a staple food in some African countries.

Table A2*
Coffee Production ('000 tonnes)

	Africa	World	A as % of World
1948-52	278.4	2221.7	12%
1952-56	393.0	2526.0	16%
1961-65	988.2	4409.6	22%
1970	1311.9	3872.6	34%
1972	1287.7	4566.7	28%
1974	1241.2	4715.3	26%
1976	1234.0	3644.6	34%
1978	1090.0	4583.0	24%
1979	1144.0	4972.0	23%

Major African Producers: Ivory Coast, Ethiopia, Uganda, Zaire, Kenya, Cameroon, Madagascar, Angola.

Palm Products

The dramatic decrease in Africa's share of world output of palm oil and kernels is probably due almost entirely to the investment strategies of a single transnational corporation. Unilever found that it could produce better oil more cheaply in Malaysia than in Africa and from the mid-1960s, increased its investments there.** Malaysia now produces almost half of the world's palm products. Although developed on a commercial scale as a plantation crop in Africa, smallholders also grow palm for sale. It is a useful crop, and all parts of the plant can be used. The pulp left over after extracting oil from palm is called 'cake' and is used as animal feed.

Table A3
Production of Palm Products:
Oil and Kernels ('000 tonnes)

Oil:	Africa	World	A as % of World
1952-56	976.5	1202.0	81%
1961-65	1153.2	1513.6	76%
1970	1120.1	1963.7	57%
1972	1158.0	2424.8	48%
1974	1220.2	2951.7	41%
1976	1295.3	3498.3	37%
1978	1323.2	4029.8	32%
1979	1337.0	4533.0	29%

* The sources for this and the subsequent Tables 2-9 are the UN Statistical Yearbooks 1979, and the New African Yearbook 1981-82.

** See Unilever company profile, and Unilever and Zaire, in Chapter 14, Agribusiness in Africa.

190

(continuation of Table A4)

Kernels:	Africa	World	A as % of World
1952-56	813.0	974.0	83%
1961-65	778.6	1062.5	73%
1970	736.3	1195.2	61%
1972	661.3	1201.0	55%
1974	716.8	1356.9	53%
1976	734.1	1523.6	48%
1978	774.9	1602.5	48%
1979	727.0	1683.0	43%

Major African Producers: Nigeria, Benin, Zaire, Cameroon, Sierra Leone, Ivory Coast, Guinea, Angola.

Cocoa

The major producing countries within Africa in 1979 were Ivory Coast 36 per cent, Ghana 28 per cent, Nigeria 19 per cent and Cameroon 12 per cent,[3] although cocoa is also grown in Togo and in smaller quantities elsewhere. Cocoa has traditionally been a smallholder crop in Africa, and even in 1927 Ghanaian small farmers produced 210,000 tonnes valued at £11.7 million.[4] Ghana was the leading African producer until 1979, when Ivory Coast overtook it.

The leading African producers are also the world's largest exporters, as hardly any cocoa is consumed locally. For example, in 1976 Africa grew 65.7 per cent of the world's cocoa, but accounted for 75.6 per cent of world exports. These exports are almost entirely in the form of beans, reflecting the difficulty which African countries have in establishing the processing plants which add value to the crop. Cocoa beans are processed into three main products: paste, butter and powder. Some African countries, particularly Ghana and Nigeria, now process cocoa paste and butter, however by far the largest proportion of exports are still in the form of beans. Cocoa is processed, turned into chocolate-based products and sold under brand names such as Cadbury's, Rowntrees or Nestlé's in the major industrialised countries.[5]

Table A4

Cocoa Production ('000 tonnes)

	Africa	World	A as % of World
1948-52	499.3	765.1	65%
1952-56	517.0	827.0	63%
1961-65	930.3	1245.0	75%
1970	1092.5	1519.2	72%
1972	1014.8	1434.1	71%
1974	1017.2	1551.7	65%
1976	854.4	1372.9	62%
1978	899.0	1472.0	61%
1979	971.0	1585.0	61%

Major African Producers: Ivory Coast, Ghana, Nigeria, Cameroon.

Tea

Tea production has increased slowly but surely since the war, and Africa's share of world production rose during the 1960s, mainly at the expense of India and Sri Lanka. Much of the increase in production has been due to the involvement of smallholders in tea growing, particularly in Kenya. However, tea has traditionally been a plantation crop, and many large foreign-owned plantations still operate, e.g. Brooke Bond, Finlays, Lonrho and Unilever all own tea estates in Africa. Tea must be processed shortly after picking. All plantation or tea growing areas have a factory nearby to turn the green leaf into the familiar black particles of leaf for drinking. This is then packed into large tea crates and exported to Europe for packaging into consumer-sized portions, labelling and selling under branded names.

Table A.5

Tea Production ('000 tonnes)

	Africa	World	A as % of World
1948-52	19.8	639.0	3%
1952-56	26.7	667.0	4%
1961-65	59.6	1084.8	5%
1970	100.5	1026.0	10%
1972	118.9	1085.0	11%
1974	147.9	1175.0	12%
1976	151.2	1230.0	12%
1978	174.4	1445.0	12%
1979	201.0	1821.0	11%

Major African Producers: Kenya, Malawi, Mozambique, Uganda, Tanzania.

Groundnuts (peanuts)

Africa grows a large percentage of the world's crop, although it is now smaller than previously. 'Groundnut' is the generic term for a plant with tuber-like parts, the peanut being the most common example. These small bean-like plants are widely grown in Africa, having been a traditional protein-rich food in many parts of the continent. Their commercial use is in providing oils for cooking, soap making or industrial use. As with palm, the fibre left over after extracting the oil is called 'cake', and is used for animal feed. The economies of some African countries are tied to ground-nut exports: Gambia earned 90 per cent of its foreign exchange from the crop (in 1976) and has devoted *73 per cent of its arable land* to growing it. In the mid-1970s Guinea Bissau earned 60 per cent of its foreign exchange from the crop and Senegal 50 per cent.

Table A.6

Groundnut Production ('000 tonnes)

	Africa	World	A as % of World
1961-65	5348.6	15876.3	34%
1970	5167.4	18408.9	28%
1972	4960.7	15988.1	31%
1974	5321.9	17485.6	30%
1976	5211.0	17894.6	29%
1978	5170.2	18876.0	27%
1979	5522.0	19228.0	29%

Major African Producers: Senegal, Sudan, Nigeria, Zaire, Cameroon, Mali, Uganda, Malawi, Zimbabwe, Gambia, South Africa.

Timber

Africa has marginally increased its share of world timber production since the 1950s, and is an important supplier of hardwoods. Ironically, the value of African exports of roundwood are only just over half the cost of imports of finished wood products, mainly pulp and paper.[6] Africa has numerous natural forests and in many instances these are being replaced with plantation forests, generally of pine, cypress and eucalyptus. Although some countries have selectively replanted so as to maintain their natural forest,[7] others (like the Ivory Coast) are over-exploiting this valuable resource. If African production continues to expand, the pressure on natural forests will increase, as agricultural land is unlikely to be transferred to forestry, and savannah is not suited for timber production.[8] Timber is important to the export economies of Gabon, Congo, Ghana and Liberia. As firewood and charcoal are the only fuels of the vast majority of Africans, timber is very important as a natural resource.

Table A.7

Timber Production
(In million cubic metres, solid volume roundwood without bark)

	Africa	World	As a % of World		Africa	World	As a % of World
1970	329	2613	13%	1975	375	2751	14%
1971	339	2654	13%	1976	386	2870	13%
1972	347	2672	13%	1977	387	2909	14%
1973	358	2764	13%	1978	406	2955	14%
1974	366	2794	13%	1979	416	3020	14%

Major African Producers: Kenya, Nigeria, Ivory Coast, Tanzania, Sudan, Ethiopia, Gabon, Mali.

Tobacco

The main tobacco areas are in the south, particularly Zimbabwe, South Africa and, more recently, Malawi. After 1965 when Rhodesia declared UDI investment switched to Malawi and the tobacco industry expanded, displacing Zimbabwean producers from their traditional British and US markets. The Malawi government is now worried that investment will switch back to Zimbabwe. None of the black-African countries is a major manufacturer of cigarettes, although South Africa is the world's fourth-largest cigarette manufacturing country, after the USA, Netherlands and the UK.[9] However, tobacco is grown and manufactured into cigarettes as an import substitute in some countries, and British American Tobacco have established many factories for this purpose.

Table A.8

Tobacco Production ('000 tonnes)

	Africa	World	A as % of World
1961-65	223.4	4382.6	5%
1970	201.9	4675.4	4%
1972	224.7	4869.9	5%
1974	235.1	5296.9	4%
1976	271.0	5695.1	5%
1978	249.4	5710.1	4%

Major African Producers: Malawi, Zimbabwe, South Africa and Tanzania.

Cotton

Cotton is grown for local use as well as for export. It is particularly important to the economies of Chad (80 per cent of export earnings in 1976), Sudan (60-68 per cent), Mali (approximately 50 per cent), Upper Volta (approximately 46 per cent), Benin (34-48 per cent), Central African Republic (20 per cent in 1976), and Tanzania (around 11 per cent). (See Table 1). Although important to the *economies* of so many African countries, the only major cotton producer within sub-Saharan Africa is Sudan, which grows between 30 and 40 per cent of the world crop of long staple cotton, making it a more important producer than is implied by the figures in table 9. The massive Gezira Scheme makes up 12 per cent of all cultivated land in Sudan, and about half of this grows cotton.[10] The scheme was developed in the days of the Empire by British companies (the Sudan Plantations Syndicate), and partly engineered by the British Government, which saw the Sudan as "not only the finest cotton growing country in the whole of the British Empire, but, what is more important, that it can grow the sort of cotton that Lancashire requires."[11]

Table A.9
Cotton Production ('000 tonnes)

	Africa	World	A as % of World
1948-52	678	7581	9%
1961-65	925	10931	8%
1970	1337	11803	11%
1972	1292	13605	9%
1974	1247	13903	9%
1976	1053	12042	9%
1978	1113	12951	9%
1979	1157	14050	8%

Major African Producers: Sudan, Egypt.

Sugar Cane*

The economies of two African countries are based on sugar production: Mauritius (70-90 per cent of export earnings), and Swaziland (around 50 per cent). In Mauritius, 90 per cent of arable land is devoted to sugar production, almost entirely on large estates, some owned by transnational corporations such as Lonrho, others run by the State. Two out of every five Mauritian workers are employed in the sugar industry.[12] Since sugar is often the second largest item of expenditure on food import bills (after cereals), it is grown increasingly throughout Africa (usually on large estates) in an attempt to cut back on imports. Among those developing a sugar industry are Gambia, Ghana, Kenya, Nigeria, Senegal, Sierra Leone, Somalia, Sudan, Togo and Uganda.

Table A.10
Sugar Cane Production ('000 tonnes)

	Africa	World	A as % of World
1948-52	15287	278029	5%
1961-65	30835	475008	6%
1969-70	46074	595358	7%
1970-71	43499	585482	7%
1977	60027	737483	8%
1979	60214	754130	8%

Major African Producers: South Africa, Mauritius, Egypt, Mozambique, Kenya, Swaziland, Zimbabwe.

*See chapter 3, Sugar in Africa.

Other Cash Crops

Africa is the world's most important supplier of pyrethrum, a small flower which is a natural pesticide. This grows mainly in Kenya and Tanzania, and was once a crop produced on large farms with the processing and marketing monopolised by Mitchell Cotts, a UK company. However it is now grown almost entirely by smallholders.

Rubber is still an important crop in Africa. From the late 1950s onwards demand was affected by the development of synthetic oil-based products and many markets were lost to synthetic competitors. However, in 1978 there was renewed interest in rubber, partly because of its superior quality for products in expanding markets (particularly radial and heavy duty tyres), and partly because of the rising costs of oil. Liberia is still the main rubber-producing country in Africa.

In more recent years, foreign investment and aid has gone into developing new food crops for export, such as pineapples (in Kenya, Swaziland and Ivory Coast), and fresh vegetables for air-freighting to Europe (Kenya, Upper Volta, Senegal), and even flowers (Brooke Bond in Kenya). This development is examined in more detail in Chapter 1. However, it is important to stress that growing fruit and vegetables for export does not increase local supplies of these foods.

APPENDIX B

Declining and Fluctuating Prices

During the post-war period there has been a long-term tendency for primary commodity prices to fall and the prices of industrial goods to rise.[1] This trend halted for a while between 1966 and 1977, when the value of agricultural exports rose substantially. During this period the value of agricultural exports from the developing countries rose on average by 12 per cent a year, which is superficially impressive, but takes no account of changes in purchasing power. Deflating the figures by an index of the unit price of manufactured exports reduces the growth in value to only 3.4 per cent a year. Although this was a period of relative prosperity, developing country exporters of agricultural products were falling behind the major exporters in the developed world, sales from which were growing at 5.8 per cent a year in terms of real purchasing power.[2] (see table B.1).

After 1977 the purchasing power of exports from industrialised countries (largely manufactured goods) increased sharply in relation to those of underdeveloped countries, as illustrated in Figure B.1.

The implication of this is that while the relative price of primary products is falling, countries exporting agricultural commodities are compelled to increase their volume of exports in order to buy a constant quantity of manufactured goods from the outside world. However, constant increases in output almost always result in a glut and falling prices, although this may be disguised temporarily by a harvest failure or delayed by the length of time it takes to bring a tree-crop into production. Furthermore, exporters are not always free to increase their sales since many crops are subject to complicated agreements involving quotas on production. Finally, it is relevant to recall here that most African countries have increased their production of cash crops by devoting more land to them, rather than increasing the yields. If this strategy continues, it may prejudice other priorities, such as the need to increase domestic food production.

Figure B.2 shows the price since 1950 of three major African exports: cocoa, tea and coffee. The figure is based on current prices, taking no account of inflation. The rather flat curve up to the early 1970s suggests that countries exporting these products would have had considerable difficulty in keeping up with the costs of their manufactured imports. However, from 1974 prices began to rise and positively boomed in 1976-77. This bought

Table B.1

Value of World Exports of Agricultural Products*

	Average 1961-65	1970	1977	1978	1979	Average Annual Increase 1966-77 (per cent)
	(million US dollars)					
Current						
World	37,655	51,611	147,652	170,792	199,330	14.0
Developing	13,808	18,920	51,936	56,151	61,417	12.4
Developed	23,848	32,691	95,716	114,641	137,912	14.9
*Adjusted to show purchasing power***						
World	43,784	51,611	73,926	na	na	4.9
Developing	16,056	18,920	25,968	na	na	3.4
Developed	27,789	32,691	47,858	na	na	5.8

*Excluding fishery and forestry products **Deflated by UN index of unit values

Source: FAO Commodity Review and Outlook 1977-79, 1980.

windfall gains to to countries exporting the crops (Kenya wiped out its balance of payments deficit with its coffee and tea earnings in these years). Such high prices are rarely sustained for any length of time. By May 1980, cocoa had fallen back to July 1976 prices, and coffee and tea were well down. There are other consequences, too, of periods of high prices. For example, sugar reached a record price of £640 a tonne in 1974, and many African countries planned a rapid expansion of their sugar industries, both to save imports and to diversify their agriculture into what seemed like a profitable cash crop. But the prices plummeted and were low through the rest of the 70s, with only a temporary rally in 1980.[3] As a result, several governments were left with expensive sugar development projects, but low prices for sugar. Groundnuts, the major export of Gambia, Guineal-Bissau and Senegal, fell from a high price of US$740 a tonne in 1974 to US$430 a tonne in 1974, and by 1979 had recovered only slighly at US$480. Palm oil and kernels have also fluctuated a great deal since 1976.

Figure B.1

Purchasing Power of Exports, Developed and Developing Countries 1970 = 100

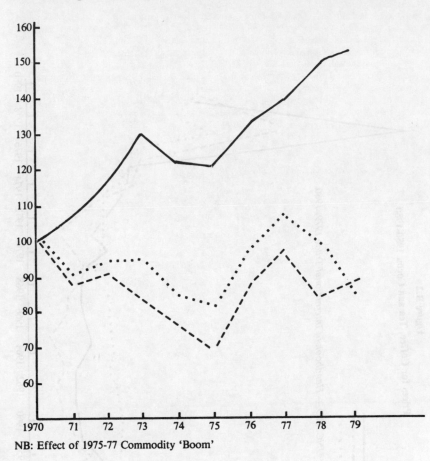

NB: Effect of 1975-77 Commodity 'Boom'

─────── *Developed Market Economies.*

─ ─ ─ ─ ─ *Least Developed Countries:* Includes Benin, Botswana, Burundi, Central African Republic, Chad, Ethiopia, Gambia, Guinea, Lesotho, Malawi, Mali, Niger, Rwanda, Somalia, Sudan, Tanzania, Upper Volta.

• • • • • • • • *Most seriously affected:* Includes Least Developed Countries, plus Ghana, Guinea Bissau, Ivory Coast, Kenya, Madagascar, Mauritania, Mozambique, Senegal, Sierra Leone.

Source: UNCTAD, Handbook of International Trade & Development Statistics, 1979 & 1980.

198

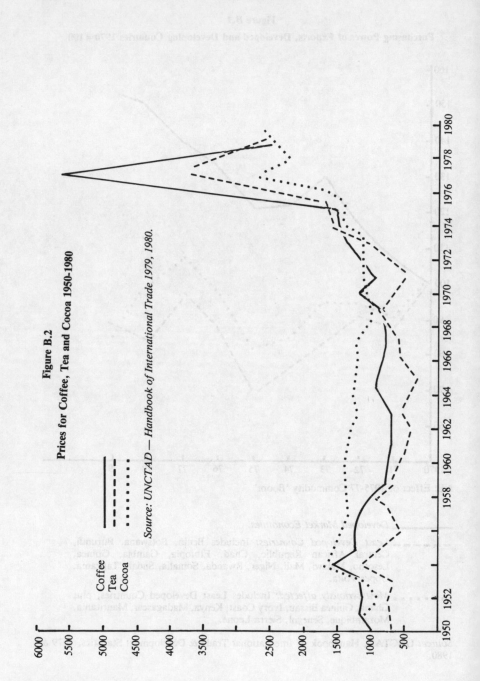

Figure B.2

Prices for Coffee, Tea and Cocoa 1950-1980

Coffee
Tea
Cocoa

Source: UNCTAD — Handbook of International Trade 1979, 1980.

Appendix C

Table C.1

Imports of Food and Animals to Selected African Countries 1972-79 (in US$1,000)

(Figures in brackets represents percentage of total imports)

Country / Major food import	1972	1973	1974	1975	1976	1977	1978	1979
Cameroon, cereals about half	24124 (8)	31858 (9)	48347 (11)	51765 (9)	65506 (7)	69831 ( )	73215 (6)	94805 (7)
CAR, half animals /¼ cereals	7271 (21)	11387 (22)	12051 (26)	15012 (22)	13896 (26)	13810 ( )	15454 (27)	15875 (2)
Chad, mainly sugar and cereals	12707 (21)	19907 (24)	24404 (28)	17549 (13)	19147 (16)	13498 ( )	14261 (12)	12615 (9)
Congo, cereals about half	10042 (11)	12339 (10)	15700 (14)	20151 (13)	20906 (13)	26950 ( )	33530 (12)	48691 (19)
Ethiopia, 74-77, cereals ¾	7943 (4)	9433 (4)	24451 (9)	20262 (7)	23094 (6)	36414 (14)	32623 (6)	56409 ( )
Gabon, cereals 33% in 1975	10002 (7)	12270 (8)	21499 (6)	42624 (10)	37345 (8)	41341 ( )	63204 (11)	59814 (8)
Gambia, cereals, some sugar	3206 (14)	6214 (15)	8374 (22)	9270 (18)	16153 (22)	14009 (19)	20539 (22)	177921 (16)
Ghana, half cereals then sugar	37213 (12)	70062 (15)	93102 (11)	65596 (8)	75252 (8)	101581 (12)	113322 (12)	113511 (9)
Ivory Coast, cereals, dairy products then sugar	90240 (20)	141657 (20)	144656 (15)	132455 (12)	133983 (10)	197931 (11)	239796 (10)	309517 (13)
Kenya, sugar and cereals	44813 (8)	47455 (8)	46912 (5)	36902 (4)	32932 (4)	29814 (2)	52362 (3)	39952 (2)
Liberia, mainly cereals	23176 (13)	30061 (15)	37761 (13)	37560 (11)	40099 (10)	54398 (11)	67310 (14)	76911 (15)
Malawi, cereals, dairy	9624 (7)	10706 (8)	12169 (6)	14763 (6)	13695 (7)	10199 (4)	11742 (3)	17255 (4)
Mali, cereals, sugar, dairy	19945 (25)	61805 (56)	100427 (56)	58135 (31)	31435 (21)	23302 (15)	31135 (14)	28540 (16)
Mauritius, mostly cereals	28276 (23)	37589 (22)	82480 (26)	72299 (21)	67596 (18)	83654 (18)	94620 (19)	102763 (18)
Nigeria, cereals, sugar	179619 (12)	218364 (12)	265939 (10)	444310 (7)	607025 (7)	989311 (9)	1470253 (11)	1256547 (10)
Senegal, cereals (50%), sugar, fruit & vegetables, dairy	73619 (26)	126065 (35)	163498 (32)	129922 (22)	148903 (23)	168118 (27)	163921 (21)	196707 (25)
Sierra Leone, cereals, sugar	22120 (18)	34887 (22)	48917 (22)	31138 (16)	30846 (19)	38290 (21)	53524 (19)	79177 (25)
Somalia, half cereals, sugar	15693 (20)	19986 (20)	28308 (20)	41725 (26)	47802 (28)	61403 (36)	42973 (18)	74342 (26)
South Africa, mostly coffee, tea, cocoa	169136 (5)	221031 (5)	311027 (4)	296240 (4)	253893 (4)	291355 (6)	258836 (4)	306833 (4)
Sudan, sugar, cereals	75330 (21)	109752 (23)	148848 (22)	166404 (17)	131207 (13)	100734 (9)	175560 (19)	157498 (14)
Tanzania, cereals, sugar	42840 (10)	37012 (7)	145980 (18)	135468 (18)	47681 (8)	62717 (8)	64329 (6)	43107 (4)
Togo, cereals, sugar	8484 (10)	11057 (11)	9459 (8)	10563 (6)	13970 (8)	40789 (14)	24771 (6)	36683 (7)
Uganda, sugar, cereals	19200 (8)	20498 (12)	27862 (13)	13999 (7)	9812 (11)	15215 (8)	4610 (2)	24506 (13)
Zambia, mostly cereals	46497 (8)	33516 (6)	61887 (8)	52003 (8)	31323 (5)	28769 (5)	27355 (4)	59472 (8)

Source: FAO Trade Yearbook, 1978, 1980.

References

Introduction

1. Esman, Milton J. *Landlessness and Near Landlessness in Developing Countries*, Cornell university, August 1978; Cohen, John M. 'Land Tenure and Rural Development in Africa' in Bates, Robert H. and Lofchie, Michael F. eds. *Agricultural Development in Africa*, Praeger, 1980, p.358.
2. See *Development Forum*, August-September 1979 for a discussion of trade between African States.
3. Kaplinsky, R. *Trends on the Distribution of Income in Kenya, 1966-70*, Working Paper No. 336, Institute for Development Studies, Nairobi, 1978.
4. "Why Famine Threatens the Sahel", in *Dollars and Sense*, No.33, January 1978.
5. Seers, Dudley, "What are we trying to measure?" *Journal of Development Studies*, 1972, pp.21-25.

Agribusiness

1. George, Susan, *Feeding the Few, Corporate Control of Food*, Institute for Policy Studies, 1979, p.60.
2. Feldman, David and Lawrence, Peter, *Social and Economic Implications of the Large Scale Introduction of New Varieties of Foodgrains, Africa Report*, preliminary draft, UNRISD, 1975.
3. *Ibid*.
4. Davidson, Basil, *Africa — History of a Continent*, Spring Books, 1978, first published 1966, p.233.
5. *New Internationalist*, October 1978, p.7.
6. Davidson, *Africa, op. cit*, pp.234 and 269.
7. *Ibid*, p.225.
8. Rodney, W., *How Europe Underdeveloped Africa*, Bogle L'Ouverture, London and Tanzania Publishing House, Dar-es-Salaam, 1972, pp.170-4.
9. Davidson, *Africa, op cit*, p.225.
10. Davidson, Basil, *Africa in Modern History*, London, Penguin, 1978.
11. Davidson, *Africa — History of a Continent, op. cit*. p.290.
12. Rodney, *op. cit*. pp.170-2.
13. Davidson, *Africa — History of a Continent, op. cit*., p.285.
14. Arrighi., "Labour Supplies in Perspective: Rhodesia", in Arrighi & Saul, *Essays on the Political Economy of Africa*, Monthly Review Press, New York, 1973, p.210.
15. Feldman & Lawrence, *op. cit*. p.103.
16. Herskovits, Melville, *The Human Factor in Changing Africa*, Vintage Books, New York, 1962, p.156.
17. Lanning, G., *African Undermined*, Penguin, London, 1979, p.258.
18. *Ibid*.
19. Wainwright, David, *Brooke Bond — A Hundred Years*, published for Brooke Bond Liebig Ltd by Newman Neame Ltd., 1969.
20. World Development Movement, *The Tea Trade*, 1980.
21. Davidson, *Africa in Modern History, op. cit*., p.126.

202

22. Rodney, *op. cit.* p.200.
23. Counter Information Services, *Unilever's World,* 1975, p.62.
24. For example in South Africa. See also the story of palm oil in Zaire.
25. Quoted in Davidson, *Africa — History of a Continent, op. cit.,* p.289.
26. Herskovits, *op. cit.* pp.409-10.
27. *African Business,* November 1978, p.37.
28. World Bank, *Zaire, Appraisal of the Oil Palm Project,* Report No. 1592-ZR, 29 March 1978.
29. Oliver, Roland and Fage, J.D., *Short History of Africa,* Penguin 1968, p.254.
30. Letter from Unilever in *One World,* No.64, March 1981.
31. UN Statistical Yearbook, 1976.
32. World Bank *op. cit.* Summary and Conclusions, p.(i).
33. Letter from Unilever, *op. cit.*
34. Most of the information in this section is taken from the World Bank document, *Report and Recommendation of the President of the International Development Agency to the Executive Directors, on a proposed credit to the Republic of Zaire for an Oil Palm Development Project,* 3 April 1978, Report No.P.2296-ZR.
35. *Ibid.,* pp.16-17.
36. These terms are set out on pages 25-28 of the World Bank *Appraisal, op. cit.*
37. Gordon, Samuel, President of Del Monte Banana Co., Quoted in George, Susan, *How the Other Half Dies,* Penguin, London, 1976, p.120.
38. Brooke Bond Annual Report, 1978.
39. Unilever booklet, *Unilever Plantations,* 1961.
40. Unilever Annual Report, 1980.
41. United Nations Centre on Transnational Corporations (UNCTC). *Transnational Corporations in Food and Beverage Processing,* UN, New York, 1980, unedited version, ST/CTC/19, p.65.
42. UNCTC, *op. cit.* p.65.
43. *Kenya Export News,* April 1979.
44. *Kenya Export News,* September 1978.
45. "Why Famine Threatens the Sahel", *Dollars & Sense,* No.33, January 1978.
46. Lappé, Frances Moore and Collins, Joseph, "Turning the Desert Green for Agribusiness", *IDOC Bullettin,* No. 56, May-June 1979, p.15.
47. "Why Famine Threatens the Sahel", *op. cit.*
48. *IDOC Bulletin, op. cit.*
49. "Nipped by the the Bud", Chasin, Barbara, *New Internationalist,* No.108, February 1982.
50. *IDOC Bulletin, op. cit.*
51. UNCTC, *op. cit.* p.95.
52. UNCTC, *op. cit.* p.95.
53. UNCTC, *op. cit.* p.95.
54. Tate & Lyle Annual Report, 1978.
55. UNCTC, *op. cit.* p.57.
56. Clairmont, F., and Cavanagh, "Stuck in a Cotton-pickin' Transnational Corner", *Guardian,* 13 August 1979.
57. *Ibid.*
58. *Sunday Times,* 21 May 1978.
59. *Business Week,* 29 August 1977.
60. *Research on TNCs,* UNCTC Report of the Secretariat.
61. Feldman and Lawrence, *Africa Report, op. cit.* p.112.
62. *Business Week,* 29 August 1977.
63. *Africa Now,* May 1981, p.107.
64. George *op. cit.* p.215.

65. *Ibid.* pp.214-234.
66. International Peace Research Association's Food Policy Study Group, *Circular Letter VII,* 1/80, p.19.
67. Linear, Marcus, "Zapping Africa's Flies", *Vole,* March 1981.
68. *Ibid.* p.14.
69. *Ibid.* p.14.
70. *Ibid.* p.17.
71. Lappé, Frances Moore and Collins, Joseph, *Food First,* Ballantine Books, September 1979, p.47.
72. UNCTC, *op. cit.* p.57.
73. *Ibid.* pp.95-118.
74. *Ibid.* p.118.
75. *Ibid.* pp.125-7.
76. Langdon, S., *Multinational Companies in the Political Economy of Kenya,* PhD thesis, December 1975, chapter 9.
77. See for example, Kaplinsky, R., *Breakfast Cereals in Kenya,* paper from the Institute for Development Studies, Nairobi, Kenya.
78. Langdon, *op. cit.*
79. Langdon, *op. cit.* chapter 9.
80. *One World,* March 1978, p.11.
81. UNCTC, *op. cit.* p.73.
82. UNCTC, *op. cit.* p.57.

Coffee

1. Quarterly Statistical Bulletin on Coffee, October-December 1980, Vo.4, No.4, p.3.
2. Fisher, B.S. *The International Coffee Agreement: A Study in Coffee Diplomacy,* Praeger, 1972, p.3
3. Payer, C. "Coffee". In: Payer, C. ed. *Commodity Trade of the Third World,* Macmillan, 1975, p.154.
4. Fisher, B.S., *op. cit.* p.3.
5. Fisher, B.S. *op. cit.* p.3.
6. *Revista do Comercio de Cafe,* "The Buyers from Brazil". Rio de Janeiro. October 1979, p.19.
7. Singh, S. *et. al. Coffee, Tea & Cocoa, Market Prospects & Development Lending, World Bank Staff Occasional Papers, No.22, 1977, p.24.*
8. Carlson, K.L. Thvilum, O., *The World Coffee Economy & the Price of Coffee.* The Arhus School of Business Administration & Economics, May 1979, p.10.
9. Sivetz, M. *Coffee: Origin & Use, 2nd ed.,* Coffee Publications, Corvallis Oregon, 1977, p.2.
10. *World Coffee Survey,* UNFAO, Rome 1968, p.7.
11. Quarterly Statistical Bulletin, *op. cit.* p.8.
12. FAO, *op. cit.* p.178.
13. Payer, C., *op. cit.* p.155.
14. Report to the Congress by the Comptroller General of the United States, *Coffee Production & Marketing Systems,* 28 October 1977, p.21.
15. Whetham, E. *Agricultural Marketing in Africa,* OUP 1972, pp.91-2.
16. Fitch, Bob and Oppenheimer, Mary, *Ghana, End of an Illusion,* Monthly Review Press, NY, 1966.
17. Whetham, E., *op. cit.*
18. Report to Congress, *op. cit.* pp.24-25.
19. Stainer, Robin, "Dearer Cup of Coffee", *Guardian,* 15.2.82.
20. International Coffee Organisation, Press Release PR50/81, 18 September 1981.

21. Decision of the International Coffee Council concerning coffee export quotas for coffee year 1981/2. International Coffee Council 36-16(E) 2 October 1981, London.
22. *Guardian*, 15.2.82, *op.cit.*
23. Campaign Co-op, *The World in Your Coffee Cup*, Revised Ed. 1980. Campaign Co-op, London 1980. p.10.
24. Payer, C., *op. cit.* p.32.
25. *Ibid.* p.32.
26. *Ibid.* p.161.
27. Bloch, Dan, "Boca Ratan 1980: A Record Attendance as Spirits Revive". *Coffee International*, Vol.7, No.2, 1980, p.31.
28. *Revista do Comercio de Cafe, op.cit.* p.19.
29. Report to the Congress, *op. cit.*
30. *Revista do Comercio de Cafe, op.cit.* p.19.
31. Campaign Co-op, *op. cit.* p.15.
32. George, Susan, "Nestlé Alimentana SA: the limits to Public Relations". *Economic and Political Weekly*, Vol.13, No.37, 16 September 1978, Bombay.
33. "Uganda Coffee Ban Widens", *Financial Times*, 19 May 1978.
34. This entire section is based on Masini, J. Ikonicoff, M. Jedlicki, C., Lanzarotte, M. *Multinationals & Development in Black Africa. A Case Study in the Ivory Coast.* ECSIM. Saxon House, 1979, pp..113-146.
35. This section is based on *The World in Your Coffee Cup*, first ed. September 1976, p.24, 2nd ed. pp.17, 19 and *Africa Now*, May 1981, pp.97, 98.
36. Singh, S. *op. cit.*
37. *Africa Now, op. cit.* pp.97, 98.

Sugar

1. *The Future of Sugar*, Part 3 of Sugarworkers popular report of the International Sugarworkers Conference, published by GATTFLY, Toronto, February 1978.
2. Hagelberg, G.B., *Outline of the World Sugar Economy*, Institut für Zuckerindustrie, Berlin, 1976.
3. Hagelberg, G.B., *Structural and Institutional Aspects of the Sugar Industry in Developing Countries*, Institute für Zuckerindustrie, Berlin 1976, p.38.
4. Hagelberg, *Ibid.* p.40.
5. "Move to halt sugar fall". *Guardian*, 18.5.81.
6. "African Sugar Producers face threat as EEC reviews policy", *New African*, August 1981. p.45.
7. Tate & Lyle Annual Report 1979.
8. United States Department of Agriculture (USDA) *Sugar and Sweetener Report*, Vol.4, No.4, April 1979.
9. *African Business, July 1979.*
10. *South*, No.17, March 1982.
11. "Speculators Won't Grow Fat on Sugar", *Guardian*, 19.3.80.
12. *South*, No.17, March 1982.
13. "Spiralling Sugar Prices lead to cuts in demand", *Guardian*, 9.2.81.
14. "Third World Sugar Forecast", *African Business*, January 1981.
15. FAO Trade Yearbook 1978.
16. Kaplinsky, R., *Inappropriate Products and Techniques, the Case of Breakfast Cereals in Kenya*, Review of African Political Economy, No.14, 1979.
17. *Kenya Export News*, August 1978.
18. Swainson, Nichola, *Foreign Corporations and Economic Growth in Kenya*, Ph.D. thesis, University of Sussex (1978), p.199.
19. Hagelberg, G.B. *Sugar Industry in Developing Countries, op. cit.* p.22.

20. Hagelberg, G.B., *ibid*. p.25.
21. Hagelberg, G.B., *Sugar Industry in Developing Countries, op. cit.*
22. *International Sugar Journal*, January 1980.
23. "Little Success with Six", *Sudanow*, October 1980.
24. *South*, March 1982.
25. *The Economist*, 18 March 1978.
26. *South*, March 1982.
27. *New African*, January 1977.
28. *New African*, January 1978, p.50.
29. The information in this paragraph is taken from *Sudanow*, October 1980, *op. cit.*
30. *African Business*, July 1979, p.4; and *African Business*, April 1979, pp.25-6.
31. *African Business*, August 1979.
32. *African Development*, October 1976.
33. *GATT-Flyer*, No.4, January 1977.
34. *African Business*, August 1979.
35. Interview in *Afrique Industrie*, quoted in "Ivory Coast Reaps Bitter Harvest", *African Business*, August 1979,
36. Booker McConnell company information on the Mumias sugar scheme.
37. *African Business*, April 1981, p.65.
38. "Brazil avoids hiccups with alcoholic car fuels", *New Scientist*, 18.9.80.
39. "Brazil turns to Sugar Power", *Financial times*, 11.1.80.
40. "Brazil's drive for cars run on alcohol may misfire", *Guardian*, 20.7.81.
41. *New Scientist*, 18.9.80, *op. cit.*; and *Financial Times*, 11.1.80, *op. cit.*
42. "Put a Sunflower in your Tank", *New Scientist*, 26.2.81.
43. "Discord over Energy Conference threatens North-South Debate, *New Scientist*, 16.7.81.
44. Estimated by Professor Fernando Homem de Mello, of Sao Paulo University, an expert on Brazil's agriculture, quoted in the *Guardian*, 20.7.81, *op. cit.*
45. *New Scientist*, 26.2.81, *op. cit.*
46. Bennett, Gavin, "The Great Gasahol Goof", *Autonews*, March 1981.
47. "Sticky End for Molasses", *New Scientist*, 10 June 1982, p.690.
48. *African Business*, February 1981, p.35.
49. "Green petrol . . . a possible palliative for the oil crisis, *Financial Times*, 4.6.79.
50. "Kenya-Flowers Before Food", *New African*, March 1981.
51. Hagelberg, G.B., *Sugar Industry in Developing Countries, op. cit.*
52. William's, 1971, *International Sugar Journal*, Vol.77, 1975, p.293, quoted in Hagelberg, *op. cit.* p.22.

Kenya

1. Central Bureau of Statistics, Ministry of Finance & Planning, Nairobi, *Integrated Rural Survey*, 1974-5.
2. Memo to the Ambassador of 18.8.78, on Smallholder Agricultural Production in Kenya — Overview. Quoted in USAID Country Development Strategy Statement, Kenya, 1980-84, January 1979.
3. Central Bureau of Statistics, *Integrated Rural Survey, op. cit.* See also ILO/UNDP, *Employment, Incomes & Equality in Kenya*. Geneva, 1972, p.76.
4. Maitha, J.K., "The Kenyan Economy", chapter 2, in Heyer, Judith; Maitha, J.K. and Senga, W.M., eds., *Agricultural Development in Kenya, an Economic Assessment*, OUP, Nairobi, 1978.
5. These reasons have been quoted in many articles, but see in particular the Government of Kenya's Food Policy Paper, 1981, reported in the "Kenya Survey", *Guardian*, 8 June 1981.

206

6. *Ibid.*
7. Miller, Charles, *The Lunatic Express,* Ballantine Books Inc., New York, 1971, p.195.
8. Hughes, A.M., *East Africa, Kenya, Tanzania, Uganda.* Penguin, Harmondsworth, 1969, p.90.
9. For background, see for example, Oliver, Roland & Fage, J.D. *A Short History of Africa.* Penguin, Harmondsworth 1968, p.202; and Kariuki, J.M., *Mau Mau detainee.* Penguin, Harmondsworth, 1963, p.27.
10. These figures are drawn from Hinga, S.N. and Heyer, Judith. *The Development of Large Farms,* chapter 7 in Heyer *et. al. op. cit.;* and the *New African Yearbook,* 1979.
11. Hinga & Heyer, chapter 7 in Heyer *et. al., op. cit.*
12. Economist Intelligence Unit, Special Report No.99. *Kenya: Economic Prospects to 1985,* by Martin Godfrey, EIU, London 1981, quoted on page 9.
13. Coffee Board of Kenya Annual Reports, 1976-78.
14. EIU Report, *op. cit.*
15. Central Bureau of Statistics, Ministry of Economic Planning and Community Affairs, Nairobi. *Economic Survey,* 1979.
16. Coffee Board of Kenya Annual Report 1979.
17. Interview with R.J.G. Ballard, Managing Director of Brooke Bond Liebig Kenya Ltd., February 1980.
18. Kenya Tea Development Authority Annual Reports 1976-78.
19. Swainson, Nicola. *Foreign Corporations and Economic Growth in Kenya,* PhD thesis for Institute of Development Studies, Sussex University, 1978. Now published as the *Development of Corporate Capitalism in Kenya, 1918-77,* Heinemann Educational Books, London, 1980.
20. Interview with R.J.G. Ballard, *op. cit.,* February 1980.
21. Interview with Ministry of Agriculture official, January 1980.
22. World Development Movement, *The Tea Trade.* 1980.
23. This and much of what follows is taken from Nicola Swainson, *The Development of Corporate Capitalism in Kenya, 1918-1977.* Heinemann Educational Books Ltd., London, 1980. pp.250-264.
24. *BBLK News,* No.26, September 1979.
25. Jórgensen, Jan Jelmert, "Multinational Corporations and the Indigenization of the Kenyan Economy". In: Widstrand, C., *Multinational Firms in Africa,* Scandinavian Institute of African Studies, Uppsala, 1975, p.153.
26. Swainson, PhD thesis, *op. cit.*
27. Swainson, *Development of Corporate Capitalism in Kenya, op. cit.*
28. Interview with R.J.G. Ballard, *op. cit.* February 1980.
29. Brooke Bond Liebig Kenya Ltd., Annual Report, 1979.
30. *Kenya Farmer,* October 1979.
31. *Kenya Export News,* March, 1979.
32. *East African Standard,* 14.9.55.
33. *East African Standard,* 5.12.59.
34. Lappé, Francis Moore & Collins, J., *Food First,* Ballantine Books, 1979, pp.289-90.
35. *East African Standard,* 20.12.65.
36. *East African Standard,* 8.9.67.
37. Swainson, PhD thesis, *op. cit.* p.205.
38. Swainson, *ibid,* p.206.
39. *Kenya Export News,* March 1979.
40. *East African Standard,* 3.1.80.
41. For a full assessment of the benefits and otherwise of Del Monte to the Kenyan Economy, see Kaplinsky, R., *Export Oriented Growth: A Large Internatinal Firm in*

a Small Developing Country. (Draft, but later published in World Development in 1979).

42. Kabala Kabunda, M.K.K. "Multinational Corporations and the Installation of Externally-oriented Economic Structures in Contemporary Africa: the Example of the Unilever-Zaire Group". In: Widstrand, *op. cit.* p.303.
43. *Topics,* January/February 1977, the magazine of Overseas Private Investment Corporation, Washington.
44. Interview with Ministry of Agriculture, January 1980.
45. *Ibid.*
46. *Kenya Export News,* January 1979.
47. *Milling Feed & Fertiliser,* April 1979, p.22.
48. *Ibid.*
49. *Nestlés in Developing Countries,* Nestlés, Alimentant SA, Vevy, 1975, p.98.
50. Néstles, *op. cit.* p.99.
51. INFACT Questionnaire, 1980.
52. *Guardian,* 18.5.81.
53. Langdon, S., *Multinational Corporations in the Political Economy of Kenya,* PhD thesis for the Institute of Development Studies, Nairobi, 1975, Chapter 2.
54. *Guardian,* 11.6.79, "Kenya special". Article by H. Okoth-Ogendo.
55. Economist Intelligence Unit Report, *op. cit.* p.12.
56. Morrison, C., quoted in Kaplinsky, R., *Trends on the Distribution of Income in Kenya, 1966-70.* Working Paper No.336, Institute for Development Studies, 1978, p.16.
57. Kaplinsky, R., IDS Working Paper, No.336, *op. cit.* p.16.
58. EIU Report, *op. cit.* p.13.

Tanzania

1. Hyden, Goran, *Beyond Ujamaa in Tanzania, Underdevelopment and an Uncaptured Peasantry,* Heinemann Educational Books, London, 1980.
2. Von Freyhold, Michaela, *Ujamaa Villages in Tanzania, Analysis of a Social Experiment,* Heinemann Educational Books, London, 1979, p.12.
3. Hatch, John, *Tanzania, a Profile,* Pall Mall Press, London, 1972, pp.85 and 86.
4. Hyden, *op. cit.* p.48.
5. Von Freyhold, *op. cit.* pp.33 and 34.
6. Hyden, *op. cit.* chapter 3.
7. Barker, Jonathan, "The Debate on Rural Socialiam", in Bismark, U. Mwansasu and Cranford Pratt, *Towards Socialism in Tanzania,* Tanzania Publishing House, Dar-es-salaam, 1979, pp.97-99. Much of the information in this section is based on a summary of Ujamaa in this paper.
8. Hyden, *op. cit.* chapter 4.
9. *New African Yearbook,* 1981-82.
10. Ellis, Dr Frank, *Agricultural Pricing Policy in Tanzania, 1970-79, Implications for Agricultural Output, Rural Incomes and Crop Marketing Costs, 1980,* Economic Research Bureau, University of Dar-es-Salaam.
11. Hyden, *op. cit.* p.133.
12. *New African Yearbook,* 1981-82.
13. Hyden, *op. cit.* p.138.
14. *Guardian,* 1 December 1980.
15. *New African,* January 1981, p.14.
16. This is one of the major arguments of Hyden, *op. cit.*
17. Von Freyhold, *op. cit.* p.22.
18. Personnel communication to the author.

19. "Food Aid Drawbacks", *Africa Now,* May 1982, p.17.
20. Musoke, Dr Issa Kahoko S., *The Impact of Agricultural Development Measures on Tanzania's Rural Economy and Social Structure,* University of Dar-es-Salaam, Department of Sociology, November 1979, p.36.
21. *Daily News,* Dar-es-Salaam, 2.3.80, p.1 and 3.3.80, p.3.
22. Von Freyhold, *op. cit.* pp.30-31.
23. USAID, *Country Development Strategy Statement,* Tanzania, FY 1981, January 1979, p.31.
24. British Agricultural Export Council, *Country Notes,* Tanzania.
25. *New African,* January 1979. The figures were worked out by UNIDO for a project to support village smiths.
26. "Tanzania: Which Way?" *New African,* February 1981, p.30.
27. Barker, *op. cit.* p.101.
28. Boesen, Jannik, from "Ujamaa to Villagisation", in Mwansasu & Pratt, *op. cit.* p.130.
29. "Tanzania: Which Way?" *New African,* February 1981.
30. *Guardian,* 2.12.80.
31. Von Freyhold, *op. cit.* p.109.
32. "Food Aid Drawbacks", *Africa Now,* May 1982. p.17.
33. Von Freyhold, *op. cit.* p.109.
34. *Ibid.* p.109.
35. Much of what follows is based on discussions with Dr Frank Ellis of the Economic Research Bureau, University of Dar-es-Salaam, and of Barbara Dinham's own discussions with Tanzanians during a visit in 1980. Other sources have been referenced.
36. Dr Frank Ellis provided this example.
37. *Guardian,* 2 December 1980.
38. Ellis, *op. cit.* p.18.
39. *New African Yearbook,* 1981-82.
40. World Bank, *World Development Report, 1981,* August 1981, p.83.
41. "World Bank — Help of Hindrance?" *New African,* June 1980.
42. "Compromise in Tanzania", *New African,* September 1980.
43. "Tanzania Survey, World Bank — Help or Hindrance?" *New African,* June 1980.
44. Von Freyhold, *op. cit.* p.111.
45. *Africa Now,* May 1982, *op. cit.*
46. Neersø, Peter, "Tanzania's Policies on Private Foreign Investment". In Widstrand, C. (ed.) *Multinational Firms in Africa.* Scandinavian Institute of African Studies, Uppsala, 1975, p.178.
47. Coulson, Andrew, "The Automated Bread Factory", in ed. Coulson, Andrew, *African Socialism in Practice, The Tanzanian Experience,* Spokesman, Nottingham. 1979.
48. Hyden, *op. cit.*
49. *New African,* June 1980, World Bank, *op. cit.*
50. "Strangulation of Africa", interview with Rene Dumont, *New African,* August 1981.
51. Barker, *op. cit.* p.120.

Agribusiness and Africa's Food Crisis

1. United States Department of Agriculture, Economic Statistics and Co-operatives Services, International Economics Division, Africa and Middle East Branch *Food Problems and Prospects in Sub-Saharan Africa — The Decade of the 1980s.* September 1980. p.1.

2. International Economics Division of the Economics and Statistical Service, US Department of Agriculture, *World Food Aid Needs and Availabilities,* 15 March 1981. p.4.
3. *Ibid.*
4. *Ibid.*
5. United States Department of Agriculture, ESCS, IED, Africa and Middle East Branch, *op. cit.* p.1.
6. *Ibid.*
7. *Ibid. p.9.*
8. *FAO Regional Food Plan for Africa,* ARC/7815, Rome, June 1978.
9. International Food Policy Research Institute (IFPRI), *Food Needs of Developing Countries.* IFPRI, Washington DC, December 1977.
10. United States Department of Agriculture, Economics, Statistics and Co-operatives Service, *Structural Issues of American Agriculture,* AER-438, November 1979.
11. USDA, ESCS, IED, Africa and Middle East Branch, *op. cit.* p.5.
12. *Ibid.*
13. International Economics Division of the Economics and Statistical Service, USDA, *op. cit.* p.21.
14. Seidman, Ann, *Eliminating Rural Poverty,* World Bank, World Development Report, 1979. OUP August 1982.
15. For examples of this approach as well as detailed criticism of it see Franke, Richard W. and Chasin, Barbara H. *Seeds of Famine,* Allanheld, Osmun & Co, 1980. pp.112-120; George, Susan, *How the Other half Dies,* Penguin, 1976, p.53-68; Lappé, Francis Moore and Collins, Joseph, *Food First,* Ballantine, 1978, p.13-53.
16. USDA, ESCS, IED, Africa and Middle East Branch, *op. cit.* p.43.
17. Cohen, John M. 'Land Tenure and Rural Development in Africa' in Bates, Robert H., and Lofchie, Michael F. eds. *Agricultural Development in Africa,* Praeger, 1980, p.358.
18. USDA, ESCS, IED, Africa and Middle East Branch, *op. cit.* p.121.
19. United Nations, *World Population Trends and Policies.* 1977 Monitoring Report, New York, 1979, cited *ibid,* p.12.
20. *Ibid.* p.12.
21. *Ibid.* p.27.
22. USDA, ESCS, IED, Africa and Middle East Branch, *op.cit.,* p.53.
23. The information on Continental's activities in Zaire is from Morgan, Dan, *Merchants of Grain,* Viking Press, 1979. p.226-254.
24. *Ibid.* p.4.
25. Lappé, Frances Moore, Collins, Joseph and Kinley, David. *Aid as Obstacle,* Institute for Food and Development Policy, 1980. p.93-110.
26. George, Susan, *Feeding the Few: Corporate Control of Food,* Institute for Policy Studies, 1979. p.64.
27. *Ibid.*
28. United Nations Centre on Transnational Corporations, *Transnational Corporations in Food and Beverage Processing,* United Nations, New York, 1981. p.33.
29. Morgan, Dan, *op. cit.* p.232.
30. UNCTC, *op. cit.* p.35.
31. USDA, ESCS, IED, Africa and Middle East Branch, *op. cit.* p.172.
32. Feldman, David and Lawrence, Peter, *Africa Report,* United Nations Research Institute for Social Development, 1975, unpublished. p.189.
33. *African Business and Economic Review,* Vol.1, No.17, 1 May 1980. p.127.
34. Advertisement for Business Guide to World Aid Funds and Projects in *African Business and Economic Review,* Vol.2, No.20, July 16-August 1, 1981.
35. USDA, ESCS, IED, Africa and Middle East Branch, *op. cit.* p.101-105.

210

36. *Guardian,* 23.9.81.
37. Kinley, David, Levinson, Arnold and Lappé, Frances Moore, "The Myth of 'Humanitarian' Foreign Aid", *The Nation,* 11-18 July 1981. p.43.
38. Dumont, Professor René and Mottin, Marie France, *Towards Another Development in Rural Zambia,* Government Printer of the Republic of Zambia, 1980.
39. Africa Research Bulletin, May 15-June 14, 1980, Lusaka *Times of Zambia,* 13.1.81.
40. *Ibid.*
41. "Operation Food Production Causes Protests", *African Business,* October 1980, p.25.
42. *Economist,* 1.11.80.
43. Dumont, René, *op. cit.*
44. *African Business. op. cit.*
45. Franke, Richard W. and Chasin, Barbara H. *op. cit.* p.148-164.
46. *Ibid.* p.148.
47. *Ibid.* p.192-194.
48. *Ibid.* p.219-226.
49. *Ibid.*
50. Holdcroft, Lane E. "The Role of External Aid". *African Report,* July-August, 1981. pp.15-18.
51. Feldman, David and Lawrence, Peter, *Africa Report, op. cit.* pp.105-108.
52. *Ibid.* pp.22-24.
53. Franke, Richard W. and Chasin, Barbara H. *op. cit.* pp.191-2.
54. *Ibid.*
55. Berg, Elliot, *Marketing, Price Policy and Storage of Food Grains in the Sahel: A Survey,* Ann Arbor: University of Michigan Centre for Research on Economic Development, 1977. Vol.II, p.40.
56. Franke, Richard W. and Chasin, Barbara H. *op. cit.* p.192.
57. *Ibid.*
58. *African Business and Economic Review,* Vo.2, No.10/11, February 16/March 1, 1981. p.68.
59. Abalu, G.O.I. and D'Silva, B., "Nigeria's food situation: Problems and Prospects", *Food Policy,* February 1980, p.49-60.
60. *African Business and Economic Review, op. cit.;* Obe Ad'obe "Growing Dangers of the Green Revolution", *Guardian* 11.9.1980.
61. Pamphlet of the African Development Group, Washington D.C., 1981.
62. *Ibid.*
63. United States Department of Agriculture, Office of International Co-operation and Development, "US Business to Co-operate in Nigerian Agriculture", *Fact Sheet* Nigeria FS-1, November 1980.
64. *African Business and Economic Review, op. cit.* p.69.
65. Olsen's *Agribusiness Report,* New York, Vol.2, No.6, December 1980; *African Business and Economic Review, op. cit.* p.68.
66. Pope, George J. "US Farm Exports to Nigeria Could Hit $1 Billion by 1985", *Foreign Agriculture,* United States Department of Agriculture, Foreign Agricultural Service, February 1982, p.4.
67. Chapman, Rod, "Nigerian Oil Crisis Forces Imports Ban", *Guardian,* 24.3.82.
68. *Guardian* 11.9.80 *op. cit.*
69. Oculi, Okelli "Bougeoise Verte Centre Paysans" *Le Monde Diplomatique,* Issue 332, November 1981.
70. *Ibid.*
71. Esman, Milton J, *Landlessness and Near-Landlessness in Developing Countries,* Centre for International Studies, Cornell University, August 1978.

211

72. USDA, ESCS, IED, Africa and Middle East Branch, *op. cit.* p.50.
73. Esman, Milton J. *op. cit.* p.9 and p.16.
74. United States Department of Agriculture, International Economics Division, Economics and Statistics Service, Africa and Middle East Branch, *Current Agricultural Dilemmas in Gabon,* March 1981.

Unilever

1. Annual Report, Unilver, 1974.
2. Annual Report, Unilever, 1978.
3. *Unilever's World,* CIS Anti-Report, No.11, Counter Information Service, 1975, p.72.
4. Annual Report, Unilever 1981.
5. Annual Report, Unilever 1978, p.27.
6. *Unilever's World, op. cit.* p.45.
7. Kabala Kabunda, M.K.K. 'Multinational Corporations & the Installation of Externally-oriented Economic Structures in Contemporary Africa. In: Widstrand, K. Multinational Corporations in Africa, Upsaala, 1975, p.303. *Unilever and World Development,* Unilever, p.16.
8. Wilson, C. The History of Unilever. Cassell 1968, quoted in: *Unilever's World, op. cit.* p.64.
10. UAC International, supplement to Unilever Report & Accosunts 1975.
11. Fieldhouse, D.K. *Unilever: Portrait of a Multinational.* Croom Helm, London, 1978, p.62.
12. *Unilever's World, op. cit.* p.62.
13. *Unilever's World, op. cit.*
14. *Unilever's World, op. cit.* p.62.
15. International Bank for Reconstruction & Development (IBRD). *Zaire, Appraisal of the Oil Palm Project,* Report No. 1592-ZR, 29 March 1978.
16. *Plantations,* Unilever, 1961.
17. Minutes of Unilever Special Committee, October 1960, quoted in- Fieldhouse, *op. cit.*
18. UAC International, supplement to Unilever report & Accounts, 1975.
19. *Unilever's World, op. cit.*
20. *Unilever & World Development,* Unilever, 1977.

Tate & Lyle

1. Hugill, A. *A Sugar & All That . . . A History of Tate & Lyle.* Gentry Books, London 1978. Much of what follows is based on Hugill's account of Tate & Lyle. Mr Hugill is a retired director of the company.
2. Hugill, A. *op. cit.* p.111.
3. Hugill, A. *op. cit.* p.205.
4. Tate & Lyle Technical Services Ltd. *Capabilities & Experience,* 1979.
5. Hugill, A. *op. cit.* p.309.
6. *New African,* February 1978, p.60.
7. Hugill, A. *op. cit.* p.280.
8. Tate & Lyle Limited, *Group Report to Employees,* 1978.
9. Tate & Lyle, Annual Report, 1978.
10. Tate & Lyle, Annual Report, 1978.
11. Tate & Lyle Limited, *Group Report to Employees,* 1978.
12. See Hugill, A. *op. cit.*

212

Booker McConnell

1. *New African*, August 1978.
2. *African Development*. No.5. 1976.

Lonrho

1. Hambros Company Guide, 1979.
2. Cronje, S., M. Ling & G. Cronje, *Lonrho, Portrait of a Multinational*, Penguin. London 1976. This and much of what follows is based on this book.
3. Cronje *et. al., op. cit.* Chapter 5.
4. Cronje, *et. al., op. cit.* pp.94.95.
5. Report of the Department of Trade, *Inquiry into Lonrho*, 1978.
6. Report of the Department of Trade, *Inquiry into Lonrho*, 1978, p.42.
7. *The Economist*, 18 March 1978.
8. Lonrho Annual Report, 1978.
9. *African Business*, October 1978, p.37.
10. Cronje, *et. al., op. cit.*
11. *African Business*, December 1979, p.14.
12. *African Business*, December 1979, p.14.
13. *African Business*, April 1979.

Appendix A

1. Feldman, David and Peter Lawrence, *Africa Report*, UNRISD, 1975, unpublished, Chapter IV.
2. *Statistical and Economic Bulletin for Africa*, UNECA, No.12, December 1979.
3. *UN Statistical Yearbook*, 1979.
4. Hindin, Rita, *Plan for Africa*, Fabian Society, 1941.
5. *Statistical and Economic Bulletin for Africa*, UNECA, *op. cit.*
6. Plumptree, Robert, in a discussion of the Forests of Africa, 17 September 1979, taken from FAO statistics.
7. *Ibid.*
8. Centre for Agricultural Strategy, *Strategy for the UK Forest Industry*, CAS Report 6, February 1980, p.103.
9. *UN Statistical Yearbook*, 1979.
10. Parliamentary Debates, Fifth Series, Vol.50, 1913, Col.17, quoted in Barnett, Tony, *The Gezira Scheme, an Illusion of Development*, Frank Cass, 1977, p.7.
11. Barnett, Tony, *The Gezira Scheme, op. cit.*, p.5.
12. World Development Movement and London Refineries Trade Union Committee pamphlet, undated.

Appendix B

1. Feldman, David and Peter Lawrence, *Africa Report*, UNRISD, 1975, Unpublished, Chapter IV.
2. *FAO Commodity Review & Outlook 1977-79*.
3. *Financial times*, 17 May 1980.

Index of Companies

214

216

Index, General

222